School Consultation
Conceptual and Empirical Bases of Practice
SECOND EDITION

Issues in Clinical Child Psychology

Series Editors: **Michael C. Roberts**, *University of Kansas, Lawrence, Kansas*
Lizette Peterson, *University of Missouri, Columbia, Missouri*

CHILDREN AND DISASTERS
Edited by Conway F. Saylor

CONSULTING WITH PEDIATRICIANS: Psychological Perspectives
Dennis Drotar

HANDBOOK OF ADOLESCENT HEALTH RISK BEHAVIOR
Edited by Ralph J. DiClemente, William B. Hansen, and Lynn E. Ponton

HANDBOOK OF CHILD ABUSE RESEARCH AND TREATMENT
Edited by John R. Lutzker

HANDBOOK OF CHILD BEHAVIOR THERAPY
Edited by T. Steuart Watson and Frank M. Gresham

HANDBOOK OF CHILDREN'S COPING: Linking Theory and Intervention
Edited by Sharlene A. Wolchik and Irwin N. Sandler

HANDBOOK OF DEPRESSION IN CHILDREN AND ADOLESCENTS
Edited by William M. Reynolds and Hugh F. Johnston

HANDBOOK OF PSYCHOTHERAPIES WITH CHILDREN AND FAMILIES
Edited by Sandra W. Russ and Thomas H. Ollendick

HANDBOOK OF RESEARCH IN PEDIATRIC AND CLINICAL CHILD
PSYCHOLOGY
Edited by Dennis Drotar

INTERNATIONAL HANDBOOK OF PHOBIC AND ANXIETY DISORDERS
IN CHILDREN AND ADOLESCENTS
Edited by Thomas H. Ollendick, Neville J. King, and William Yule

MENTAL HEALTH INTERVENTIONS WITH PRESCHOOL CHILDREN
Robert D. Lyman and Toni L. Hembree-Kigin

SCHOOL CONSULTATION: Conceptual and Empirical Bases of Practice,
Second Edition
William P. Erchul and Brian K. Martens

SUCCESSFUL PREVENTION PROGRAMS FOR CHILDREN
AND ADOLESCENTS
Joseph A. Durlak

A Continuation Order Plan is available for this series. A continuation order will bring delivery of each new volume immediately upon publication. Volumes are billed only upon actual shipment. For further information please contact the publisher.

School Consultation

Conceptual and Empirical Bases of Practice

SECOND EDITION

WILLIAM P. ERCHUL

North Carolina State University
Raleigh, North Carolina

and

BRIAN K. MARTENS

Syracuse University
Syracuse, New York

Kluwer Academic/Plenum Publishers
New York, Boston, Dordrecht, London, Moscow

Library of Congress Cataloging-in-Publication Data

Erchul, William P.
    School consultation: conceptual and empirical bases of practice/William P. Erchul
and Brian K. Martens.—2nd ed.
        p.   cm. — (Issues in clinical child psychology)
    Includes bibliographical references and index.
    ISBN 0-306-46691-0
        I. School psychology—United States.   2. Psychological consultation—United
States.   3.
    Educational consultants—United States.   I. Martens, Brian K.   II. Title.   III. Series.

    LB 1027.55 .E73 2002
    370.15—dc21

                                                                        2001054190

The authors and publishers are grateful to the following publishers and copyright holders for permission to reprint material in this book: Educational Publishing Foundation and the Division of Consulting Psychology of the American Psychological Association, for permission to reproduce Table 1 (p. 7) from G. Caplan, R. B. Caplan, & W. P. Erchul, "Caplanian Mental Health Consultation: Historical Background and Current Status," which appeared in Vol. 46 of the *Consulting Psychology Journal: Practice and Research*. Copyright © 1994 by the Educational Publishing Foundation and the Division of Consulting Psychology. The Society for the Psychological Study of Social Issues, for permission to reproduce Table 3 (p. 238) and Figure 4 (p. 240) from B. H. Raven, "The Bases of Social Power: Origins and Recent Developments," which appeared in Vol. 49 of the *Journal of Social Issues*. Copyright © 1993 by The Society for the Psychological Study of Social Issues.

ISBN: 0-306-46691-0

© 2002 Kluwer Academic / Plenum Publishers
233 Spring Street, New York, N.Y. 10013

http://www.wkap.nl/

10   9   8   7   6   5   4   3   2   1

A C.I.P. record for this book is available from the Library of Congress

To Ann
   —WPE

To Rosemarie
   —BKM

Preface

Consultation is an indirect model of delivering psychological services. Within this model, a specialist (consultant) and staff member (consultee) work together to optimize the functioning of a client in the staff member's setting and to increase the staff member's capacity to deal with similar situations in the future. In schools, for example, a psychologist may consult with a teacher about a student in the teacher's classroom. The practice of school consultation has burgeoned since its formal introduction into public education during the 1960s. Today, graduate training programs in various specialties of psychology and education require coursework in consultation, and many professionals in these areas spend some portion of their day engaged in consultation.

Consultation can be a powerful tool in delivering psychological services in schools, but only when the consultant possesses a requisite level of skill and sophistication. In preparing this volume, we envisioned its major purpose as reducing the level of naivete typically experienced by the beginning school consultant. Toward that end, we offer a systematic approach to school consultation that targets much of the information needed for one to consult in a competent manner. The reader should note that our use of the somewhat ambiguous term *school consultant* is intentional and recognizes that consultants working in schools today represent a variety of professional disciplines. The primary intended audiences for this book, however, are clinical child psychologists and school psychologists, although psychologists having other specialties are likely to find its content useful. A clear secondary audience is educational specialists, including counselors, special educators, and school social workers. What the reader must have to benefit from our approach is a solid background in psychology, a content area of expertise from which to draw, and well-developed human relations skills.

We believe the overall method of school consultation detailed in this book is different from others that have been published previously. In stating that it is different, we are not claiming that it is wholly original. Our goal instead has been to incorporate the most useful conceptual and/or empirically validated principles of known consultation approaches into a single model that is particularly relevant to school-based practice. More specifically, the model of school consultation we promote attempts to integrate aspects of the historically separate models of mental health consultation and behavioral consultation, along with principles of social power, interpersonal influence, social support, and organizational psychology. In our model, the effective practice of school consultation is linked to the accomplishment of three interrelated tasks—the problem-solving, social influence, and support and development tasks.

Structurally, this volume is comprised of three major sections. The first of these consists of three chapters that describe foundational information, including using interpersonal influence in consultation (Chapter 2) and understanding the school as a setting for consultation (Chapter 3). The second section, comprised of Chapters 4 to 6, documents important processes and outcomes of school consultation. Chapters 4 and 5 present our integrated model of consultation, focusing on elements of mental health consultation, behavioral consultation, professional support, problem solving, social influence, and the organizational context. Moving away somewhat from these core elements, Chapter 6 offers advice on how to select school-based interventions and how to assess their effectiveness in terms of treatment outcome, integrity, and social validity. Chapters 7 through 9 form the third section. Key participants in school consultation, teachers and students, are described in Chapters 7 and 8, respectively. Chapter 9 contains a transcribed school consultation case study, conducted and analyzed by the first author. Chapter 10 is an epilogue that reviews important points and looks ahead to the future practice of school consultation.

We have been very heartened by the positive reactions of students and colleagues to the first edition of *School Consultation: Conceptual and Empirical Bases of Practice*. For example, Hintze (1998) wrote: "In reviewing the text, I found myself reflecting on what was being proposed from a variety of perspectives: 'how much easier this is going to make my teaching,' 'this is just the type of book students have been asking for,' 'that's exactly what I experienced as a practitioner,' or 'I wish I had a book like this when I was being trained.'" We hope that readers of the second edition will find it just as useful. New to this edition are the topics: implications of the IDEA Amendments of 1997 for school consultation; additional approaches to the support and development task; methods for conducting a functional behavioral assessment; a listing of instructional interventions; teacher shortage, recruitment, and retention issues; prereferral intervention teams and programs; strategies to increase teacher skill transfer and maintenance; and the inclusion of new research studies that inform the effective practice of school consultation.

We have heard that one of the strengths of the earlier volume lay in its concise presentation of many topics germane to school consultation. We have retained that emphasis in the revised edition but also acknowledge there is much more to consultative practice than a single source can adequately cover. Therefore, instructors selecting this book for their graduate-level courses may wish to supplement it with another. We suggest the following sources for deeper coverage of indicated topics: Caplan and Caplan, (1993/1999; mental health consultation); Kratochwill and Bergan (1990; behavioral consultation); Sheridan, Kratochwill, and Bergan (1996; conjoint behavioral consultation); Marks (1995; entry issues); Witt, Daly, and Noell (2000; functional assessment); and Telzrow and Tankersley (2000; IDEA Amendments of 1997).

Books are seldom the result only of their authors' efforts, and with this in mind, we wish to express our gratitude to several individuals. Priscilla Grissom and Lynne Myers are thanked for their careful proofreading and editing efforts. We also appreciate Blair Johnson's help in preparing Figure 5.1.

We continue to be intellectually sparked by the scholarly contributions of Gerald Caplan and Bertram H. Raven. Gerald Caplan, Professor Emeritus of Psychiatry at Harvard Medical School and originator of the modern practice of mental health consultation, has been a primary influence on our understanding of the interpersonal, organizational, and preventive aspects of consultation. Bert Raven, Professor of Psychology Emeritus at the University of California, Los Angeles, and renowned social psychologist, has greatly enhanced our view of the role that social power and interpersonal influence play in consultation. We are grateful to these gentlemen for both their kindness and insights into human behavior that led us to develop our integrated model of school consultation.

We also wish to acknowledge the many talented doctoral students with whom we have collaborated over the years. The diligent efforts and insights of Seth Aldrich, Scott Ardoin, Tracy Bradley, Sandy Chafouleas, Teri Chewning, Sheila Clonan, Ed Daly, Ami Dombalis, Priscilla Grissom, Andrea Hiralall, Richard Hollings, Mary Cathryn Murray, Lynne Myers, Susan Smith Scott, and Michelle Whichard have contributed immeasurably to the development of our model.

Finally, Bill Erchul would like to thank his wife, Ann Schulte, for the ongoing support of his research, administrative, consulting, and musical activities as well as for her incisive thoughts on school consultation that she freely shares. Brian Martens would like to thank his wife, Rosemarie, for her energy, intuition, and voice of reason which bring much needed balance to work and family.

WILLIAM P. ERCHUL
BRIAN K. MARTENS

Contents

PART ONE: BACKGROUND

1. Introduction to Consultation   3

The Effectiveness of Human Services Consultation   5
Historical Influences on the Human Services Consultant
    Role   7
Historical Influences on the School Consultant Role   10
Reconceptualizing Consultation for Today's Schools   13
Consultation Versus Collaboration   16
The Rest of the Book   18

2. Promoting Change in Schools   19

Changing Beliefs, Attitudes, and Behaviors within
    Consultation   20
General Strategies for Effecting Changes in Human
    Systems   27
The Bases of Social Power and Their Application to
    School Consultation   29
Other Means of Influence   40
A Power/Interaction Model of Interpersonal Influence
    and Its Application to School Consultation   44

3. The School as a Setting for Consultation   49

Organizational Traditions in the Public School System   50
The Service Structure of Public Schools   58
School Consultation from an Administrative Perspective   66

PART TWO: CONSULTATION PROCESSES AND OUTCOMES

4. **Bases of an Integrated Model of School Consultation**   73

Community Mental Health and Mental Health Consultation
   Bases   73
Behavioral Psychology and Behavioral Consultation
   Bases   82
Summary of the Bases of an Integrated Model of School
   Consultation   89
Achieving Entry in School Consultation: Entering the
   Service Delivery Network   89

5. **Model Description and Application**   97

A Critical Appraisal of Consultation Models   98
An Integrated Model of School Consultation   103

6. **Selecting and Evaluating School-Based Interventions**   119

Effectiveness of Intervention Alternatives   120
Implementation Issues   128
Evaluating Intervention Outcomes   135

PART THREE: KEY PARTICIPANTS IN CONSULTATION

7. **Teachers as Consultees**   141

Perspectives on Teachers and Teaching   142
Perspectives on Teachers and School Consultation   148
Increasing the Effectiveness of Consultation with Teachers   155
Providing Consultative Support to Teachers   160

8. **Students as Clients**   163

Legislation Governing Service Delivery in the Schools   164
Educational Approaches to Classification   167
A Contextual Model of Student Achievement   177

9. **Consultation Case Study**   183

First Interview: Tuesday, September 21   184
Second Interview: Tuesday, September 28   191
Third Interview: Tuesday, October 19   199

10. Epilogue: The Effective Practice of School Consultation   **203**

The Limited Utility of Psychoeducational Evaluation   204
The Emergence of School-Based Consultation Teams   204
Changes to IDEA   205
Reconceptualizing School Consultation   206

References   213

Author Index   235

Subject Index   243

About the Authors   249

I

Background

1

Introduction to Consultation

> Consultation...denote[s] the process of interaction between two professional persons—the consultant, who is a specialist, and the consultee, who invokes his help in regard to a current work problem with which the latter is having some difficulty, and which he has decided is within the former's area of specialized competence. The work problem involves the management or treatment of one or more clients of the consultee, or the planning or implementation of a program to cater to such clients. (Caplan, 1963, p. 470)

We begin with psychiatrist Gerald Caplan's definition of consultation, not because it is the best definition for our purposes, but rather because it provides a starting point, both historically and conceptually, from which to view the role of the school consultant. Historically speaking, perhaps the earliest systematic approach to human services consultation began in 1949 in Israel where Caplan and his small clinical staff were assigned the challenging task of attending to the mental health needs of 16,000 adolescent immigrants. Complicating this assignment were the facts that these adolescents were housed at more than 100 residential institutions, transportation within the country was often problematic, and there were about 1,000 initial requests for assistance. In confronting these obstacles to the traditional model of referral/diagnosis/psychotherapy of individual clients, Caplan reasoned that available professional resources would need to be used more effectively (Caplan, 1970).

In response to these circumstances, a different model of delivering mental health services emerged. Rather than meet individual clients at the clinic in Jerusalem, Caplan and his staff traveled to the many institutions and met there with the referred teenagers and their caregivers (later termed *consultees*). Supportive, collegial discussions with the caregivers about the adolescents often resulted in the caregivers returning to work with a new, enhanced perspective that led to their more effective management of client problems. By concentrating his staff's professional energies on consultative activities that improved the functioning of caregivers, Caplan believed that the mental health of many more clients could be positively affected than was possible through traditional one-on-one therapy. He also found that much more pertinent information was obtained when meeting with caregivers on-site as opposed to a clinic (Caplan & Caplan, 1993/1999).

Conceptually, Caplan's 1963 definition and later elaborations (Caplan, 1964, 1970; Caplan & Caplan, 1993/1999) specify the unique and essential features of the mental health consultation relationship. These features distinguish consultation from the relationships and contracts inherent to other professional activities such as supervision, teaching, and psychotherapy. First, the consultative relationship is essentially triadic, with the involvement of a consultant and one or more consultees and clients. Consultees typically lack the training and experience that consultants possess, and may be professionals or paraprofessionals representing various fields, including education, nursing, law or medicine. Second, the optimal working relationship is coordinate and nonhierarchical; ideally, there is no power differential between consultant and consultee. Third, consultee work-related challenges rather than personal problems form the basis for consultative discussion. Fourth, the consultant has no administrative responsibility for or formal authority over the consultee. Thus, the ultimate professional responsibility for the client's welfare remains with the consultee, not the consultant. Fifth, the consultee retains the freedom to accept or reject whatever guidance the consultant may offer. In other words, consultation is considered to be a voluntary relationship. Sixth, messages exchanged between consultant and consultee are to be held in confidence, unless the consultant believes someone will be harmed if silence is maintained. Finally, consultation has a dual purpose—to help the consultee with a current professional problem and to equip the consultee with added insights and skills that will permit him or her to deal effectively with similar future problems, preferably without the consultant's continuing assistance.

Gerald Caplan's historical and conceptual contributions to the practice of consultation are unprecedented (Erchul, 1993a). Nothwithstanding, it is also true that the field of consultation has progressed considerably from these early beginnings, benefiting along the way from the views of many other theorists, practitioners, and researchers. Today, consultation maintains a high profile within school, clinical, community, counseling, and organizational psychology, as well as related mental health fields (e.g., social work, psychiatric nursing) and many areas of education (e.g., special education, school counseling). For example, a school psychologist may consult with teachers about effective management strategies in order to prevent classroom disruptions. A clinical psychologist may be contracted initially to conduct psychological testing in a school, but later may be asked to consult with special education teachers who instruct adolescents with impulse control problems. A community psychologist may consult with elected officials about ways to reduce violent crime in the downtown area at night. A counseling psychologist employed at a university counseling center may consult with residence hall advisers to help them identify and assist those students who do not effectively handle the pressures of university life. A special educator may consult with a classroom teacher about how to instruct a student who has a moderate learning disability.

There are many external indicators of the growth and popularity of consultation in the human services. Searching the PsychINFO database (1990–2000) using the word *consultation*, we found 4607 references in a key word search and 1104 references in a title search. Well over 100 books on human services consultation have been published since 1967, including more than 20 since 1990. There are currently three professional journals that focus primarily on aspects of consultation: *Consultation: An International Journal*, *Consulting Psychology Journal: Practice and Research*, and *Journal of Educational and Psychological Consultation*. There are several other journals that routinely publish articles on human services consultation, including *American Journal of Community Psychology*, *Journal of Primary Prevention*, *Journal of School Psychology*, *School Psychology Quarterly*, and *School Psychology Review* (Zins, Kratochwill & Elliott, 1993). With respect to practice issues, school psychologists typically spend about 20% of their time engaged in consultation and report that consultation is one of the most (if not the most) preferred of their service delivery activities (Fagan & Wise, 2000).

This short introduction establishes a context for the rest of this chapter and foreshadows the content of chapters that follow. Other topics examined in Chapter 1 are the efficacy of consultation, historical antecedents of the general human services consultant role and the specific school psychological consultant role, our definition of school consultation and assumptions as authors, and a brief comparison of mental health consultation and collaboration.

THE EFFECTIVENESS OF HUMAN SERVICES CONSULTATION

As helping professionals, we live in an era that increasingly promotes the use of "empirically supported interventions" (Kratochwill & Stoiber,

2000; Stoiber & Kratochwill, 2000). Thus, before investing the required time and energy in learning how to consult, the reader might ask, "Does consultation work?" In other words, is there empirical evidence indicating that positive effects accrue to clients and consultees when a specialist works directly with one or more consultees who in turn work directly with one or more clients? Before providing an answer, it is important to note first that consultation research is difficult to conduct, and regrettably, many studies are flawed, both conceptually and methodologically (Alpert & Yammer, 1983; Fuchs, Fuchs, Dulan, Roberts & Fernstrom, 1992; Gresham & Kendell, 1987; Gresham & Noell, 1993; Pryzwansky, 1986). As just one example, because consultation represents an attempt to benefit a third party (client) through change in a second party (consultee), one often cannot determine whether client change resulted from consultant effort or some other factor instead.

Accepting this less-than-ideal state of consultation outcome studies, however, there is ample evidence indicating that consultation is an effective treatment. Some of this evidence is based on *meta-analysis,* a statistical method for summarizing the effects of a treatment across large numbers of original research studies that investigated the treatment (Smith & Glass, 1977). For each study included in a meta-analysis, the change in performance due to a particular treatment is calculated as the mean of the treatment group minus the mean of the control group divided by the standard deviation of the control group. These *effect size* (ES) *statistics* are then averaged across studies examining a common treatment procedure to indicate the mean effectiveness of that procedure in standard score units. For example, an ES of 1.0 would indicate that the treatment group, on average, outperformed the control group by one standard deviation unit on whatever outcome measure was used (e.g., teacher rating of student, achievement test score). Translating this ES = 1.0 example to percentile ranks, the mean score of the treatment group could have fallen at the 84th percentile and that of the control group, the 50th percentile. A negative ES would indicate that the treatment group scored lower than the control group, whereas a zero ES would indicate there was no group difference.

Medway and Updyke (1985) examined the results of 54 controlled studies of psychological consultation published from 1958 to 1982 that were conducted in schools, clinics, and other organizations. These studies collectively reported 83 consultee outcome measures and 100 client outcome measures. Medway and Updyke's key findings included: (1) the average ES was .55 for consultees and .39 for clients; (2) consultees demonstrated functioning/satisfaction greater than 71% of untreated controls; and (3) clients had outcome measure scores that were more favorable than 66% of their controls.

The effectiveness of consultation is arguably greater when one focuses on results obtained from school consultation research only. For example, Sibley (1986, reported in Gresham & Noell, 1993) found average ESs of .60 for consultees and .91 for clients across 63 studies of school consultation. Adapting meta-analytic procedures for single-case designs, Busse, Kratochwill, and Elliott (1995) reported an average client ES of .95 for 23 cases of teacher consultation. Though not a meta-analysis, Sheridan, Welch, and Orme (1996) completed a comprehensive review of 46 school consultation outcome studies published from 1985 to 1995 and noted that 67% of all reported outcomes were positive, 28% were neutral, and only 5% were negative. Thus, outcome research on consultation published over nearly four decades has consistently documented the efficacy of the approach.

HISTORICAL INFLUENCES ON THE HUMAN SERVICES CONSULTANT ROLE

In order to understand the modern-day context for consultation within psychology and related fields, it is necessary to review some of the historical factors beginning in the 1950s that led to its acceptance and adoption as a significant role for many specialists. Here we present some relevant and intertwined theoretical, professional, and pragmatic considerations.

Theoretical Issues

Thomas Szasz's (1960) conceptualization of psychopathology is often credited with challenging the assumptions of traditional psychological treatment, which was strongly aligned with the medical model (Hersch, 1968). In what Szasz termed the "myth of mental illness," mental illness does not reflect an organic disease entity as much as problems with living that are psychosocial in nature. It is therefore important to assess behavior as normal or abnormal within a social, situational, and moral context rather than only within an individual's psyche. Importantly, this view suggests that normal and abnormal behavior share the same processes of development, maintenance, and change. On a broader level, Szasz's revolutionary outlook demystified psychopathology and the role of the psychiatrist, as well as emphasized the role of social institutions in the development of abnormal behavior.

A second, related issue concerns the rise of sociological and ecological models of abnormal behavior. The medical model, as applied to psychological treatment, began to lose support in the 1950s when sociological research substantiated clear linkages between the occurrence of mental illness and variables such as socioeconomic status, education, nutrition, and dysfunctional social networks. For example, Hollingshead and Redlich (1958) documented that aggressive, rebellious, and psychotic behavior was much more prevalent in the lower socioeconomic classes than middle and upper classes. These developments drew attention to variables outside the traditional individual-centered realm of mental health professionals, and provided credibility to nontraditional intervention programs by allied health professionals.

A third theoretical issue that facilitated the development of the human service consultant role was the rise of behavioral psychology. By the mid-1960s, psychoanalysis had begun to decline and behavior therapy was on the upswing. The behavioral perspective, in contrast to psychodynamic thought, views abnormal behavior as a function of environmental events and emphasizes learning and learning-based therapies. These therapeutic processes are specific, and mental health paraprofessionals (e.g., teachers, parents) can be trained to use many of them. Furthermore, behavioral treatments demonstrate relatively large, positive treatment effects. Very importantly, the emergence of behavioral psychology brought therapy out of the clinic setting, making possible the closer monitoring of treatment implementation and outcome. It also broadened the scope of potential clients and potential change agents (Gutkin & Curtis, 1982; Hersch, 1968; Tharp & Wetzel, 1969).

Professional Issues

There are at least three professional issues relevant to the emergence of the human service consultant role. The first is the problem with the clinical diagnosis of psychopathology, stemming from the early demonstrations that client assignment to specific DSM I and II diagnostic categories was generally unreliable (e.g., Zubin, 1967), and that symptomotology often failed to discriminate among diagnostic categories (e.g., Zigler & Phillips, 1961). Also, because the client's socioeconomic status rather than his or her diagnosis was shown to be the best predictor of type of treatment received (Hollingshead & Redlich, 1958), many began to question the utility of diagnosis by highly trained mental health professionals prior to treatment (Hobbs, 1964).

Second, there was a failure on the part of mental health professionals to specify therapeutic goals and processes. As more therapies became available in the 1960s, it became less clear whether the overriding goal of psychological treatment was to reduce inner stress, cure mental illness, reorganize the patient's personality, remove symptoms, or promote mental health. With respect to therapeutic processes, active treatment components often were not identified or, in the case of behavior therapy and existentialism, polar opposite concepts were advanced as critical for treating mental illness (Hersch, 1968). Confusion for the field and the public ensued, with one result being the greater acceptance of nontraditional forms of therapy, such as encounter groups (Lieberman, Yalom & Miles, 1973).

Third, the lack of demonstrated therapeutic outcomes for psychotherapy (Eysenck, 1952) led some to question its value and, in some cases, pursue other treatment options. One impact of Eysenck's findings, then, was to legitimize other forms of helping relationships, including basic human relations training (Carkhuff, 1969) and mutual help groups (Caplan & Killilea, 1976). Eysenck's classic study also focused psychology's efforts on demonstrating the benefits of psychotherapy, which others later documented (e.g., Smith & Glass, 1977).

Pragmatic Issues

One might specify three pragmatic reasons why the consultant role emerged in psychology and allied fields. First, there was the realization that there were insufficient numbers of trained mental health professionals to implement the medical model on a large scale (Albee, 1959). Even if there had been adequate personnel, there was the concern that psychotherapy as a means of addressing widespread mental health problems was ineffective and inefficient. As Hobbs (1963) stated, "A profession that is built on a fifty-minute hour of a one-to-one relationship between therapist and client ... is living on borrowed time" (p. 3). Complicating this situation was the discovery that the majority of individuals who needed help often failed to contact service providers (Hersch, 1968).

Second, during the 1960s there was a growing awareness of the differential delivery of mental health services among the rich and poor. Sociological research indicated that more serious mental health problems and risk factors were significantly overrepresented in the lower classes, but irrespective of diagnosis, the poor client received a quick treatment such as electric shock and the rich client received extended (and often costly) psychotherapy (Hollingshead & Redlich, 1958). During this time it seemed as though psychotherapy was appropriate only for a circumscribed client population—one that was young, attractive, verbal, intelligent, and successful (YAVIS).

Third, there were demonstrations of the successful use of paraprofessionals in various studies, suggesting that less formally trained individuals could contribute meaningfully to the prevention and treatment of mental disorders. In particular, researchers showed that parents, teachers, and teacher assistants could be trained to modify children's behavior in specific settings (e.g., Cowen et al., 1975; Hobbs, 1966).

The culmination of all the above factors, which illustrate dissatisfaction with the traditional means of delivering mental health services, was a revolution termed the *community mental health movement*. This movement was officially sanctioned in 1963 when President Kennedy signed into law the Community Mental Health Centers Act (P.L. 88-164) and continued until federal funds were reduced or reallocated in the early 1980s. Most importantly for our purposes, P.L. 88-164 specified consultation as one of five essential services that community mental health centers had to provide in order to receive federal monies. This provision gave consultation formal recognition and legitimized the placement of consultants in mental health agencies and schools. The community mental health movement also is acknowledged for its emphasis on: (1) population-oriented prevention (i.e., primary, secondary, and tertiary); (2) social support systems, which can lessen the risk of mental illness through the sharing of tasks and mobilization of resources; and (3) crisis intervention, which establishes a brief timeframe for action (Erchul & Schulte, 1993; Gallessich, 1982; Schulberg & Killilea, 1982).

HISTORICAL INFLUENCES ON THE
SCHOOL CONSULTANT ROLE

Other notable trends occurred within public education and school psychology from the 1940s to the present. These trends have served more directly to increase the need for psychologists and other professionals who consult with school personnel about educational and psychological issues.

Changes in Special Education Service Delivery

In the 1940s and 1950s, children with disabilities generally were excluded from education, as there was no mandate to serve this population. During this era, school psychology was viewed as the attempt to apply concepts and methods from clinical psychology to school adjustment problems. Beginning in the 1960s, state and federal funding became available to support special education programs, and school psychologists assumed the role of diagnostician. The passage of several states' laws that protected the educational rights of children with disabilities led to the authorization in 1975 of P.L. 94-142, the Education for All Handicapped Children Act (re-named the Individuals with Disabilities Education Act [IDEA], P.L. 102-119, in 1990). This law increased the number of children to be served and required multidisciplinary team evaluation procedures as well as a continuum of services to be provided in schools. Although many of these services were of a pull-out variety (where students with disabilities were sent to special classrooms), through its "least restrictive environment" provision, the law did provide the impetus for mainstreaming efforts. *Mainstreaming* refers to the integration of children with disabilities into regular education classes. P.L. 94-142/IDEA broadened the potential role of school psychologists to include consultation, but at the same time institutionalized the school psychologist's primary role as "gatekeeper" for special education. (Fagan & Wise, 2000; Reynolds, Gutkin, Elliott & Witt, 1984). The 1997 amendments to IDEA (P.L. 105-17; IDEA 97) suggest an expanded role for school psychologists relative to consultation (e.g., Hoff & Zirkel, 1999), a topic we return to in Chapters 6, 8, and 10.

Many changes were observed in public education in the 1980s. Perhaps as a result of state and federal cuts in the education budget, there emerged a greater focus on teacher accountability and a major rethinking of national educational goals, with a decided emphasis on outcomes. Within special education, there was rapid growth evidenced in mildly handicapped populations, particularly the specific learning disability category. Responses to this trend included increased mainstreaming efforts and the *Regular Education Initiative* (REI), a movement whose adherents believe that most mildly disabled students can and should receive instruction in the regular classroom. It should be clear that mainstreaming and REI emphasize the provision of consultative support to regular education teachers (Lloyd, Singh & Repp, 1991; Reschly, Tilly & Grimes, 1999).

Now, in the early 2000s, other relevant developments in U.S. public education are apparent. There is increased concern over school violence and discipline problems, a greater appreciation for cultural differences in schools, and a renewed interest in improving home-school relationships. The debate continues over how to serve students with disabilities most effectively. Advocates of *zero reject* models of inclusion argue that students with disabilities cannot be excluded from a free, appropriate public education, and others believe that original pull-out programs remain the best option. There has been a movement away from hierarchical skill development, as in the case of whole language instruction wherein creative writing assignments supplant phonics and grammar instruction. Another trend is seen in the realm of student assessment, where emphasis has been placed on more direct forms of assessment rather than on multiple-choice standardized tests. Authentic or portfolio assessment, for example, typically involves careful examination of student work samples, exhibits, or products to determine whether specified performance skills have been mastered (Christenson & Sheridan, 2001; Furlong, Morrison & Pavelski, 2000; Gelzheiser, Meyers & Prusek, 1992; Gopaul-McNicol, 1992). These and other emerging issues strongly suggest there will be a need for school-based consultants for years to come.

Problems with the Gatekeeper Role in School Psychology

As noted earlier, P.L. 94-142/IDEA is credited with establishing the school psychologist's primary role as gatekeeper for special education. Although this role has provided a secure funding base and clear responsibilities to children with disabilities, it also has made individual child assessment the primary professional activity for many school psychologists, thereby reducing involvement in intervention and prevention activities (Tindall, 1979). Dissatisfaction with the gatekeeper role, and the unworkability of the system of psychological service delivery that results from it, has the field of school psychology looking for other options, including increased consultation with school personnel (Reschly, 1988).

There are numerous problems associated with the school psychologist's service as gatekeeper. Practical and logistical issues include increased caseloads and backlogs of outstanding assessments; lengthy delays for receipt of services; the likelihood of students in need of services deemed ineligible for them; and the high cost of evaluation-placement relative to other available services, such as the Title I reading program. There is also the realization that commonly used standardized tests have poor psychometric properties, and the results obtained from them are often of little use in making programming decisions and monitoring student progress. Within the ranks of school psychologists, there is dissatisfaction over the reality that most are trained broadly but used narrowly. With the effectiveness of special education placements being questioned, it is understandable that organizations such as the National Association of School Psychologists have pressed for an expanded role for school psychologists. Much more positively, there is a growing body of research demonstrating the manipulable influences on academic achievement and the educational applications of behavior analysis and intervention. This type of research certainly holds promise for the greater involvement of psychologists in school consultation (Fagan & Wise, 2000; Martens, Witt, Daly & Vollmer, 1999; Reschly, 1988; Reynolds et al., 1984).

RECONCEPTUALIZING CONSULTATION FOR TODAY'S SCHOOLS

Historical Summary

Some of the more critical developments distilled from our historical review are presented in the following 10 points:

1. Over time, there has been a greater emphasis placed on social and situational determinants of behavior.
2. There is often no clear connection between assessment and treatment, suggesting that formal diagnosis and classification are unnecessary for effective treatment.
3. There has been a growing reliance on therapeutic methods other than traditional psychotherapy.
4. Human services have been delivered increasingly in naturalistic settings rather than clinic settings.
5. Direct care providers, rather than highly trained specialists, increasingly have been viewed as primary change agents.
6. The aims of population-oriented prevention can be served well through the provision of social support.
7. Crisis intervention has shown that effective psychological services can be delivered within a short time frame.
8. Experience with IDEA's multidisciplinary team approach has suggested a clear benefit to sharing expertise and information among professionals representing different specialties.
9. The specification of treatment goals, procedures, and outcomes has become increasingly important as accountability for services looms larger in education and psychology.
10. Within school psychology, many commonly used standardized assessment tools have been shown to lack adequate psychometric properties, and thus are of little value in deciding on programming options and in monitoring client progress.

Our Definition of School Consultation

These 10 points constitute a strong rationale for the delivery of psychological and educational services in schools via a consultation approach. As a step toward operationalizing this approach, we offer the following definition:

> School consultation is a process for providing psychological and educational services in which a specialist (consultant) works cooperatively with a staff member (consultee) to improve the learning and adjustment

of a student (client) or group of students. During face-to-face interactions, the consultant helps the consultee through systematic problem solving, social influence, and professional support. In turn, the consultee helps the client(s) through selecting and implementing effective school-based interventions. In all cases, school consultation serves a remedial function and has the potential to serve a preventive function.

Assumptions of Our Approach to School Consultation

The approach to consulting in schools presented in this book draws on our experiences as practicing consultants and researchers of processes and outcomes associated with psychological consultation. In presenting this approach, we wish to alert readers to our biases:

1. We promote a scientist-practitioner viewpoint by providing guidance for consultative practice whenever possible that is based on research findings rather than conjecture. As the title of the book implies, we believe our approach is based on solid conceptual ground and, where possible, relevant empirical findings.

2. We view successful school consultation as involving a combination of social influence and professional support within a problem-solving context. We refer to the resulting approach as an "integrated model of school consultation." What is specifically integrated in the model are two theoretically distinct approaches to consultation (i.e., Caplan's mental health consultation [1970; Caplan & Caplan, 1993/1999] and Bergan's behavioral consultation [1977; Bergan & Kratochwill, 1990]), as well as two general approaches to consultative practice (i.e., social influence and professional support) regarded by some as mutually exclusive concepts.

3. We believe that our approach is most appropriate for use by external consultants. An *external* consultant is often defined as one who spends most of his or her time at a site other than the one that is the setting for consultation, although how consultees view the consultant frequently is a key factor as well (Brown, Pryzwansky & Schulte, 2001). A clinical psychologist, for example, may spend two afternoons each week consulting in schools but is physically housed the rest of the time in a mental health center and thus may be regarded as an external consultant. School psychologists often are difficult to characterize as internal or external consultants because they are more appropriately placed on an internal-external continuum (Alpert & Silverstein, 1985). For example, one school psychologist may be assigned full time to a single school (internal); another may consult only two days each month with a particular school but has done so for 18 years, so is considered a regular staff member (external and internal). A third school psychologist may have considerable administrative responsibilities but consults occasionally with teachers at

an elementary school. Because teachers perceive her as a central office staff member, she is perhaps most accurately considered an external consultant.

Our approach to consultation fits best with external consultants because internal consultants are generally better served by methods of *collaboration* (see, for example, Caplan & Caplan, 1993/2001; Friend & Cook, 1992; Pryzwansky, 1974, 1977). This issue is explored later in this chapter.

4. We believe the elements of Caplan's mental health consultation approach are useful for understanding relationship and system-level issues within consultation. Many others (e.g., Brown et al., 2001; Davis & Sandoval, 1992; Heller & Monahan, 1977; Marks, 1995; Meyers, Parsons & Martin, 1979) have offered similar endorsements.

5. Because of their documented effectiveness, we believe psychological interventions employing behavior analytic principles are well suited for use by professionals in school settings. Our view, developed more fully in Chapter 6, is shared by others writing about school consultation, including Bergan (1977), Bergan and Kratochwill (1990), Sugai and Tindal (1993), and Vernberg and Reppucci (1986).

Topics Not Addressed in Our Approach to School Consultation

The integrated model put forth in this book will prove useful to school consultants when applied to many situations, but does not claim to be equally useful to all. Important applications not addressed in this book include the following:

1. The approach is not an organization development model, although it assumes a basic understanding of the school as an organization. For example, in Chapter 3 we describe the school and its importance as a setting for consultation, but we do not offer guidance on how the consultant can then engage in typical organization development activities such as survey feedback and team-building.

2. Although we apply an ecological framework to understanding the classroom and school as systems, we do not apply this framework to understand the family as a system, despite its clear importance to the overall effort of school consultation. Others who offer this valuable perspective include Christenson and Conoley (1992), Christenson and Sheridan (2001), and Sheridan, Kratochwill, and Bergan (1996).

3. It is not our intention to provide comprehensive coverage of any single consultation model, as other authors have in comparable books (see, for example, Brown et al., 2001; Dougherty, 2000; Gallessich, 1982). As noted previously, we emphasize and draw on major elements of two well-established models, Caplan's mental health consultation and Bergan's behavioral consultation.

4. Although we recognize the significance of multicultural and cross-cultural factors in school consultation (e.g., Ingraham, 2000; Ramirez, Lepage, et al., 1998), we do not explicitly incorporate these factors into our integrated model because the underlying research base currently is too underdeveloped to inform consulting practices from a scientist-practitioner viewpoint.

5. We do not provide an introduction to the basic interviewing and supportive communication skills considered prerequisite to any helping relationship but focus instead on more advanced skills involving problem solving and social influence. Helpful references with regard to mastering these core skills include Dillard and Reilly (1988), Egan (1994), and Goldstein and Higginbotham (1991).

CONSULTATION VERSUS COLLABORATION

Before ending this chapter, we pose a critical question: Should you "consult" or "collaborate"? Due to the evolution of the consulting role, the answer is not as straightforward as one might think, and, in fact, has generated considerable debate (Erchul, 1999; Gutkin, 1999a, 1999b).

The original idea of the mental health consultant was of a clinically trained professional whose home base was outside the consultee's work setting (cf. Caplan, 1970). As the practice of consultation grew, however, mental health consultants were being hired more often as regular staff members of organizations such as schools and hospitals. With the rise of this internal consultant role came challenges to some time-honored beliefs regarding consultation, including most of those mentioned at the beginning of this chapter in relation to Caplan's approach.

Several examples illustrate these challenges. First, a school psychologist working as an internal consultant may find it difficult to serve non-hierarchically in a school when he or she possesses more knowledge about learning, instruction, and behavior management than some teacher-consultees. In addition, an internal consultant may see it as unacceptable for a consultee to reject an expert viewpoint about a situation when the consultant shares responsibility for the outcome, and when the two are under pressure to bring about change in a difficult-to-manage client or program. Because of institutional realities and the clear need to share relevant information among interested parties, strict confidentiality of communications often cannot be observed when a consultant is internal. Finally, organizational factors often force an internal consultant to adopt a "hands-on" direct action approach rather than a facilitative, advisory approach. Recognition of these constraints of the internal consultant's role has led to the development of a different mode of interprofessional communication termed *mental health collaboration* (Caplan & Caplan, 1993/1999; Caplan, Caplan & Erchul, 1994, 1995). Table 1.1 summarizes the key distinctions between mental health consultation and collaboration. We readily acknowledge that this definition of collaboration may differ from others reported in the literature (e.g., Welch & Tulbert, 2000).

Table 1.1. **Mental Health Consultation and Mental Health Collaboration Contrasted on Key Dimensions**

Dimension	Mental health consultation	Mental health collaboration
Location of consultant's home base	External to the organization	Internal to the organization
Type of psychological service	Generally indirect, with little or no client contact	Combines indirect and direct services, and includes client contact
Consultant–consultee relationship	Assumes a coordinate and nonhierarchical relationship	Acknowledges status and role differences within the organization, and thus the likelihood of a hierarchical relationship
Consultee participation	Assumes voluntary participation	Assumes voluntary participation, but acknowledges the possibility of forced participation
Interpersonal working arrangement	Often dyadic, involving consultant and consultee	Generally team-based, involving several collaborators
Confidentiality of communications within relationship	Assumes confidentiality to exist, with limits of confidentiality (if any) specified during initial contracting	Does not automatically assume confidentiality, given organizational realities and pragmatic need to share relevant information among team members
Consultee freedom to accept or reject consultant advice	Yes	Not assumed to be true, as a collaborator's expertise in his or her specialty area is generally deferred to by team
Consultant responsibility for case/program outcome	No	Shares equal responsibility for overall outcome, and primary responsibility for mental health aspects of case or program

The point of this brief discussion is that the true internal consultant may profit more from using methods of mental health collaboration than consultation. In fact, Caplan (1993a) has forcefully asserted that mental health collaboration eventually must replace mental health consultation as the most frequent mode of interprofessional communication used by mental health specialists who are staff members of an organization. Until that time, however, we believe that internal consultants can benefit greatly from the integrated model of consultation presented in this book.

THE REST OF THE BOOK

A major purpose of this book is to reduce the level of naiveté typically experienced by the beginning school consultant. Toward that end, we attempt to provide a systematic approach to consultation that emphasizes the information necessary for one to practice competently as a school consultant.

The book is divided into three sections. The first section is comprised of three chapters that describe important background information, including how one can produce change employing social influence (Chapter 2) and what it takes to understand the school as a setting for consultation (Chapter 3). The second section, consisting of Chapters 4 to 6, explains significant processes and outcomes of school consultation. Chapters 4 and 5 focus on the integrated model of consultation, emphasizing the elements of professional support, problem solving, social influence, and the organizational context. Recognizing that a mutually respectful relationship between professionals is a necessary but not sufficient condition for effective school consultation, Chapter 6 provides guidance on how to select interventions and how to evaluate their effectiveness relative to treatment outcome, integrity, and social validity.

The third section includes Chapters 7 to 9. Key participants in school consultation, teachers and students, are the focus of Chapters 7 and 8, respectively. Chapter 9 offers a three-session school consultation case study and includes a frank, retrospective analysis of the directions taken by the consultant during each interview. An epilogue chapter, summarizing important points and looking toward the future practice of school consultation, concludes the volume.

The role of school consultant has been characterized as that of change agent (Conoley, 1981b). To realize this role fully, the consultant must understand how to accomplish change through the application of social power and interpersonal influence, and this is the focus as we proceed to Chapter 2.

2

Promoting Change in Schools

The central purpose of this chapter is to demonstrate that a primary role of the consultant is to serve as a change agent in the school. By "change," we are referring to the purposeful alteration of beliefs, attitudes, and/or behaviors of children, adolescents, and adults who are part of the school setting. Given our definition of consultation presented in Chapter 1, the psychologist acts in a direct, face-to-face manner to change the beliefs, attitudes, or behaviors of the adults who are consultees. In turn, consultees work with students, intervening directly in classroom-based problems. To serve as an effective change agent, the consultant needs to understand issues of social power and interpersonal influence and how both relate to the consultant/consultee relationship.

We begin by offering a rationale for why it is important to focus on consultee change in consultation. Next, the unique nature of the psychologist-teacher consultative relationship is examined, and issues surrounding social influence in consultation are explored. We then present three frameworks for understanding and promoting change: (1) Chin and Benne's (1969) general strategies for effecting change in human systems; (2) J. R. P. French and Raven's (1959; Raven, 1965) bases of social power model; and (3) Raven's (1992, 1993) power-interaction model of interpersonal influence. Elements of these frameworks are applied throughout the chapter to the practice of school consultation.

CHANGING BELIEFS, ATTITUDES, AND BEHAVIORS
WITHIN CONSULTATION

The Need for Consultee Change

The phrase, "psychological services in schools," historically has meant delivering direct clinical services to children and adolescents, including psychological assessment, counseling, and psychotherapy (Fagan & Wise, 2000; Reynolds, Gutkin, Elliott & Witt, 1984). However, a more recent theme in the school psychology literature is that the provision of comprehensive school psychological services depends on the psychologist's ability to offer indirect services to adult caregivers (Conoley & Gutkin, 1986; Gutkin & Conoley, 1990). The term *indirect services* refers to psychological services in which a party other than the psychologist is the primary intervention agent providing treatment directly to clients. Examples include consultation, pre-referral intervention, inservice training, program evaluation, and research. Conoley and Gutkin have noted that the increasing viability of indirect services is due to several well-documented factors, including:

1. There are not enough fully trained professionals to offer direct therapeutic treatment to those clients who need it.
2. Lesser trained individuals, who are often readily available and less expensive to hire, can offer quality direct services to clients if given appropriate training, support, and supervision.
3. Indirect psychological services, when implemented well, can create ripple effects that may include nonprofessional or paraprofessional staff learning new skills and passing them along to others, as well as the generalization and successful application of these new skills to novel problems they will encounter in the future.

So how can the effective provision of indirect psychological services be facilitated? According to Conoley and Gutkin (1986), the successful delivery of indirect services "depend[s] to a large extent on psychologists' abilities to influence the behavior of third-party adults" (p. 403).[1] Along these lines, we contend that *influence is necessary in school consultation in order to increase the probability that teachers will function effectively as intervention agents, and engage in activities that potentially lead to the prevention of student academic failure and mental illness.*

With respect to teachers serving as effective intervention agents in their classrooms, consider some common explanations for why they may *fail* as intervention agents:

1. They may lack essential skills, such as how to observe students systematically or how to implement effective intervention strategies.

Even if teachers possess adequate skills, they may not display them for a variety of reasons.

2. They may hold unrealistic beliefs about children with special needs, such as believing that a child with a diagnosis of attention-deficit/hyperactivity disorder will never learn to read, or a student with a learning disability will not show significant academic gains until the child's home environment improves. Caplan (1970) referred to these stereotypical, self-fulfilling prophecies as "themes."

3. They may harbor unusual attitudes toward support specialists, such as what these specialists can achieve with students with disabilities in special educational placements is "magical" and simply cannot be replicated in their own classrooms (Martens, 1993b).

Thus, to address skill and performance deficits and to alter misguided beliefs and attitudes such as those listed, one can see how critical it is for consultants not only to understand interpersonal influence but also to possess the skills needed to implement influence strategies.

With respect to teachers playing a role in preventing student educational failure and promoting mental health, much of the same logic applies. For example, adoption of a classroom-based primary prevention approach (i.e., activities aimed at preventing the emergence of educational and psychological problems in all class members) may require an alteration of a teacher's perception of the value of prevention and the corresponding activities needed to achieve it. Similarly, a teacher would not be expected to effectively implement a secondary prevention approach (i.e., early detection and treatment of problems in at-risk students) unless properly trained to carefully observe student behavior. We shall return to the topic of prevention in Chapter 4; at this juncture, however, the message should be clear that effective school-based intervention and prevention activities rarely occur solely on the basis of teachers having the proper information. Rather, the exercise of influence is needed in order to achieve change.[2]

The Myth of Collaboration in Consultation

But what about "helping"? Aren't school consultants expected to assist, and even "empower," teachers instead of influence them? Shouldn't we always "collaborate" when we consult? These questions, all reasonable ones, may be summed up as, "Should the consultant control the process of consultation?" (Erchul, 1999). The somewhat surprising answer is that research shows teachers are satisfied, and indicate that they have been helped, when consultants have used verbal strategies associated with the exercise of influence to control the direction of consultation interviews.

Moreover, there is evidence that some positive effects of consultation appear to diminish when *consultees* have attempted to control the process. Other research indicates that students produce academic and behavioral gains when consultants use a prescriptive approach to school consultation. Below we present a sampling of this research.

Three studies of school-based behavioral consultation conducted by Erchul and his colleagues (Erchul, 1987; Erchul & Chewning, 1990; Witt, Erchul, McKee, Pardue & Wickstrom, 1991) demonstrated the value of the consultant's active direction of interviews. All three investigations utilized a relational communication framework, which examines how the *process* of communication occurs (e.g., through talkovers, topic changes/other's acceptance of topic changes, requests/other's compliance with requests) rather than through the actual words that are spoken. Although these studies used different relational communication coding systems, all employed methodologies that included the verbatim transcription of consultation interviews followed by the application of a particular coding scheme.

Erchul (1987) used a modified version of the Rogers and Farace (1975) coding system to study eight school consultants who worked with one consultee each across the three behavioral consultation interviews (Kratochwill & Bergan, 1990). The two key variables studied were domineeringness and dominance. *Domineeringness* is defined as the number of Person A's one-up (i.e., controlling) messages divided by the total number of A's messages. *Dominance* for A is defined as the proportion of one-down messages (i.e., acceptance of the other's control) by Person B to all one-up messages offered by A. Regrettably, it is beyond the scope of this chapter to explain the details of this and the other relational communication coding systems; suffice it to say that the assignment of one-up and one-down control codes to individual messages is based on other investigators' systematic study of interpersonal communication processes.

Three interesting findings emerged from Erchul (1987). First, consultants controlled the process of consultation across all three interviews, a finding that challenges earlier held beliefs that the relationship is supposed to be collaborative and nonhierarchical. This result led Witt (1990) subsequently to label the notion of school consultation as a collaborative enterprise as a "myth." Second, consultant dominance scores correlated .65 with consultee perceptions of consultant effectiveness, suggesting that more directive consultants were viewed more favorably by consultees. Third, consultee domineeringness scores correlated .81 with consultant perceptions of the extent to which consultees followed through with the collection of baseline (i.e., preintervention) data collection on clients. This result implies that consultee attempts to control interview direction are associated with lower consultant evaluations of consultee participation in baseline data collection.

Erchul and Chewning (1990) continued this line of research by studying 10 consultant–consultee dyads engaged in behavioral consultation. The coding system used was that of Folger and Puck (1976), which considers only requests or "bids" and responses to them. As applied to school consultation, requests typically are categorized as either dominant, dominant-affiliative, or submissive (listed from most to least controlling) and responses are categorized as accepted, rejected, or evaded. These researchers found two major results pertinent to the present discussion. First, consultants' initiation of requests outnumbered that of consultees by a ratio of more than 6 : 1 (93.5 vs. 15) and nearly all (94.6%) of consultee responses were acceptances of consultant requests. Second, all but one correlation between types of consultee requests during the first interview and consultation outcomes were negative (mean $r = .40$). This finding suggests that consultee attempts to control the process of school-based behavioral consultation are generally associated with adverse results, including perceptions of lower levels of consultant effectiveness, consultee participation in baseline data collection, and consultee participation in treatment plan implementation.

In a third study, Witt et al. (1991) explored whether consultants and consultees had equal control over determining topics for discussion across the three behavioral consultation interviews. The coding system used was that of Tracey and Ray (1984), which specifies four variables associated with topic changes: topic initiation, topic following, topic determination, and topic continuation. Of central importance to understanding this study is *topic determination*—the extent to which one is successful in changing topics of conversation, thereby providing a measure of interpersonal control in a relationship. Witt et al. found two interesting results: First, consultants successfully executed topic changes 78% of the time, compared to consultees who initiated topic changes successfully only 58% of the time, thus suggesting that interpersonal control is not equal for the two parties within school consultation. Second, whereas consultant topic determination generally was associated with positive outcomes of consultation, consultee topic determination generally was associated with negative outcomes.

In a different line of research altogether, Fuchs, Fuchs, Bahr, Fernstrom, and Stecker (1990) showed that forms of behavioral consultation in which the consultant is directive or "prescriptive" can facilitate effective classroom interventions for students having problems such as inattention, low motivation, or poorly developed academic skills. These researchers compared the effects of three levels of behavioral consultation, involving students and teachers representing grades 5, 6, and 7. All three levels of consultation included a standardized intervention package so that teachers could use a consistent strategy to address specific student behaviors. The lowest level of consultation services consisted of the first two stages of behavioral consultation (problem identification and problem analysis) but did not offer assistance in implementing or assessing the effects of the intervention. The intermediate level of consultation services offered all elements of the lowest level and added consultant visits to the classroom in order to facilitate the implementation of the treatment. The highest level of consultation services included all aspects of the intermediate level and added a component in which the consultant conducted a formative evaluation to modify the treatment if needed.

Fuchs et al.'s results indicated that the intermediate and highest levels of consultation (i.e., the more prescriptive versions) resulted in greater improvements in students' problem behaviors. Specifically, with greater consultant involvement and control over the process, (1) student behavior improved significantly relative to an untreated control group, and (2) postintervention independent observation of student behavior revealed significant decreases in the discrepancy between target student and normal peer behavior. They concluded that a prescriptive approach to consultation is highly recommended for use in schools where "stress is high, expertise in consultation is low, and consultation time is nonexistent" (p. 511). Our experience suggests that this description applies to many schools in which psychological consultation occurs.

These four investigations collectively suggest the value of the school consultant engaging in "strategic interpersonal communication" (Daly & Wiemann, 1994) and "dyadic social influence" (Barry & Watson, 1996) to direct the course of interviews and the overall process of consultation. Although alternative interpretations of these studies are possible (Gutkin, 1999a), the importance of social influence to the practice of school consultation is well-established (e.g., Gutkin, 1999b; Hughes, 1992; O'Keefe & Medway, 1997). We shall present social influence strategies and tactics consistent with our integrated model of consultation in Chapters 4, 5, and 9.

To avoid misunderstanding, we wish to clarify two points before proceeding. First, it is the process and not the content per se that is important for the consultant to control. We are not suggesting that consultants should ignore or fail to listen attentively to what consultees say; instead, consultants are to establish an interview framework in which consultees are free to respond to and elaborate on issues of mutual concern. Second, although there is value in the consultant structuring the interview format, we are not implying that the consultant frequently "tells the consultee what to do," as some have interpreted this line of research to suggest (see, for example, Henning-Stout, 1993). Crises certainly will present themselves in schools, prompting the consultant to act in a highly directive manner. However, that is neither the predominant type of school consultation studied by these researchers nor the general approach to consultation we advocate. In reality, very few school consultant messages are orders or instructions; instead, most are assertions and questions that offer support, extend previous discussion, or initiate new topics (Erchul, 1987).

The Cooperative Consultative Relationship

Although we acknowledge the importance of interpersonal flexibility and responsiveness when working with various types of consultees and situations (cf. Hughes, Erchul, Yoon, Jackson & Henington, 1997), we believe that for much school consultation, available research supports the development of a working relationship that is best characterized as "cooperative." In promoting a cooperative relationship, we first note the need for the school consultant to develop facilitative, respectful partnerships with consultees, who must feel it is safe to discuss problems arising in their professional roles. Second, once a common understanding of trust and mutual respect has been established, it is critical for the consultant to direct the process of consultation using his or her knowledge of social influence, the problem-solving process, and continued professional support. A growing behavioral consultation research base reviewed earlier suggests that the most favorable consultation outcomes occur when the consultee follows the lead of the consultant; thus, it is essential that consultees actively participate in consultation via the interview structure put in place by the consultant.

The Egalitarian Virus

Another helpful vantage point from which to view the cooperative consultative relationship is the egalitarian virus (Barone, 1995). In explaining his failure to challenge a teacher's claim that "peanut butter cures attention-deficit hyperactivity disorder" (p. 35), school psychologist Stephen Barone proposed that a disease he termed the *egalitarian virus* paralyzes otherwise competent professionals, causing them to wither in the face of strong but perhaps uninformed opinions. According to Barone, unrealistic ideas regarding the display of expertise permeate the schools today. These ideas include the belief that the specialized expertise of each staff member is directly interchangeable with that of any other, and that any person's opinion should be afforded *equal* rather than *due* consideration. The implication for school consultants who wish to maintain a cooperative relationship is to act as content experts when necessary and not downplay their specialized knowledge but, at the same time, attempt to understand and respect the consultees' unique strengths and weaknesses.

Professional Dissonance Regarding the Use of Power and Influence

We realize our view of the role of power and influence within school consultation may not be universally shared (cf. Erchul, 1992a; Gutkin, 1999a). Although some may claim that the school consultant–consultee relationship must be an "equal" one, it has been argued forcefully elsewhere that practical and organizational constraints inherent in schools typically preclude this ideal (e.g., Harris & Cancelli, 1991). Also, those who promote the value of equality within consultation may erroneously consider "equal" to mean "the same as," when the reality is that consultant and consultee have different levels of need, information, and skills, and thus different roles to perform within consultation (Zins & Erchul, 2002).

Perhaps the main reason human service consultants feel uneasy when adopting a social power perspective is that it is unrelated, and perhaps antithetical, to their professional training (Martin, 1978). To this we would add that the use of power and influence often raises difficult ethical questions for the consultant (Erchul, 1992b; Hughes, 1986; Hughes & Falk, 1981). Consider these examples: Is the consultee being "deceived" or "manipulated" when the consultant uses power and influence for the good of the client? Is the consultee's autonomy as a professional inappropriately restricted when the consultant uses influence strategies? Can the consultant's exercise of influence negatively affect important outcomes for the consultee or client? These are difficult questions for a consultant to answer, just as they are for a psychotherapist, trainer, supervisor, or teacher (e.g., Friedrich & Douglass, 1998) who uses a power–influence framework to guide his or her professional actions.

The crux of the matter is that any strategy that is effective in changing behavior can be used unethically. When a consultant uses influence strategies to alter behavior, it should be clear that these strategies must be used in a responsible and ethical manner (Kipnis, 1994). As practicing consultants, we have found it helpful to measure the responsibility of our professional actions within an *empowerment philosophy* (Rappaport, 1981; Witt & Martens, 1988). A philosophy of empowerment, as applied to consultation, relates to the belief that consultees already possess many basic strengths and eventually will solve their own problems if the consultant helps them develop those strengths by alerting consultees to existing resources and how they may be used (Dunst & Trivette, 1987). In other words, the consultant uses his or her power and influence to make consultees more powerful and influential. Within school consultation, the point has been made that frequently the consultant is attempting to solve a teacher's problem in influencing students (Erchul & Raven, 1997). In our view, making consultees more powerful and influential is a very responsible and ethical goal within the practice of consultation.

GENERAL STRATEGIES FOR EFFECTING CHANGES IN HUMAN SYSTEMS

Having established a rationale for why achieving change is important within consultation, and why the exercise of interpersonal influence is necessary to achieve this change, we step back to examine issues of change more generally. One often referenced perspective on change in human systems is that of Chin and Benne (1969). They examined philosophical views present throughout history that have undergirded numerous theories of influence and then proposed a three-part typology that captures the essence of those theories. Chin and Benne termed their resulting approaches *empirical–rational*, *normative–reeducative*, and *power–coercive*. The critical difference among the approaches is the motivation the influencing *agent* attributes to the *target* of the influence attempt.

Empirical–Rational Approach

The underlying philosophy of *empirical–rational* approaches is that people are essentially rational and will change their behavior when the change is justifiable to them on an intellectual level. In other words, if a person thinks that it is logical and important to change, he or she will do so if given the proper information. It is only ignorance and superstition that act to prevent behavior change from occurring (Chin & Benne, 1969). A consultant who uses empirical-rational approaches typically disseminates information and techniques to consultees, thus reinforcing Sir Francis Bacon's view that "knowledge is power."

Normative–Reeducative Approach

Normative–reeducative approaches assume that people are active organisms who depend on new knowledge as well as a variety of noncognitive, sociocultural determinants to arrive at a decision of whether to change. When using these approaches, therefore, the influencing agent tries to change the target's attitudes, values, and feelings at a personal level, and norms and significant relationships at the social level (Chin & Benne, 1969). For example, a consultant might rely on a facilitative consultative relationship to persuade a teacher to change a current ineffective instructional practice, or attempt to make the teacher more aware of values and norms present in the school that could affect his or her decision to adopt a new course of action. Importantly, a consultant who subscribes to these approaches believes that, in most cases, the consultee has much of the required information; the focus is on helping the consultee utilize these resources more effectively. In summary, the normative–reeducative view incorporates the empirical–rational view and adds to it a distinctively social element, thereby recognizing the importance of "knowledge *and people* as power."

Power–Coercive Approach

Although empirical–rational and normative–reeducative approaches deal with the role of power in influencing others, both types reject the notion of power as coercive and nonreciprocal. In contrast, *power–coercive* approaches generally assume that the target will change when presented with sanctions that are political or economic in nature, or when made to feel guilty or shameful for not changing. The influencing agent may take these steps when it is apparent the target believes that it is not in his or her best interests to change. Although power–coercive approaches have been associated with tyrannical leaders of the past, it is also important to note that they have formed the basis of nonviolent strategies for change such as those advocated by Henry David Thoreau, Mahatma Gandhi, and Martin Luther King, Jr. (Chin & Benne, 1969). Unless clearly serving as an advocate for a disenfranchised group (see, for example, Conoley, 1981a), a school consultant who uses power–coercive strategies will be more subtle. For instance, when a consultant informs a consultee that his or her presence in the school has been fully authorized by the principal, the consultee may interpret this message to mean that whatever guidance the consultant offers must be followed or else trouble will result.

Relevance of Chin and Benne's Strategies for the Consultant

The school consultant's job would be extremely easy if a consultee needed only the proper information in order to act on and resolve a work-related problem. Although simple, straightforward problems may be solved using only an empirical–rational approach, in our experience the problems brought to a school consultant are rarely this simple or straightforward. Having the "proper information" is helpful only to a point; often it must be augmented with other elements such as the provision of professional support, guidance, skill building, and feedback, as well as the application of influence in order to accomplish change. For this reason, we regard the exclusive use of, and overreliance on, empirical–rational change strategies in consultation as shortsighted and naive.

Instead, the skillful integration of all three approaches to effect change appears to underlie the successful practice of school consultation. How the consultant integrates these types of strategies, however, is not well established. Although an empirical basis for their application to consultation has been slow to develop, French and Raven's (1959; Raven, 1965) bases of social power model and Raven's (1992, 1993) power–interaction model of interpersonal influence do offer useful conceptual perspectives through which to view issues of influence in school consultation.

THE BASES OF SOCIAL POWER AND THEIR APPLICATION TO SCHOOL CONSULTATION[3]

An Introduction to Social Power Bases

According to Mintzberg (1983), the best known framework for examining social power is the typology of social power bases developed originally by J. R. P. French and Raven (1959) and later expanded by Raven (1965). Social influence is defined as a change in the belief, attitude, or behavior of a target of influence, which results from the action or presence of an influencing agent. Social power is the potential for this influence to occur. French and Raven's model contains six bases of power that the influencing agent (Person A) can utilize in changing the beliefs, attitudes, or behaviors of a target (Person B).

1. *Coercive power* is based on Person B's perception that Person A can punish B if B does not comply.
2. *Reward power* is based on B's perception that A can reward B if B complies.
3. *Legitimate power* is based on B's obligation to accept A's influence attempt because B believes A has a legitimate right to influence, perhaps because of A's professional role or position.
4. *Expert power* is based on B's perception that A possesses knowledge or expertise in a specific area of interest to B.
5. *Referent power* is A's potential to influence B based on B's identification with A and/or desire for such identification.

6. *Informational power* (Raven, 1965) is A's potential to influence B because of the judged relevance of the information contained in A's message. Informational power is attributed to A by A providing B with a logical explanation or new information favoring change.

Expert power and informational power are similar and can be rather easily confused. In both types, B thinks, "I will do as A suggests because that is the best way to address this problem." The critical distinction, however, is that with expert power, B thinks, "I don't really understand exactly why, but A really knows this area so A must be right"; with informational power, B thinks, "I listened carefully to A and see for myself that this is clearly the best way to address this problem."

J. R. P. French and Raven (1959; Raven, 1965) further suggested that, as compared to the other bases of social power, the changed behavior stemming from informational power can be maintained without continued social dependence upon the influencing agent. B essentially has internalized the new behavior and will continue in that manner even if B were to forget that the impetus for the change came originally from A. For the five other bases of power, the changed behavior is socially dependent upon the influencing agent (e.g., "I am doing this differently because A *has told me* to do it this way"). The form of social dependence will differ according to the power base used: "...and I feel obligated to do as A requests" (legitimate), "...A knows what is best for me" (expert), "...A has experience similar to mine, so we should see eye-to-eye on this issue" (referent), "...A will punish me if I don't do it this way" (coercive), and "A will do something nice to me if I do as A asks" (reward). For reward and coercive power, there is an additional distinction. In order for these bases of power to operate, B must believe that A is able to observe whether B has complied or not. Thus, for these two bases of power, A's surveillance of B is essential.

An initial attempt to apply J. R. P. French and Raven's social power model to the practice of school consultation was made by Martin (1978). He proposed that only expert and referent power constitute bases for a consultant's influence over a teacher-consultee. Because social psychological research has indicated that expert power tends to be highly restricted in range (i.e., only a small number of areas of expertise are usually attributed to any one person), Martin advised consultants to develop advanced knowledge of a limited number of topics, and to try to confine their consultation to these areas of "true" expertise. Because other research demonstrated that referent power has a wide range (i.e., one who has accrued referent power can potentially influence the beliefs, attitudes, and behaviors of another across many aspects of daily life), Martin suggested that consultants should develop this form of power by spending time with consultees in a variety of settings and activities in order to enhance their professional work relationship.

The main reason Martin (1978) dismissed coercive, reward, and legitimate power as irrelevant to the psychologist-teacher consultative relationship is that these types of power are associated with supervisory, hierarchical relationships. Because the psychologist hired by the school system typically occupies a staff position rather than a line authority position, these three types of power are simply irrelevant. It should be noted that Martin's analysis did not consider informational power, which J. R. P. French and Raven (1959) mentioned as a type of influence, but not a power base. Erchul and Raven (1997) have proposed an alternate view: given the further development of French and Raven's original social power model, various forms of coercive, reward, and legitimate power, as well as informational power, can play important roles in school consultation. We continue by presenting the expansion of the original model as well as Erchul and Raven's applications of the updated power model to school consultation. These ideas are previewed in Table 2.1.

Coercive Power and Reward Power: Impersonal Forms

The original forms of coercive and reward power, now called "impersonal" forms (Raven, 1992, 1993), refer to B's perception that A is capable of delivering tangible punishments and rewards, respectively. In contrast to Martin (1978), Erchul and Raven (1997) suggested that it is shortsighted to dismiss the relevance of the impersonal forms of coercive and reward power within school-based consultation. After all, an early description of behavioral consultation in schools (Tharp & Wetzel, 1969) included some concrete suggestions for how the consultant can modify the consultee's behavior through the application of positive reinforcement and punishment. Also, at some level, the consultee may be concerned about the consequences of failing to follow the suggestions offered by the consultant or failing to implement interventions developed jointly during consultation. For instance, despite the commonly assumed confidential nature of consultation, word may spread quickly through informal social networks within a school about a consultee's failures to profit from consultation. Staff members may attribute a particular consultee's long-standing failure to improve classroom management via consultation to his or her unwillingness to work effectively with the consultant. This in turn may negatively influence the consultee's future relationships with these coworkers. Fortunately, successes arising from consultation may be communicated—and possibly rewarded—through these same networks (Erchul & Raven, 1997).

Table 2.1. Further Differentiation of the Bases of Social Power (Raven, 1992, 1993) and School Consultation Examples

Further differentiated power base	Definition and consultation example
Impersonal Reward	B's perception that A is capable of delivering tangible rewards. *Example*: Consultant, very pleased with how much effort teacher has put forth in consultation, brings in a box of extra classroom supplies for her to use. Of course, the supplies are rewarding, but reward *power* stems from teacher's expectation that there will be additional supplies provided if there is further compliance.
Impersonal Coercion	B's perception that A is capable of delivering tangible punishments. *Example*: Subtly, or not so subtly, the consultant communicates the expectation that a failure to follow recommendations could lead to a negative report or poor performance review.
Positive Expert	B's perception that A possesses knowledge or expertise in a specific area of interest to B. *Example*: Teacher views consultant as knowledgeable because of her doctoral degree in school psychology.
Positive Referent	A's potential to influence B based on B's identification with A and/or desire for such identification. *Example*: Teacher is likely to follow consultant's direction in consultation because she wishes to enter the field of school psychology herself in order to consult with teachers.
Direct Information	A's potential to influence B because of the judged relevance of the information contained in A's message. *Example*: Teacher views consultant's treatment plan as likely to succeed—not because of the consultant's expertise or other factors—but because the teacher made up her mind long ago that boys with ADHD always benefit from a classroom point system.
Formal Legitimacy	B's perception that A has a right to influence based on A's professional role or organizational position. *Example*: Teacher sees consultant's role as implying the authority to make recommendations that the teacher should feel obligated to follow.
Legitimacy of Dependence	B's perception that there is an obligation to help people like A who cannot help themselves and who are dependent upon others. *Example*:

Table 2.1. *continued*

Further differentiated power base	Definition and consultation example
	Consultant asks for teacher's help in assisting a student through consultation because the student's test scores do not qualify him for a special education placement.
Legitimacy of Reciprocity	B's perception that he/she is obligated to respond in-kind for what A has done already to benefit B. *Example*: Consultant has spent several lengthy sessions with the teacher working out a reasonable intervention plan, so now teacher feels an obligation to implement the plan as well as possible.
Legitimacy of Equity	B's perception that he/she is obligated to respond to A's request due to an imbalance of expended effort and possible inconvenience incurred previously by A. *Example*: Consultant has spent much time working with teacher developing an intervention plan but teacher has failed to start implementation, causing consultant to return to classroom unnecessarily to begin what would have been an initial evaluation of the plan. Teacher, perhaps feeling guilty, begins plan implementation immediately.
Personal Reward	A's liking and personal approval of B is important to B, and B believes that approval is more likely if B follows A's recommendations. *Example*: Consultant compliments teacher for collecting baseline data for five days, as was recommended. Teacher feels good about such compliments and hopes and expects further approval for future compliance.
Personal Coercion	B is very concerned about A not liking or disapproving B, and expects that noncompliance will result in such disapproval. *Example*: Consultant expresses disapproval when teacher has not implemented the intervention as agreed upon previously. Teacher finds such disapproval painful, and expects even more severe disapproval if she does not follow subsequent recommendations.

Note. Absent from this list are negative expert, negative referent, and indirect informational power, three other forms of power discussed by Raven (1992, 1993).

Coercive and Reward Power: Personal Forms

Two newer types of coercive and reward power are labeled "personal" forms by Raven (1992, 1993), and refer to B's perception that A's personal disapproval and approval, respectively, can potentially influence B. It has been recognized for some time that approval from someone whom we like can be as rewarding as a tangible reward, just as rejection or disapproval from someone we like can serve as a powerful basis for coercive power (Raven & Kruglanski, 1970). For example, within behavioral consultation (Bergan & Kratochwill, 1990), a consultant may choose to compliment a consultee for keeping accurate baseline data on a client, but later may confront that same consultee for repeatedly failing to implement the treatment plan with integrity (Gresham, 1989). These actions may result in consultee attributions of the personal forms of reward power and coercive power, respectively. It may also be that, given the generally acknowledged supportive nature of the consultative relationship, the use of the personal form of reward power may be more frequent than the use of the personal form of coercive power (Erchul & Raven, 1997).

Legitimate Power: Position, Reciprocity, Equity, and Responsibility-Dependence

The term *formal legitimate power* refers to an agent's potential to influence a target based on the target's belief that the agent has a right to influence based on professional role or organizational position (J. R. P. French & Raven, 1959). For example, a firefighter is attributed legitimate power by those trapped in a burning building, allowing him or her to take whatever actions deemed necessary to achieve a successful rescue. The external consultant, in particular, may draw on formal legitimate power on occasion (Erchul & Raven, 1997). The consultant who relies on legitimate power ("position power") is attempting to project an image that suggests, "I am a consultant, and I am trying to do my job—to help you do your job better. As a consultee, you should feel obligated to consider what I have to offer." However, we would not expect a psychological consultant ever to be explicit in the use of legitimate position power. In all probability this blatant use of legitimate position power would be resented by the consultee, and could result in very disastrous consequences. But even if legitimate position power is not made explicit, some consultees may feel that they should follow the consultant's advice. When the consultant is a member of a healing profession, consultee attributions of legitimate power may be more likely (Gallessich, 1982).

In Raven's (1992, 1993) more recent development of the bases of power model, he has gone beyond legitimate position power to promote three other types of legitimate power. These more subtle types draw on social norms involving obligations to comply, and are termed the legitimate power of reciprocity, equity, and responsibility-dependence.

The *legitimate power of reciprocity* (Gouldner, 1960) suggests that the target should respond in kind for what the agent has done already to benefit the target. For example, the consultant might imply that considerable effort had been expended to develop an acceptable intervention plan, so the consultee should feel obligated to implement the plan as well as possible.

The *legitimate power of equity* (Walster, Walster & Berscheid, 1978) obligates the target to respond due to a perceived imbalance of expended effort and possible inconvenience incurred by the agent. For instance, a consultant might diplomatically state the idea that, because the consultee did not even try once to implement the intervention, a return trip to the school after one week to monitor student progress was unnecessary; in order to compensate the consultant, the consultee might begin the intervention as soon as possible (Erchul & Raven, 1997).

The *legitimate power of responsibility-dependence* is based on a norm that states there is an obligation to help those who cannot help themselves and who are dependent upon others (Berkowitz & Daniels, 1963). A rationale we have presented on occasion to encourage teachers to participate actively in consultation relies on the legitimate power of responsibility-dependence: "I, unfortunately, am not in a position to change the rules and regulations governing special education programs. As a result of her test scores, Sarah cannot be considered to be a student having a learning disability so she will remain in your classroom. I hope I can count on you to help me generate a plan that will meet her educational needs."

Expert Power and Referent Power: Positive Forms

The forms of expert and referent power proposed originally by J. R. P. French and Raven (1959) now are referred to as "positive" forms (Raven, 1992, 1993). As Martin (1978) argued, the positive forms of expert and referent power have great utility in explaining what happens in school consultation. With respect to the positive form of expert power, in order to be effective it is critical for the consultant to be perceived as an expert. Helping reinforce this perception is that some consultees consider the psychologist to be part of the medical community, and may believe in certain medical traditions such as "the doctor knows best" and thus attribute expert power to the consultant. The psychologist may increase the probability of being accorded expert power by limiting his or her consulting practice to a small number of areas of true expertise, offering recommendations in a confident manner, stating his or her relevant professional training and experience, and mentioning successful past consulting efforts (Erchul, 1992b; Martin, 1978).

The positive form of referent power is a concept that should be familiar to all human service professionals, though it may be more recognizable as "rapport building" or "relationship development." The consultant may be attributed referent power by getting to know a consultee and his or her work setting and demonstrating an understanding of both, pointing out similarities between himself or herself and the consultee ("You may not be aware of this, but I was a teacher once myself and know the problems you are facing"), engaging in joint decision-making, and describing him- or herself and professional activities in ways that the consultee perceives as favorable (Erchul, 1992b; Martin, 1978).

The Expert–Referent Power Dilemma

Martin (1978) observed that expert and referent power tend to mutually oppose each other. After all, expert power is based on the target's perception that the influencing agent has superior knowledge and thus is different from the target. Referent power, in contrast, grows from mutual identification or a sense of similarity. Recognizing this antagonistic relationship, Martin hypothesized that the most successful consultants are capable of striking a balance between these two power bases. In other words, a consultant should avoid being perceived as "too knowledgeable" (and thus be attributed little or no referent power), and "too similar" (and thus be attributed little or no expert power). It has been suggested that the external consultant is attributed more expert than referent power, and the internal consultant is attributed more referent than expert power (Lippitt & Lippitt, 1986; Martin, 1978).

A major challenge for the consultant appears to be to develop strategies that reduce the likelihood of expert and referent power undermining each other. The consultant who emphasizes his or her similarity and mutuality with the consultee may find it useful to suggest that he or she is also an expert, but in a gentle, nonthreatening manner. If he or she has been relying heavily on expert power, an occasional reference to common background, mutual goals, general similarity—without undermining expertise—may be helpful (Erchul & Raven, 1997).

Empirical Studies of Positive Expert and Positive Referent Power in School Consultation

According to Erchul and Raven (1997), seven empirical investigations of the positive forms of expert and referent power in school consultation have been conducted (i.e., Cienki, 1982; Crowe, 1982; Kinsala, 1985; Kruger, 1984; Martin & Curtis, 1980; Roberts, 1985; Short, Moore &

Williams, 1991). These individual researchers operationalized consultant expert power in several ways, including age (older than consultee), gender (male), professional experience (more years of experience than consultee), and academic degree (higher level than consultee). Consultant referent power was operationalized as the consultant having the same gender, and same approximate age and professional experience, as the consultee. Although we shall not critically review these investigations, it may be concluded that, in five of these studies, indicators of the positive forms of expert and/or referent power were linked to significant consultation processes and outcomes. In two other studies, no significant relationships were found. Although more research is definitely in order, these studies collectively support the view of expert and referent power as meaningful constructs within school consultation.

Expert and Referent Power: Negative Forms

Two more recently recognized types of expert and referent power (the "negative" forms) are based on the observation that sometimes the target may do exactly the opposite of what the influencing agent does or desires the target to do (Raven, 1992, 1993). Perhaps this phenomenon exists because the target recognizes the expertise of the agent but distrusts him or her because it is assumed that the agent does not have the target's best interests foremost in mind (i.e., negative expert power). Conversely, maybe the target sees the agent as someone whom he or she dislikes, or someone from whom the target would rather disidentify him- or herself (i.e., negative referent power). Negative influence also can emerge when the target believes that his or her independence, individuality, or sense of personal control is threatened. There may be a strong tendency to avoid doing what the agent requests, or to do the exact opposite. This form of negative influence is called *reactance* (Brehm, 1966; Hughes & Falk, 1981).

Though less commonly seen than their positive forms, the negative forms of expert and referent power are relevant to the practice of school consultation. Perhaps the most relevant application is that school consultants need to be aware of how an overcontrolling attempt at influence or an unpopular personal presentation can lead to nonacceptance by the consultee and to negative influence in the form of active resistance or reactance (Erchul & Raven, 1997).

Informational Power: Direct and Indirect Forms

The direct form of informational power is founded on the information or logical argument that the influencing agent presents directly to the target in order to achieve change. Unlike the other bases of social power, the resulting change in the target stems from the effectiveness of the agent's message rather than from any characteristics of the agent. In order for informational power to produce change in the target, the target must judge the message's content to be very useful and relevant to his or her situation. To clarify further, for both informational power and expert power, the target believes that the recommendation by the agent is the best thing to do. With expert power, however, the target may not really understand why it is best because he or she is relying on his or her faith in the agent's superior knowledge (Raven, 1965, 1992, 1993).

The direct form of informational power has some distinct advantages over other bases of power. First, it is often more comfortable for the target to believe that he or she is doing what the agent asks because it is understood from the agent's presentation that this is the best course of action, instead of being based on faith in the agent's expertise, an obligation to comply, or a concern about the agent rewarding or punishing the target. Second, informational power tends to be more permanent, with no surveillance required, and fewer negative side effects (Raven, 1992, 1993). Third, the direct form of informational power appears to have great potential for the consultant because it does not rest on the consultee's favorable assessment of the consultant (i.e., it is socially independent, unlike the other five power bases; Erchul, 1992b; Parsons & Meyers, 1984). The unique nature of informational power has led to its endorsement by mental health consultation pioneer Gerald Caplan (see Erchul, 1993b) and by Raven and Litman-Adizes (1986), who studied doctor–patient interactions.

On the other hand, the direct form of informational power has certain disadvantages. First, it may lead to resistance on the part of the target, depending on the way in which the agent presents it. Second, it may lead to reactance if the target believes that his or her sense of integrity is being violated. For instance, a consultee who is told, "Here are four good reasons why you should change your classroom rules to improve discipline," may respond by doing the exact opposite of what the consultant suggests (Erchul & Raven, 1997). Third, the use of the direct form of informational power may require more time in explanation and depends on the target having background to understand the bases for the recommendation (Raven, 1965). Fourth, there is some evidence that direct use of informational power may also be resisted when a subordinate attempts to influence a superior, or when a female attempts to influence a male (Johnson, 1976; Stein, 1971).

Given these apparent disadvantages of the direct form of informational power, information may be more persuasive if it is presented indirectly. Often there is a large difference between an agent directly telling a target what he or she wants and why, versus proceeding through the offering of hints and suggestions. Classic social psychological research on the effectiveness of "overheard" communications, compared to direct communications, illustrates this point (e.g., Walster & Festinger, 1962). In a similar way, Falbo and Peplau (1980) found the direct-indirect dimension particularly important in their classification of power strategies. Johnson (1976) and Tannen (1994) have noted that women are more likely to use the indirect forms of information, and men more likely to use direct information. In addition, indirect information seems particularly useful when a person in what is considered a low-power position attempts to influence someone in a superior position (Stein, 1971).

The use of the indirect form of informational power in school consultation is less clear at this time. Although consistent with the psychodynamic elements of Caplan's (1970; Caplan & Caplan, 1993/1999) mental health consultation model, others writing specifically about school consultation do not advocate techniques based on indirect communication (see, for example, Conoley & Conoley, 1992, Ch. 2). Still, the consultant who notes some uneasiness in his or her relationship with a consultee may consider using more subtle, less direct forms of informational influence. For example, in the manner of Caplan's (1970) use of parables, a consultant might say, "I have heard that at a school not far from here, a teacher has been using this method to deal with her classroom problem and has achieved some success. Perhaps you might wish to consider it." Also, given Stein's (1971) major result, a younger consultant may find the use of indirect communication helpful when consulting with a more senior teacher having many years of experience (Erchul & Raven, 1997).

A primary difficulty in the consultant's use of either direct or indirect forms of informational power would seem to be not knowing ahead of time what information the consultee will consider most important and helpful. However, to the extent a consultee can be regarded as a professional "in crisis" and therefore more open to outside influence, this issue may be far less salient. That is, the consultee beset with crisis will tend to be more open to a variety of approaches advocated by the consultant (Caplan, 1989).

Empirical Studies of Raven's (1992, 1993) Social Power Bases Applied to School Consultation

Which social power bases from Raven's expanded model do psychologists and teachers believe will be most successful in changing the behavior of a consultee who is described as initially resistant to comply with a consultant's requests? Two recent studies have addressed this question using the Interpersonal Power Inventory (IPI; Raven, Schwarzwald & Koslowsky, 1998), a 44-item self-report instrument that measures the 11 social power bases listed in Table 2.1. Erchul, Raven, and Ray (2001) used the IPI to survey 101 school psychologists and found that respondents considered direct informational, positive expert, impersonal reward, and positive referent power to be the four most effective bases when consulting with an initially resistant teacher. Building on this methodology, Erchul, Raven, and Whichard (in press) polled a national sample of school psychologists and elementary school teachers with consulting experience. In their psychologist subsample, the top four most effective bases were direct informational, positive expert, positive referent, and personal reward power. In their teacher subsample, direct informational, positive expert, legitimate dependence, and positive referent power were perceived as the most effective power bases for a consultant to use when consulting with an initially resistant teacher. Across these studies, then, it may be concluded that psychologists and teachers similarly acknowledge the effectiveness of direct informational, positive expert, and positive referent power to explain processes and outcomes of school consultation.

Groupings of Social Power Bases: The Soft vs. Hard Distinction

Analyzed in a slightly different way, these results support the general effectiveness of soft bases over hard bases (Bass, 1981; Yukl & Falbe, 1991). *Soft* bases are considered to be more subtle, positive, and non-coercive, and include positive expert, positive referent, direct informational, legitimate dependence, and personal reward power. *Hard* bases are more overt, punitive, and "heavy handed," and include legitimate reciprocity, impersonal coercive, legitimate equity, impersonal reward, personal coercive, and legitimate position power (Raven et al., 1998). In both Erchul et al. (2001) and Erchul et al. (in press), respondents indicated the use of soft bases would be more effective than hard bases when consulting with an initially resistant teacher. To illustrate, direct informational, positive expert, and positive referent power—the top-rated bases—are all soft power bases.

OTHER MEANS OF INFLUENCE

Invoking or Reducing the Power of Third Parties

Another way an influencing agent can effect change in a target is to invoke the power of a third party, either by referring verbally to the third party, or by asking directly for help from the third party (Raven, 1992, 1993). For example, a school consultant could invoke the power of a third party by making reference to another staff member whom the consultee respects (e.g., "I know you think Ms. Anderson is an exemplary teacher. Have you ever noticed what she does to solve these sorts of problems?"). Alternately, the consultant could request assistance from the third party on behalf of the consultee (e.g., "I know that Mr. Benjamin has extensive experience implementing token economy programs in classrooms. Let me see if he would be able to meet with us next time"). Because of the generally assumed confidential nature of consultation, however, it is not recommended that the school principal's legitimate power be invoked. To do so could perhaps irreparably damage the working relationship between consultant and teacher (Erchul & Raven, 1997).

The agent also can influence a target by reducing the power of a third party who might block the recommended change. This action may be achieved by undermining the third party's expertise or legitimacy, suggesting that he or she is not a desirable model, or questioning the underlying logic of his or her persuasive appeal (Raven, 1992, 1993). Particularly to the extent school consultation is practiced in a multiple consultee or group context (see, for example, Caplan & Caplan, 1993/1999), the strategy of reducing the power of a third party would appear to be of value. The well-documented finding that the group yields substantial power supports this position (e.g., Ford & Zelditch, 1988; Lewin, 1952). As just one example, the consultant working with a group of consultees may consider exercising expert power to counter a pessimistic consultee's argument that only direct services such as counseling and not indirect services such as consultation can help students with disabilities. Through referent power and personal coercive power, other group members may help to persuade this consultee that indirect services also can be effective (Erchul & Raven, 1997).

Preparatory Devices: Setting the Stage for Social Influence

As the influencing agent evaluates his or her bases of power, the agent may decide that a specific form of power may work in a particular situation, but will require some additional preparation in order to be maximally effective (Raven, 1992, 1993). This preparation may necessitate the use of self-presentational strategies (Jones & Pittman, 1982) or management impression tactics (Schlenker, 1980). In this section, we briefly present what Raven (1992, 1993) has termed stage-setting devices. We caution that, although these devices appear to apply to the practice of school consultation, they require further investigation relative to their suitability and effectiveness.

If coercion is to be employed, then it may be important for the influencing agent to demonstrate to the target not only that the means are available for coercion, but also that the agent is willing to follow through with punishment if necessary. The agent then might resort to mild intimidation as a preparatory strategy. If reward power is to be used, then the agent must mention the availability of rewards to the target. If the agent intends to use personal reward by offering approval or personal coercion by showing disapproval, then the agent may try first to ingratiate him- or herself with the target by complimenting or flattering the target. If legitimate position power is chosen for use, the agent might subtly state that, for example, he or she is the supervisor who shoulders the ultimate responsibility for the job, so the target should comply with forthcoming requests. To prepare for legitimacy based on the reciprocity norm, the agent may do a favor for the target, expecting a later return (Raven, 1992, 1993).

If the influencing agent will be relying on expert power, then some demonstration of his or her superior knowledge may be useful as a stage-setting device. Physicians, attorneys, and other professionals often promote their expertise by displaying their extensive professional libraries, diplomas, awards, etc. Finally, for referent power, the agent must demonstrate communality with the target. Helping professionals typically lay the groundwork for the exercise of referent power by getting to know their clients, particularly their likes, dislikes, and aspirations—all of which provide a basis for establishing communality. Table 2.2 summarizes Raven's (1992, 1993) preparatory devices.

Given the differential appropriateness of social power bases for the school consultant, we would expect some of these preparatory devices to be used more than others and some not at all. For example, the acknowledged importance of developing and maintaining rapport with consultees suggests that setting the stage for using referent power, personal reward power, and personal coercive power may be critical. It is also essential that the consultant be perceived as an expert, so he or she might tactfully communicate to the teacher something about his or her experience and training in the area over which consultation will occur. Perhaps less frequently seen would be preparation for the use of legitimate power. However, a possible application of legitimate position power would be with a resistant consultee who has refused to act on plans developed in consultation. In this case, the consultant might subtly convey that she is a consultant who has been brought into the situation to offer assistance, so that the teacher should feel some obligation to try out these plans. Similarly, to prepare for legitimacy based on the equity norm, the consultant might first make reference to the long hours that she has logged

Table 2.2. Examples of Preparatory Devices for the Use of Social Power

Preparing the stage or scene:
  Displaying diplomas, library, photos with celebrities (expert)
  Wearing laboratory coat, stethoscope, etc. (expert)
  Arranging of podium or desk, chairs (legitimate)
Enhancing or emphasizing power bases:
  References to agent's ability to control rewards; punishments; formal role as supervisor, teacher, doctor, etc. (legitimate)
  Intimidation, presenting fearful image (coercion)
  Ingratiation, via compliments, etc., to increase target's attraction to agent (personal reward, personal coercion, referent power)
  Self-promotion, emphasizing superior knowledge (expert)
  Emphasizing communality of background, identification, goals (referent)
  Doing a favor for target (reciprocity), emphasizing one's dependence upon target (responsibility), telling of one's selfless dedication and sacrifice, reference to some harm which target imposed on agent (equity)
  Making a request that target would not be likely to accept, to induce guilt, in preparation for other request (legitimacy of equity)
  Presenting background information, which can subsequently serve to enhance informational influence
Minimizing target:
  Subtle "put-downs" which decrease target's self-esteem or confidence, so as to increase agent's informational, expert, or legitimate power
Minimizing opposing influencing agents:
  Reducing expertise, reference, legitimacy, etc., of others who may support the target's current position or mode of behavior

Note. From "The Bases of Power: Origins and Recent Developments," by B. H. Raven, 1993, *Journal of Social Issues, 49*, p. 238. Copyright © 1993 by The Society for the Psychological Study of Social Issues. Reprinted with permission.

traveling around to various schools in order to study many client problems, so as to help this particular consultee develop possible solutions to a current pressing problem (Erchul & Raven, 1997).

The Mode of Influence

The effectiveness of an influence attempt appears to stem not only from the power base employed, but also from how the influencing agent chooses to deliver it (Raven, 1992, 1993). At one extreme, the agent may attempt to influence using a loud, forceful, threatening, or sarcastic tone. At the other extreme, the agent may use a soft, friendly, or humorous manner. A sophisticated influencing agent may soften a coercive influence attempt by employing a light, humorous delivery. It would seem that a consultant's choice of words, body language, and facial expression can affect the manner in which the consultee responds, both in present compliance and in future interactions with the consultant (Erchul & Raven, 1997; Ng & Bradac, 1993).

Perhaps the high priority placed on establishing and maintaining mutually respectful interpersonal relationships within school consultation (e.g., Meyers et al., 1979), make it unlikely that a consultant would try to change a consultee using a harsh or threatening manner. On the other hand, the use of humor, nonthreatening forms of request, and a polite manner have been demonstrated to enhance successful influence, and it is expected the same would hold true within school consultation (Baxter, 1984; Goffman, 1967; Holtgraves, 1992; Holtgraves & Yang, 1990). Therefore, it is important for consultants to look at how an influence attempt is presented, in addition to the social power base it represents (Erchul & Raven, 1997).

A POWER/INTERACTION MODEL OF INTERPERSONAL INFLUENCE AND ITS APPLICATION TO SCHOOL CONSULTATION

The complex picture of the many choices and stages in the implementation of social power may be seen in Raven's (1992, 1993) power/interaction model of interpersonal influence, which is displayed in Figure 2.1. In describing this model, we present the process of influence from motivation to implementation and subsequent readjustment of the influencing agent. It is our approach first to describe each step in a generic way and then to comment on it with specific reference to the practice of school consultation.

The Motivation to Influence

On the left side of Figure 2.1, there is a variety of motivational factors for the influencing agent to consider prior to engaging in an influence attempt. These factors then lead the agent to assess the various bases of power and other forms of influence that might be available. For example, the consultant is encouraged to examine what motivates him or her to influence consultees as a part of consultation. Is it ultimately to benefit clients? Is it to make consultees function more competently in their professional roles? Or, less positively, is it mainly for personal gain (e.g., financial, affiliative, status, etc.)?

In the upper middle of the figure, the bases of power and other preparatory devices that might be in the agent's repertoire can be seen. As mentioned previously, the school consultant may find the use of certain

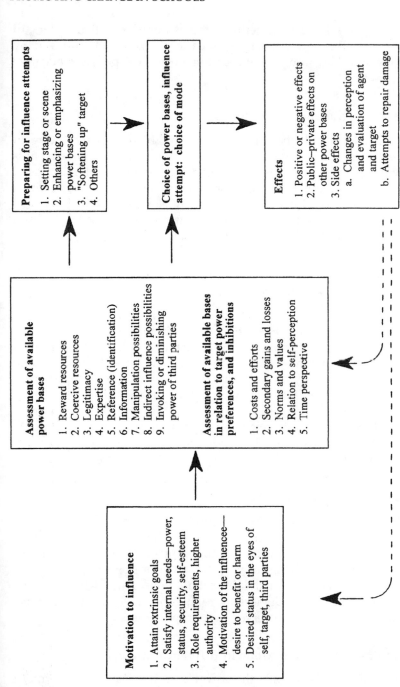

Figure 2.1. Model of power/interaction from the perspective of the influencing agent. From "The Bases of Power: Origins and Recent Developments," by B. H. Raven, 1993, *Journal of Social Issues, 49,* p. 240. Copyright © 1993 by The Society for the Psychological Study of Social Issues. Reprinted with permission.

power bases and related stage-setting devices more likely than others. In our experience, the power bases perhaps least likely to be utilized by school consultants are impersonal coercion, negative expert, and negative referent power.

Assessment of Available Power Bases[4]

Having determined what bases of power might be available, the agent must assess these possible courses of action in terms of their effectiveness in achieving change. What is the likelihood the agent would be successful or unsuccessful using various power bases? For example, the consultant who has not worked with a particular consultee previously may be successful using more expert power than referent power. A consultant who is already well known to all school staff may believe the reverse to be true.

Assessment of the Available Bases in Relation to Target, Power, Preferences, and Inhibitions

The agent also must examine the cost-benefit ratio of the influence attempt. For example, influence that stems from informational power may require more time and effort to establish than is available. Coercion has the costs of maintaining surveillance, inviting possible hostility, and perhaps violating one's personal value system or accepted social norms. Legitimate power based on dependence (i.e., "I need your help") may lead to loss of respect and may imply an obligation to return the favor. A consultant obviously must weigh these possible risks and benefits. As noted earlier, school psychologists tend to see soft bases as more effective than hard bases (Erchul et al., 2001).

Preparing for the Influence Attempt

In looking at the upper right of Figure 2.1, it can be seen that the various preparatory or stage-setting devices are introduced at this point. These devices include setting the scene, emphasizing or enhancing the agent's power resources, diminishing the target or opposing influencing agents. As discussed previously, the school consultant is likely to use some of these preparatory devices more than others, and some may not be used at all due to their perceived inappropriateness.

Choice of Power Bases and Mode in Influence Attempts

The agent chooses not only the power base, but also the power mode (i.e., the manner or tone in which the influence attempt is delivered). As

Raven (1992, 1993) observed, the mode of influence at times may be more important than the basis of power. Due to the nature of the school setting and their role within it, consultants are generally restricted in their mode choices, relying mainly on soft, friendly, or humorous approaches. It is unlikely that a school consultant would be seen as effective when using a loud, forceful, and sarcastic manner.

Assessing the Effects of Influence

After the influence attempt, the agent evaluates its effects. Was it successful? Is there some sign that the target has accepted the influence by altering his or her behavior in accordance with the outcome sought by the agent? Has the target internalized the change, or is the change clearly socially dependent? Is surveillance by the agent important for the change to continue, or will the target revert to earlier behavior patterns as soon as the agent is unable to continue to monitor the target's degree of compliance? If the influence attempt was unsuccessful, then the agent may reevaluate power resources, reassess the possibility of future success, and try again.

In assessing the effects of influence, the consultant may ask, "How has the consultee changed?" For instance, if the main goal of the influence attempt was to increase the probability of a consultee collecting accurate baseline data on a client for a week, the consultant will want to assess the degree of consultee follow-through with data collection. Perhaps more importantly, over the span of several consultations with this same consultee, the consultant will want to see whether the collection of baseline data becomes internalized or instead consistently requires the consultant's surveillance in order to occur.

CONCLUSION

With few exceptions, this chapter has presented social influence issues nearly exclusively from the perspective of the influencing agent, or for our purposes, the consultant. It is clear, however, that it also would be valuable to study these issues more extensively from the perspective of the target or consultee (Raven, 1992, 1993). Due to space limitations, we cannot provide such an analysis but wish to convey that such an analysis would produce meaningful implications for the school consultant, as others have presented before (e.g., Martin, 1978; Sandoval, Lambert & Davis, 1977). An effective consultant often will find it advantageous to be open to influence from the consultee, in part because it may strengthen the consultant's power. For example, listening attentively to the consultee may increase the legitimate power of reciprocity (e.g., "I listened to you before, so please hear me out this time"). Being open to the consultee's influence also may increase mutual attraction and result in increased personal reward and personal coercive power (Erchul & Raven, 1997).

Though a key component, the practice of school consultation involves more than a one-on-one relationship between a consultant and consultee. Consultation occurs within an organizational context and thus it is critical for the consultant to understand the structure and function of the consultee's workplace. In Chapter 3 we consider some of the fundamental elements of the school as an organization.

NOTES

1. Along with "behavior," we would add that influencing "beliefs" and "attitudes" is equally important, as it remains a debatable point whether beliefs and attitudes lead to behavior change, or vice-versa.
2. We wish to emphasize that all of us—not just teachers—often require a level of influence beyond basic information in order to change our beliefs, attitudes, and behaviors.
3. This section of Chapter 2 draws on an article co-authored by William P. Erchul and Bertram H. Raven (Erchul & Raven, 1997). The article, in turn, draws on two previous articles by Raven (1992, 1993) for its explication of the power/interaction model of interpersonal influence. We would like to thank Bert Raven for his insight and support in applying social power concepts to the practice of school consultation, and credit him for many of the ideas included here.
4. Because of space limitations, we have chosen to omit "manipulation possibilities," "indirect influence possibilities," and "the effects of feedback on the agent," topics that are discussed by Raven (1992, 1993) and included in Figure 2.1.

3

The School as a Setting for Consultation

In the early 1800s, children who were fortunate enough to receive an education did so in one-room schoolhouses. Attendance was sporadic and often depended on the availability of a teacher and the completion of chores around the home or farm. Together with a small number of friends and neighbors, the children who were present each day would be instructed in the fundamentals of reading, writing, and arithmetic using whatever materials were available and at whatever pace was necessary to accommodate their divergent skills. Following the industrial revolution of the late 1800s, it became fashionable to view schools as "factories" and children as "raw materials" who one day would become products capable of meeting the demands of an industrialized society (Cubberley, 1916). Compulsory education, child labor laws, and waves of immigrants entering the United States in the early 1900s produced staggering increases in school enrollments and corresponding increases in state and federal expenditures on public education (Fagan & Wise, 2000).

Today, the American educational system is one of the largest institutions in society employing more than 4 million teachers, administrators, and support personnel and meeting the needs of more than 44 million children (Apter, 1977; Grant & Snyder, 1986). As with any large organization, public education has come to rely on an extensive bureaucracy as a means of accomplishing its service delivery goals. One-room schoolhouses have been replaced by thousands of elementary and secondary campuses nationwide with vast administrative networks responsible for overseeing their operation. Similarly, a handful of children working with a single teacher for the entire school day has been replaced by regular education classes of 30 or more students, compartmentalized instruction, prereferral intervention programs, counseling and social skills training, and both push-in and pull-out special education services. Within this network of service options, school consultation represents only one of a variety of alternatives available to teachers in their efforts to accommodate students with special needs.

We believe that an appreciation for schools as organizations and a familiarity with the range of services they offer is crucial in order to enter the service delivery network and to function effectively as a school consultant. Toward these goals, the chapter begins by discussing the characteristics of schools and schooling that have evolved from three very different traditions in organizational thinking: (1) Weber's classical theory of bureaucracy; (2) the human relations movement; and (3) organizational behavior theory. Next, we depict the range of services that are offered in a typical school building and describe the process by which children are identified and deemed eligible for placement in special education. Known as the refer-test-place sequence, this approach continues to dominate as an administratively sanctioned solution to the problem of failure in regular education. The chapter concludes by describing the role that school consultation plays in augmenting more traditional special education services, discussing the utilization of school consultation services from an administrative perspective, and identifying three paradoxes of consultation service delivery. We believe that these paradoxes stem from the dynamic interplay of teaching as an intensive technology and schools as bureaucratic organizations.

ORGANIZATIONAL TRADITIONS IN THE PUBLIC SCHOOL SYSTEM

Classical Organizational Theory

In response to the often arbitrary and capricious manner in which human service organizations were managed at the turn of the century, Max Weber, a German sociologist, formulated a theory of the efficient, impartial administrative apparatus known as *bureaucracy* (Owens, 1981). A basic tenet of Weber's theory was that if each individual in an organization was trained with the technical expertise to complete one task, administration could assume the function of coordinating these tasks in a rational and impersonal manner. This approach would allow workers to go about their jobs unencumbered by the burdens of decision making, enabling the organization to handle an extensive client base while ensuring uniformity in the services that were provided. Weber's principles for an efficiently run bureaucracy were uniquely suited to the increasingly popular assembly line approach of mass production, and were summarized by Owens (1981) as follows (p. 11):

1. A division of labor based on functional specialization;
2. A well-defined hierarchy of authority;
3. A system of rules covering the rights and duties of employees;
4. A system of procedures for dealing with work situations;
5. Impersonality of interpersonal relations;
6. Selection and promotion based only on technical competence.

By the mid-1900s, Weber's principles of bureaucratic administration had been adopted by a large number of American industries including public education. Because the bureaucratic approach emphasized relationships among job roles rather than people, its application required certain assumptions about the nature of organizations and placed certain restrictions on an organization's ability to adapt to changing circumstances. In many respects these assumptions have proven to be inconsistent with the business of schools and schooling, and suggest why alternative approaches to service delivery such as school consultation are often slow to take root (M.D. Cohen, March & Olsen, 1972). First and foremost, bureaucracies are appropriate for organizations with clearly defined goals and objectives. A clear, common goal not only enlists the support of all employees, but provides a criterion by which the organization's success can be measured. Although government policy statements reflect a consensus over the general goals of public education (e.g., the America 2000 initiative, outcome-based education), attempts to implement these policies are often thwarted by a lack of agreement concerning specific educational objectives (Fagan & Wise, 2000; Morison, 1992). Our experience in the schools suggests that pluralistic goals also exist at the district and building levels. For example, regular education teachers may perceive their goal as seeing to it that the majority of children in their classroom master enough of the curriculum to be promoted to the next grade. In order to accomplish this goal, the effective teacher is required to integrate various managerial and instructional practices into a workable system which is characterized by a group-oriented focus (Gettinger, 1988). Support personnel, in turn, may perceive their goal as encouraging teachers to accommodate a wider diversity of student skills through individualized instruction, whereas school administrators might view both goals as being subordinate to budget accountability.

Second, in order to have a division of labor based on functional specialization, the job to be completed must be capable of being broken down into component tasks. By doing so, each employee has a limited sphere of responsibility, is required to make few decisions throughout the work day that are not dictated by standard operating procedures, and can be replaced by others who have similar skills with no loss of efficiency. *Outside of the classroom* schools are organized in ways that reflect many of these bureaucratic characteristics, including a graded system of progress through the secondary level, compartmentalized instruction where children change teachers for different content areas, and the use of itinerant substitute teachers who temporarily replace regular teachers as needed. *Inside the classroom*, however, teachers are afforded a great deal of independence and are responsible for dealing with a wide variety of student-related issues (e.g., planning lessons and making presentations, arbitrating student quarrels) (T.B. Gutkin, personal communication, March 22, 1984).

Third, bureaucracies are appropriate for organizations that rely on downward lines of communication between administrators and workers. This "top-down" approach is the way in which changes in procedure are instituted, and it makes lateral communication between departmental units at the same level relatively unimportant. In the public schools, innovative teaching approaches or new curriculum materials are rarely developed and disseminated by teachers during the course of their day-to-day instructional activities. Rather, as noted by Axelrod (1993), university-based educational researchers are typically responsible for promoting teaching practices, publishing companies are responsible for promoting curriculum materials, school boards are responsible for adopting basal series to be used throughout the district, and building principals are responsible for instituting disciplinary procedures. In short, educational innovations tend to occur in a top-down fashion within school districts, reducing the speed and flexibility with which these organizations can adapt to changing circumstances. Because school consultation often occurs at the request of teachers serving on the "front lines," it represents an approach to change that occurs in a bottom-up fashion. As with many bureaucratically run organizations, schools may not have adequate procedures in place for supporting or disseminating consultation as an innovative practice that originates from within (Piersel & Gutkin, 1983).

Related to the issue of vertical information flow, successful school consultation often requires a coordination of efforts and services laterally between various individuals and units within the school building. For example, consider the task of implementing a home-based reinforcement program as a positive behavioral support for a student classified as emotionally disturbed. In a school that adheres to the traditional pull-out approach to service delivery, the student might be placed on a part-time basis in a special education resource room and receive speech as a related service two hours a week. Once the child's program is in place, it is unlikely that the speech therapist, resource teacher, and regular classroom teacher will meet regularly to coordinate their respective activities. Successful implementation of the home-based reinforcement program would require that these individuals plus the child's parents meet to establish and review goals for behavior change, that a system be put in place for monitoring the child's behavior in different settings, that reports of behavior be collected at the end of the day and sent home to the parents, and that the parents act on these reports accordingly (e.g., Witt, Hannafin & Martens, 1983).

The Human Relations Movement

Classical theory focuses on the formal administrative structure of organizations in the absence of individuals. In contrast, the human relations movement grew out of an appreciation for the informal social interactions that arise among individuals despite this formal structure (Owens, 1981). Proponents of the human relations movement believe that members of organizations interact with each other and form alliances based on social psychological variables, and many times these patterns differ from those sanctioned by the formal bureaucratic structure. In order to understand how an organization actually functions, one must look beyond its organizational chart and take into account such issues as organizational climate, group norms, leadership style, and behavioral regularities.

Organizational climate is a term used to describe the informal, social environment of an organization that reflects the values of its members and influences the nature of their interactions and behavior (Halpin, 1966; Tagiuri & Litwin, 1968). Two important determinants of the organizational climate in schools are the principal's leadership style and the group norms of the teaching staff. The relationship of principals' leadership style to the utilization of school consultation services was examined in a study by Bossard and Gutkin (1983). In this study, school consultants were assigned to 10 elementary schools over a 14-week period. At the end of the 14 weeks, the consultant and teaching staff at each school completed the Leader Behavior Description Questionnaire (LBDQ) (Halpin, 1966), which contains two subscales: Consideration and Initiating Structure. According to Halpin:

> Initiating Structure refers to the leader's behavior in delineating the relationship between himself [sic] and members of the work group, and in endeavoring to establish well-defined patterns of organization, channels of communication, and methods of procedure. Consideration

refers to behavior indicative of friendship, mutual trust, respect, and
warmth in the relationship between the leader and members of his
staff. (p. 86)

In addition, the skills of each consultant were rated by experts
uninformed to the purposes of the study, and the utilization of consultation services in each school was calculated as the total number of consultation contacts divided by the number of teachers on staff. Results
indicated that differences in consultant skill, principal Consideration, and
principal Initiating Structure accounted for 70% of the variance in the
number of consultation contacts across the 10 schools. Interestingly, the
number of consultation contacts correlated positively with the leadership
variable of Consideration ($r = .32$) and negatively with the variable of
Initiating Structure ($r = -.35$).

The group norms of teaching staff refer to the often unspoken
values and rules for behavior that are adopted in a given school building
(Owens, 1981). According to Sarason (1971, 1996), one way of assessing
the group norms present in a school is to observe the *behavioral regularities*
of teachers and students. Behavioral regularities refer to the ways in
which things actually get done versus the ways in which things are supposed to get done. These recurrent patterns of behavior evolve over time
based on an interaction between the educational goals of teachers, the
physical environment and resources of the school, the leadership style of
the principal, and the time constraints under which teachers operate.
When examining the behavioral regularities present in a school building,
Sarason suggests that the school consultant ask two questions: "What is
the rationale for the [observed] regularity?" and "What is the universe
of alternatives that could be considered [to achieve the same outcome]?"
(p. 64). Asking these questions encourages a suspension of personal
values in our attempts to understand organizations and can represent an
important first step in the process of affecting organizational change.

To illustrate, the astute school consultant might observe the following behavioral regularities in a large, suburban elementary school: (1)
teachers pack up their belongings and leave the school building immediately after the children leave; (2) during instructional periods, the
halls of the school are empty and teachers rarely if ever enter each
other's classroom; (3) the principal does all of the talking during faculty
meetings and most of her comments are concerned with building procedures, student discipline, and the need to raise standardized test
scores; and (4) a large proportion of children (almost 13% of the student
population) are receiving special education services. Given these regularities, what might one conclude about the organizational climate of
the school? Clearly, the building principal values a smoothly running

school and is interested in competing favorably with other buildings in the district. Her behavior during faculty meetings also suggests that she would likely obtain a high score on Halpin's Initiating Structure scale. In response to the principal's bureaucratic management style, teachers concern themselves with their own classrooms, are reluctant to offer informal help to their colleagues, and essentially "punch out" at the end of the school day. When learning problems arise in the classroom, teachers at our hypothetical elementary school are encouraged to "go through the proper channels" by making a referral to the pupil service team.

An interesting arena in which to observe behavioral regularities in service delivery is the multidisciplinary team meeting. As mandated by the Individuals with Disabilities Education Act (IDEA), decisions about a child's eligibility for special education and related services are to be made by a team of professionals in cooperation with the child's parents or legal guardians. As we discuss later in the chapter, after completing an individual evaluation of the student, the evaluation team typically communicates its findings and recommendations to parents during a formal meeting often referred to as a staffing. A number of researchers have examined the behavioral regularities that occur during staffings, and we believe these findings have important implications for school consultants in their attempts to understand the culture of the school. A summary of these behavioral regularities appears below.

1. The average time allotted for meetings was approximately a half hour (Goldstein, Strickland, Turnbull & Curry, 1980; Pfeiffer, 1981) whereas allowing enough time for the staffing accounted for the most variance in participant satisfaction (Witt, Miller, McIntyre & Smith, 1984).
2. Parents, social workers, and principals were ranked high in perceived status before the meeting (3rd) and low on actual contributions (9th) after the meeting (Gilliam, 1979).
3. The most influential team members were those with the most knowledge of available placement options in the school (Pfeiffer, 1980).
4. Special education resource teachers assumed primary responsibility for conducting the meeting and developing the student's individualized education plan (IEP) (Goldstein et al., 1980).
5. Satisfaction with the meeting was related to participation and tended to be highest for the school psychologist and special education teacher (Yoshida, Fenton, Maxwell & Kaufman, 1978).
6. In all but one instance, students' IEPs were completed prior to the meeting (Goldstein et al., 1980).

7. There was a tendency for the evaluation team to recommend less restrictive placements when such recommendations were based on criterion-referenced rather than norm-referenced assessment data (Goldbaum & Rucker, 1977).
8. When parents were present at meetings there was a tendency for more school staff to be present and for them to make more recommendations (Singer, Bossard & Watkins, 1977).
9. Majority vote and resolution by the school psychologist were the most frequently used methods of resolving conflicts (Hyman, Duffey, Caroll, Manni & Winikur, 1973).
10. Overall parent satisfaction with the meeting was high (Goldstein et al., 1980; Witt et al., 1984).

Behavioral regularities also occur *within* classrooms, and these regularities can be related systematically to different instructional arrangements. By conceptualizing learning as a social process, researchers in this area have identified five *activity segments* that can be used to describe how learning typically occurs in American classrooms; recitation, teacher-directed small groups, seatwork, sharing time, and student-directed small groups (Weinstein, 1991). Activity segments refer to instructional arrangements that contain implicit rules for interaction and which partially dictate teacher and student behavior. According to Weinstein, children who are successful in classrooms are able to discriminate among various activity segments based on physical arrangement or subtle teacher cues, and understand the types of behavior appropriate to each. Characteristics of the three most common activity segments discussed by Weinstein are summarized below (the interested reader is referred to the original article for a complete description and review of supporting research).

Recitation

This activity segment affords teachers the highest degree of control over student interaction and occurs when teachers lecture or present new material to the class as a group. From the teacher's perspective, recitation requires that a certain amount of material be covered while asking for and commenting on responses from students. Students must attend to the material being presented as well as any interactions that occur, are relegated to making brief responses to teacher questions, and must identify when and how to compete for floor holding rights. Observational studies have suggested that teachers who are most effective during recitations call on children randomly to respond, require choral responding, and use alerting statements to introduce a new topic (e.g., "You won't believe what happens next.") (Brophy, 1983; Kounin, 1970).

Teacher-Directed Small Groups

Small-group arrangements are commonly used in the elementary grades for instruction in reading. By dividing the class into groups of children with similar skill levels and meeting with these groups in sequence, teachers are able to balance the practical requirement of maintaining a group-oriented focus while providing more individualized instruction (i.e., more frequent or elaborate prompting, modeling, praise, and feedback). The role of small groups in teachers' efforts to individualize instruction was demonstrated in a study by Allington (1980) who found that teachers tended to correct students' reading errors in ways that promoted comprehension in high-achieving groups, but tended to focus on decoding errors in low-achieving groups.

Seatwork

Independent seatwork in which students sit quietly at their desks reading, answering questions in workbooks, or completing teacher-made worksheets constitutes a significant portion of the school day in both regular and special education classrooms (Ysseldyke, Christenson, Thurlow & Bakewell, 1989). Because seatwork activities require students to complete assignments in the absence of teacher direction, behavioral regularities tend to involve cyclical patterns of engagement, off-task behavior, and teacher intervention, as well as attempts to solicit assistance from the teacher or peers (e.g., deVoss, 1979).

Organizational Behavior Theory

Thus far in the chapter we have depicted the organization of schools as reflecting many of the characteristics of a formal bureaucracy while at the same time supporting an informal network of implicit alliances and behavioral regularities. Although schools differ in the balance achieved between these often conflicting perspectives, at the heart of any educational system is the technology used by teachers to accomplish their instructional goals. Organizational behavior theory represents an attempt to examine the relationship between the technology used by an industry and the linkages imposed by this technology among its various departmental units (Owens, 1981).

The technology of schooling has been characterized from a number of perspectives including process-product research (e.g., Gettinger, 1988), information-processing models (Doyle, 1985), and direct instruction (Becker, 1988). Common to all of these perspectives is the realization that effective classroom instruction is an intensive activity that requires thoughtful planning, systematic execution, and ongoing monitoring of student-related outcomes (e.g., Martens & Kelly, 1993). The intensive technological aspects of instruction are reflected in the fact that teachers are required to perform a variety of operations during the course of the school day, are given a great deal of autonomy in determining what goes on in their classrooms, and receive little by way of direct supervision from principals. As summarized by Sarason (1971, 1996), even though teachers spend almost all of their time in contact with children, the absence of adult contact makes teaching a lonely profession.

To what extent is the intensive technology of teaching appropriate for the often bureaucratic structure of schools? As discussed by Owens (1981), there are three ways to describe the interdependencies between individuals and departments in an organization; sequential coupling, reciprocal coupling, or pooled coupling. *Sequential coupling* occurs when each worker is responsible for performing a relatively few number of operations on the product before passing it on to the next individual who in turn makes his or her contribution. Using assembly lines for mass production exemplifies the sequential coupling approach. *Reciprocal coupling* occurs when workers perform a number of operations on the product while passing it back and forth. The process of preparing a manuscript for publication in which the initial draft that is written by the author is edited by the publisher and then returned to the author for revisions would be an example of the reciprocal coupling approach. *Pooled* or *loose coupling* describes organizations in which "members share resources in common but otherwise work independently" (Owens, 1981, p. 29). Schools represent loosely coupled organizations in that teachers share the physical space and resources of their building but function independently in their respective classrooms. Unfortunately, pooled coupling can also be used to describe the relationship between regular education, special education, and related services such as speech and language. In a typical pull-out model of service delivery, each of these entities may be scheduled to work with the child for a portion of the school day with few explicit attempts to coordinate efforts, a situation termed by Giangreco (1989) as "programmatic isolation."

THE SERVICE STRUCTURE OF PUBLIC SCHOOLS

Available Services

When it comes to the range of services offered in schools, there is no such thing as the typical building. Rather, each school is unique as a function of size, location (e.g., rural, urban), community demographics, amount of parental involvement, number of staff, and administrative priorities. Because a great deal of school consultation occurs with elementary-age children, this section focuses on the types of services one might find in a school housing grades K (kindergarten) through 6. The school we will be describing—let's call it the Bartlett F. Sloane Elementary School—represents a composite of several buildings with which the authors are familiar. Although hypothetical, we believe that Sloane Elementary provides a useful vehicle through which to characterize the diversity of services available in the public school setting.

Sloane Elementary is located in a moderately sized city in the Northeast. It has a total enrollment of 470 students and employs 60 administrators, teachers, and support personnel who receive assistance from 15 volunteer aides. A detailed accounting of Sloane Elementary's demographics is presented in Table 3.1. As shown in the table, approximately equal percentages of Caucasian and African-American students attend Sloane, whereas there is a small but significant number of Native American students (almost 5% of the student population). Over half of the students receive free or reduced-price lunch, which often provides a rough indication of parents' socioeconomic status, and no students at Sloane require services in the English as a Second Language program. The bulk of administration at Sloane is handled by the principal and vice principal with the aid of two secretaries and an attendance monitor. There are four regular education teachers per grade level (including a pre-K classroom), seven special education teachers, and a full complement of support personnel including a librarian (also known as media specialist),

Table 3.1. Demographics of Sloane Elementary School

	Enrollment
By grade:	K (55); 1 (55); 2 (70); 3 (70); 4 (80); 5 (70); 6 (70)—Total: 470
Ethnicity:	Caucasian (47%); Black (48%); Hispanic (.5%); Native American (4.5%)
Other:	Free lunch (65%); special education (15%); out-of-school suspension (6%)

	Teaching and Support Staff
Regular education:	Pre-K (1); K (3); 1 (4); 2 (4); 3 (4); 4 (4); 5 (4); 6 (4)—Total: 28
Regular education support personnel:	Librarian, instructional specialist, music teachers (2), art teacher, gym teacher, nurse, computer lab teacher
Special education:	Self-contained (5); resource (2)—Total: 7
Special education support personnel:	Speech therapist, adapted physical education teacher, social worker, school psychologists (2), occupational therapist, physical therapist, school counselor

instructional specialist, speech therapist, nurse, social worker, psychologist, occupational therapist, and adapted physical education teacher.

Regular Education at Sloane

The four teachers at each grade level are organized into teams, with the role of team leader changing annually. Grade-level teams are responsible for assigning students to classrooms, determining the need for remedial or enrichment programs, adopting supplementary curriculum materials (e.g., supplies for science experiments), and arranging supervision for student teachers from the local university who function as teaching assistants. By virtue of the Adopt-a-School Program, student teachers at Sloane receive a small stipend for training that comes out of monies supplied by local businesses. Low-achieving students who are not yet eligible for special education services at Sloane can receive remedial assistance through several mechanisms: (1) the School-Wide Peer Tutoring Program in which students complete work assigned during each class period with the help of a high-achieving peer; (2) the Computer Lab room where students can engage in intensive drill and practice sessions in basic reading and math skills; and (3) the After School Program where students are given the opportunity to complete homework with the benefit of additional instruction and assistance from a teacher. For those students who have mastered the basic curriculum material and could benefit from opportunities to extend and apply what they have learned, Sloane provides enrichment programs in reading (the School Newsletter), writing (the In-School Mail Delivery System), and math (the School Store). Consistent with other schools in the district, students classified as "gifted" at Sloane are transported to another building two half-days a week for specialized instruction. Sloane also participates in a district-wide program designed to expose students to the history and traditions of other cultures, such as that of the Native Americans. Participation in these enrichment programs is dependent on satisfactory progress in all content areas and requires nomination from at least two teachers with the exception of the gifted program. Students' eligibility for the gifted program is based on teacher referral and individual evaluation.

Special Education at Sloane

Four of the five self-contained classrooms at Sloane can generally be distinguished by the teacher-to-student ratio, the presence of a full-time assistant, and the severity of students' handicapping conditions. These characteristics combine to produce a graded hierarchy of restrictiveness with respect to students' placements. Students attend each of these class-rooms for the majority of the school day with the exception of specials (e.g., music, art, gym) or mainstreamed subject areas as indicated on their IEPs. The least restrictive self-contained classroom includes 15 children and one teacher, and is devoted almost exclusively to students with learning disabilities or those students who have received more restrictive place-ments in the past but are transitioning back to regular education. The majority of students with other mild handicapping conditions for whom a self-contained placement is appropriate are served in a second classroom that contains 12 students, one teacher, and one teacher's assistant. Students with multiple handicaps or those who are moderately to severely mentally retarded, attend a classroom containing a total of six students, one teacher, and one teacher's assistant. A similar arrangement is used for students classified as "severely emotionally disturbed." The fifth self-contained classroom at the school is used to house one of the district's two magnet programs for students with autism. Approximately 15 children between the ages of 4 and 7 years attend the classroom for training in independent living and basic communication skills.

Sloane combines both pull-out and push-in approaches to the delivery of special education resource services. Students receiving resource services are provided assistance and remedial instruction for only a portion of the school day while spending most the day alongside their regular education peers. The two resource teachers at Sloane share one classroom that small groups of eligible students attend for an hour a day (pull-out services). When not instructing students in the resource room, the teachers team teach with their regular education counterparts who have significant numbers of mainstreamed special education stu-dents (push-in services). A similar approach to service delivery is taken by the speech therapist who has her own office in the building.

Support Services

The principal at Sloane is a strong advocate of community outreach efforts and as a result, the school offers a number of instructional and counseling groups for both students and parents. In the evenings, the school library and cafeteria double as classrooms for courses offered through the district-wide Adult Education Program (e.g., Intermediate Guitar and Tai Chi) as well as a 3-week parent training course offered by the school psychologist. Approximately 60 students are involved in one or more counseling groups addressing such issues as social skills training, anger control, or growing up in a single-parent household. These groups are run by the school psychologist and school counselor, who also provide individual counseling to a small number of students as indicated in their IEPs.

Several conclusions can be drawn from the above description of our hypothetical elementary school. First, what goes on inside the school in many ways reflects what goes on outside the school in terms of community demographics, parental values, and the involvement of local businesses. Second, consistent with the notion of schools as loosely coupled organizations, a variety of activities occur in any given school building, and these activities require a coordination of space, materials, and schedules. Third, the majority of services offered in the schools can be depicted as falling under one of two administrative units—regular or special education. Although housed in the same facilities, these units maintain separate administrative structures, receive separate lines of funding, and employ their own teaching staff. For the majority of students who fail in regular education classrooms, receiving additional services depends on the school's ability to document that a prereferral intervention was attempted, identify that a learning or adjustment problem exists, determine whether the student's needs make them eligible for individualized instruction under one or more handicapping conditions, and assign the student to a special class teacher who is responsible for designing an appropriate educational program. This process is known as the *refer-test-place sequence*, and is described in the following section.

The Refer-Test-Place Sequence

It was suggested earlier in the chapter that one outcome of the bureaucratic structure of schools and the large numbers of children they serve is an emphasis by teachers on group approaches to instruction. As discussed at length in Chapter 8, this emphasis by teachers on group instructional approaches inevitably collides with the diversity of skills and behaviors which students bring to the classroom setting to virtually insure that some children will fail in regular education (Apter, 1977). Although most students in each classroom across the country will achieve at sufficient levels to be promoted to the next grade, for some children a significant discrepancy develops between their performance and the teachers' performance expectations (Shinn, 1989). At this point, many school districts require teachers in cooperation with a building-level team to provide instructional or behavioral support to students in the form of a prereferral intervention program (McDougal, Clonan & Martens, 2000). If the student's performance does not improve significantly as a result of such intervention, the teacher then communicates his or her concerns to a building-level evaluation team by completing a referral. Referral forms typically ask for student demographic information (e.g., name and address of parent or guardian, dominant language, any special services received), a description of the student's problem or reason for referral, information concerning the student's current achievement levels (e.g., standardized test scores, teacher estimates of level in the curriculum), relevant medical information, and any attempts made by the teacher to resolve the problem. The completed referral is usually reviewed by a member of the building team who then schedules the referring teacher to present and discuss the child's case at a weekly team meeting.

Three aspects of the referral component are important because they have implications for the subsequent role played by support personnel. First, because student failure results from an interaction of student skills and the demands of the curriculum, changing either of these variables would be likely to increase student achievement (Christenson & Ysseldyke, 1989). Unfortunately, many teachers and school support personnel tend to attribute academic failure to variables inside the child, whereas curriculum demands and instructional practices are viewed as constants (e.g., Martens, Kelly & Diskin, 1996; McKee & Witt, 1990). As a result, placement in special education is seen as the only viable alternative. Second, teachers often finally decide to refer a child following several months of documented failure in the regular education curriculum and in the context of regular classroom activities (e.g., Reschly, 1988). It is not uncommon for evaluation team members, however, to eschew this information when making eligibility decisions in favor of results from standardized, norm-referenced tests (Gresham, Reschly & Carey, 1987). Third, teachers typically refer students for evaluation after making several attempts to resolve the problem on their own (e.g., Ysseldyke, Pianta, Christenson, Wang & Algozzine, 1983) or in consultation with a prereferral intervention team. Although unsuccessful, these instructional and behavioral accommodations can provide information about the severity of the student's problem and may have implications for the teacher's willingness to be involved in future service delivery efforts (e.g., Martens, 1993b).

Once a student is formally referred to the evaluation team for additional consideration, district personnel have up to 90 days by law to complete a comprehensive psychoeducational evaluation, communicate their findings and recommendations to the board of education, and arrange appropriate special education services. Parental consent must be obtained before initiating the evaluation which, depending on the nature of the referral, may involve any of the staff members listed in Table 3.1. When conducting the evaluation, IDEA mandates that tests and assessment procedures be administered in the student's dominant language and be valid for the specific purposes for which they are used. IDEA also states that no single procedure can be used as the sole criterion for determining a student's eligibility for special services, and students are to be assessed in all areas related to their suspected disability. In actuality, individual psychoeducational evaluations typically include a series of interviews with the child's parents and teachers, a review of the student's permanent school records, systematic and anecdotal observations in the classroom setting, and either the collection of work samples or the administration of curriculum-based assessment probes (e.g., Shinn, 1989). Because of the student-centered focus adopted by many evaluation teams, it is also common practice to administer a battery of standardized, norm-referenced tests to assess the student's functioning relative to others in such areas as general intelligence, adaptive behavior, achievement, language, and social behavior.

After data collection is complete, the evaluation team is responsible for drafting a report that describes the assessment results, summarizes the student's current performance levels, and indicates whether the child is eligible for classification as a handicapped student consistent with state regulations (see Chapter 8 for a complete description of various handicapping conditions). In addition, the report makes recommendations to the receiving special education teacher concerning approximate levels in the curriculum at which to begin instruction, strategies the teacher might find useful in developing the student's IEP, and any related services the student should receive such as speech or physical therapy.

With the evaluation report in hand, one or more members of the building-level team, a designated special education representative, and the child's parents or legal guardians participate in a staffing meeting. During this meeting, the findings and recommendations of the evaluation team are discussed with parents and a decision is made concerning the student's eligibility for special education services. If all parties are in agreement with this decision, the student's IEP is completed or approved by those in attendance by documenting the following information: (1) classification status; (2) annual goals and short-term instructional objectives as well as evaluation criteria and procedures; (3) recommended program, date of initiation, and amount of time per day; (4) placement; and (5) any specialized equipment or related services. The school district is required to provide the agreed upon special education services, usually within 30 days of the receipt of the recommendation. At any point during the proceedings, the child's parents are free to disagree with the actions taken by the school and request an impartial hearing to have their child's case reviewed. In addition, parents may obtain a second opinion of their child's case by seeking an independent evaluation at the school's expense.

The Role of Consultation

Cuts in state education budgets across the country have made it increasingly apparent that not all children who fail in regular education can be placed in special education classrooms. Similarly, special education teachers are facing larger numbers of students with disabilities in their classrooms, making it more difficult to deal effectively with all of the children with whom they come in contact. We believe that these realities of special education service delivery create several opportunities for school consultants to become involved in traditional refer-test-place models.

Our experience in the schools has suggested that regular education teachers are quite knowledgeable about the range of student abilities in their classrooms and can quickly identify those students who are at imminent risk of failure. Unlike their low-achieving peers, these students may have considerable difficulty mastering grade-level curriculum objectives, often engage in severe problem behavior, and challenge teachers in their efforts to meet the needs of other children in the classroom. We have observed two behavioral regularities with respect to these students that have important implications for the school consultant: (1) after trying everything deemed reasonably possible within the constraints of their classroom, teachers will refer these students for evaluation at some point during the year; (2) once these students have been referred, teachers will battle vehemently for them to be classified and placed outside their classroom (see Witt & Martens, 1988, for another perspective on this issue). How can these regularities create opportunities for school consultation? On the one hand, if the goal of consultation is to help teachers intensify their efforts to accommodate their most problematic students, the consultant should be prepared for a great deal of teacher resistance. Going along with teachers' wishes *in this instance*, however, may be viewed as a supportive move by the consultant and may be effective at enlisting teacher cooperation in future consultation cases via the principle of reciprocity discussed in Chapter 2.

When consulting over students who are not the lowest achievers in the classroom, teachers may be more willing to attempt an intervention program because it is unlikely that these children will be found eligible for special services. The consultant must realize, however, that time is on the teacher's side. That is, in the absence of additional services or accommodations, some of these low-achieving students will fall far enough behind their peers to warrant referral. At their best, school consultation services may prevent an eventual referral by enabling the student to perform at levels consistent with their peers. Even in the worst of circumstances, however, consultation is likely to forestall a referral while valuable treatment outcome data are being collected in the regular classroom setting.

Over time, the delivery of school consultation services may actually enhance the effectiveness of special education by reducing the numbers of children who are referred and placed. For example, Gutkin, Henning-Stout, and Piersel (1988) examined the long-term effects of a prereferral intervention model in which school consultation was added as an intermediate step in the referral process. In the 4 years following implementation of the program, outcome data revealed that the percentage of referred children who met their educational objectives, and therefore were not evaluated, increased from 21 to 61%. Interestingly, the percentage of students who were evaluated and deemed eligible for special education placement increased from 69 to 82% during the same time period. These latter data suggest that not only were building-level teams conducting workups on fewer numbers of students, but more of these children were actually recommended for services rather than returned to the regular education classroom following a costly evaluation.

SCHOOL CONSULTATION FROM AN
ADMINISTRATIVE PERSPECTIVE

Factors Influencing the Use of Consultation Services

Numerous school districts across the country now routinely implement prereferral intervention programs as a means of supplementing traditional special education services (Flugum & Reschly, 1994; McDougal et al., 2000; Rosenfield, 1992). As noted by Ponti et al. (1988), these programs represent attempts to view consultation as "an integral part of the educational service delivery system rather than as a separate service provided by individual practitioners" (p. 90). Attempts such as these to institutionalize school consultation practice have met with varying degrees of success as a function of the need to overcome several barriers to innovation at an organizational level. Three of these barriers are particularly common and include support from administration, consistency with traditional services, and documentation of beneficial effects on students.

Because district and building administrators (e.g., principals, vice principals, directors of special education) have authority over resource allocation and make decisions concerning such issues as class schedules and teacher release time, garnering the support of these individuals is crucial for successful school consultation (McDougal et al., 2000). As noted by Piersel and Gutkin (1983), a resistant administrator will in all likelihood ensure the failure of a prereferral intervention model. Given the bureaucratic structure of schools, however, administrators who are merely tolerant of consultation or who offer only moderate levels of support may be equally damning. The greatest barrier to consultation services identified by school consultants themselves is lack of sufficient time (e.g., Costenbader, Swartz & Petrix, 1992). By lack of time, consultants usually refer to difficulties scheduling uninterrupted meetings with teachers given their busy class schedules, and the challenges of providing consultation services while managing other professional duties (e.g., evaluation caseloads, counseling groups). Inside the classroom, lack of time for teachers may refer to difficulties working individually with a single student while adequately supervising the rest of the class during independent seatwork. Unless the building principal is willing to actively support school consultation by, for example, providing release time for teachers or assigning part-time aides to classrooms, efforts to implement agreed upon intervention programs may actually be viewed as punishing from the teacher's perspective (Piersel & Gutkin, 1983).

In order to ensure that school consultation is being provided in ways that are consistent with and augment traditional services, Ponti et al. (1988) suggest that a needs assessment be conducted prior to program implementation. As discussed in Chapter 4, conducting a needs assessment is part of successful entry into the schools and involves "mapping" the formal and informal services available in the building, identifying key administrative personnel, and evaluating gaps in the service delivery network. Such gaps may refer to high numbers of children who are referred for failure in the regular classroom but are deemed ineligible for special education, a lack of continuity or duplication of effort in the refer-test-place process, or effective services that are underutilized because school staff are unaware of their existence. McDougal et al. (2000) suggest that consultation services also be evaluated formatively throughout implementation using such means as focus groups, roundtable meetings, surveys, and direct observation. Information collected from these sources can be used to revise the way consultation services are delivered (e.g., computerized referral forms) or to arrange additional staff training in key areas (e.g., instructional interventions).

Finally, school consultation may be viewed as incompatible with more sequentially coupled special education services because its utilization and effectiveness is more difficult to document (Piersel & Gutkin, 1983). Funds for special education are typically allocated based on the number of students with handicaps in a given district. As the number of these students increases, the district can be expected to receive a corresponding increase in state and federal funds. Consultation services, on the other hand, may be directed toward children in both regular and special education classrooms, typically involve multiple contacts with any given teacher, and often have no formal relationship to district funding. For example, in New York State there is a small amount of money available to schools under the category of Educationally Related Support Services (ERSS). These funds were used in the past to obtain additional services for regular education students such as social skills training or counseling. In recent years, several districts have required support personnel to document the amount of time they spend in consultation activities, enabling a portion of these funds to be used to support prereferral intervention services.

The Three Paradoxes of School Consultation

We conclude this chapter with a discussion of three paradoxes that continue to pervade the delivery of school consultation services. A paradox is defined as a statement that is seemingly absurd or contradictory, yet is in fact true. The dynamic tension between schools as bureaucracies and teaching as an intensive technology often places the school consultant in situations that call for seemingly contradictory actions in their attempts to deliver services. Understanding consultation from the perspective of both administrators and teachers can be helpful in resolving these situations to the mutual satisfaction of all parties involved.

Paradox 1: Although Teachers Are Frequently Exposed to Innovative Educational Practices, Change Occurs Slowly in Schools

Educational innovations are typically developed by individuals outside the school setting, adopted by district administrators, and passed on to building principals for dissemination downward to teachers. Teaching is an intensive technology, however, and teachers maintain high levels of autonomy over what goes on in their classrooms. As a result, many innovations that are supposedly adopted in schools using a top-down model fail to be implemented at the level of the classroom (Sarason, 1971, 1996). This means that attempts to implement a prereferral intervention model that have administrative backing but do not involve teachers and support personnel as planning team members will probably not succeed (McDougal et al., 2000). Similarly, informal attempts by individual support personnel to implement school consultation services are likely to run counter to the generally accepted model of top-down change. As an innovation developed from within the school, consultation services in this case must be disseminated upward through the administrative hierarchy before they receive organizational approval. Although bureaucracies are well suited for moving information downward from administrators to workers, they often have few mechanisms in place for going in the reverse direction. As a result, "grass-roots" attempts to implement school consultation services in the absence of administrative approval may also be likely to fail.

Paradox 2: Most Teachers Want to Be Involved in Responding to Children's Learning and Adjustment Problems, but Schools Are Run in Ways That Limit This Involvement

In a survey of 171 teachers from 12 public and parochial schools, Gutkin (1980) found that 96% of the respondents judged the involvement of teachers in developing intervention programs for difficult-to-teach students as being "quite" or "very" important. As noted earlier in the chapter, teachers will typically attempt several instructional modifications before referring a child for evaluation, and Algozzine, Ysseldyke, Christenson, and Thurlow (1983) found that from a range of available services, teachers prefer those activities which they themselves can implement. Our own experiences in the schools have suggested that most teachers are indeed genuinely invested in the welfare of their students.

Despite their high levels of commitment, teachers come in contact with a large number of students during their career and are typically held accountable for the achievement of groups rather than individuals. In contrast, school consultation often requires teachers to modify their instructional practices to meet the needs of individual students. Tensions occur when teachers desire to make these accommodations, but are expected to do so in the absence of building-level supports or against the group-focused values of building administrators.

Paradox 3: For School Consultation to Become a Stand-Alone Service Delivery Option, One Must Decrease the Bureaucratic Nature of Schools or Increase the Bureaucratic Nature of School Consultation

In several ways, the principles of school consultation are at odds with those of classical organizational theory. First, the voluntary, cooperative nature of the consultative relationship falls outside the typical hierarchy of authority between building administrators and teachers. Second, when teachers change their behavior as a function of the consultant's problem solving, social influence, and professional support activities, this tacitly increases the number of individuals to whom the teacher is required to report. Third, during the course of their interactions with teachers, it is not uncommon for school consultants to arrange alternative service delivery configurations such as that described in the home-based reinforcement example. The exception principle of classical theory states that when the same or a similar problem arises repeatedly, solutions to this problem should be established as standard operating procedures (Owens, 1981). Because each child presents a unique set of circumstances to the teacher and consultant, it may be difficult to establish a standard set of routines in meeting their individual needs. In schools characterized by high levels of principal Consideration (Halpin, 1966) and group norms that promote creative professional behavior, teachers may be more willing to deviate from "standard operating procedures." By contrast, principals who strive to initiate a bureaucratic structure in their schools may take a dim view of such activities, unless they can be shown to facilitate the traditional special education model. In these schools, providing consultation services in a more sequentially coupled fashion by developing standard procedures for accepting consultation referrals, a standard pool of effective intervention options, and a standard set of measures for evaluating outcomes are likely to be consistent with the prevailing organizational climate (McDougal et al., 2000).

In this chapter, we attempted to describe the operation of schools from an organizational perspective and to provide the reader with an appreciation for the range of services that are offered. In Chapter 4, we begin discussion of our integrated model of school consultation by analyzing the historical antecedents of consultation as a service delivery approach and describing the principles associated with the two major consultation models—mental health consultation (Caplan, 1970; Caplan & Caplan, 1993/1999) and behavioral consultation (Bergan, 1977; Bergan & Kratochwill, 1990).

II

Consultation Processes and Outcomes

4

Bases of an Integrated Model of School Consultation

In this chapter we present the underlying bases of the integrated model of school consultation, which is described in detail in Chapter 5. Bases associated with community mental health are the concepts of population-oriented prevention, crisis, and social support as well as Gerald Caplan's model of mental health consultation (Caplan, 1970; Caplan & Caplan, 1993/1999). Bases associated with behavioral psychology are problem solving, behavior modification in applied settings, and John R. Bergan's model of behavioral consultation (Bergan, 1977; Bergan & Kratochwill, 1990). Other important bases are social power and interpersonal influence. Finally, we address the issue of laying the groundwork for successful entry into school and classroom settings. After reading Chapter 4, one should understand the bases of and rationale for the integrated model of school consultation presented in Chapter 5.

COMMUNITY MENTAL HEALTH AND MENTAL HEALTH CONSULTATION BASES

After World War II, mental health professionals explored new ways of promoting mental health and preventing mental illness in the public at large, a perspective known as the community or preventive approach. This approach—later legitimized by federal legislation and popularized during the community mental health movement—was founded on the concepts of epidemiological strategies, a primary prevention orientation, and community-wide social support systems (Schulberg & Killilea, 1982).

One of the key originators of the preventive approach is child and community psychiatrist Gerald Caplan (see, for example, Caplan, 1961, 1963, 1964, 1970, 1986, 1989; Caplan & Caplan, 1980, 1993/1999). Caplan's early professional career in Israel (1948–1952) and later work at Harvard University (1952–1977) saw the development of models and techniques that were integral to the community mental health movement (Erchul & Schulte, 1993). In this opening section, we describe four models commonly associated with Caplan: population-oriented prevention, crisis, support systems, and mental health consultation.

Population-Oriented Preventive Model

For many years, the traditional practice of psychiatry concerned itself with the long-term psychoanalysis of individual patients. In the 1940s, therefore, it was a radical departure for Gerald Caplan to advocate for a population-oriented approach that viewed prevention as the ultimate goal (cf. Caplan & Bowlby, 1948). Interestingly, the basis for the population-oriented preventive model is not found within psychiatry, but rather within the field of public health. While a Harvard faculty member in the early 1950s, Caplan attended lectures on conceptual models within public health and epidemiology presented by faculty colleagues. Caplan specifically credits Hugh R. Leavell (e.g., Clark & Leavell, 1958) with the conceptual development of primary, secondary, and tertiary prevention within public health practice (Erchul, 1993b). Caplan (1961, 1964) later developed a new model of prevention in the mental health field that incorporated this now familiar typology of prevention.

Primary prevention relates to decreasing the incidence (i.e., rate of occurrence over time, or new cases) of a disorder by defeating the harmful factors before they produce the disorder in the population. Within public health, primary prevention may be accomplished through interventions that target health promotion, such as education, or specific protection, such as vaccination (Clark & Leavell, 1958). In adapting this concept, Caplan (1964) noted that the primary prevention of mental disorders may result from social action (including attempts to increase physical, psychosocial, and sociocultural supplies to the population) and interpersonal action (including attempts to maximize the mental health professional's benefit to the population). In Caplan's (1986) current model—the "recurrent themes model of primary prevention"—past risk factors (biopsychosocial hazards) interact with intermediate variables (competence, reactions to crisis, and social supports) to produce outcomes of good or poor mental health. Interventions intended to achieve primary prevention include community social action, consultation, collaboration, education, crisis intervention, and support systems intervention.

Secondary prevention refers to actions intended to decrease the prevalence of a disorder, with prevalence signifying the percentage of the population that has the disorder at a given time. Its aim is to reduce the rate of old and new cases, generally accomplished by shortening the duration of the disorder (Caplan, 1964). Secondary prevention efforts typically focus on an at-risk group—a segment of the population that may be very likely to develop a particular disorder under certain conditions. (Primary prevention efforts, in contrast, focus on the entire population.) As an example, children of recently divorced parents may be considered an at-risk group for behavioral and emotional problems. Other examples of secondary prevention efforts are the Head Start program and the Primary Mental Health Project (Cowen & Hightower, 1990).

Tertiary prevention refers to attempts to decrease the extent of impairment in the population currently afflicted (Caplan, 1964) or increase the degree of ongoing role-functioning in the population that already has recovered (Caplan, 1989). Tertiary prevention may be achieved through rehabilitation or disability limitation efforts (Clark & Leavell, 1958). The purpose of tertiary prevention is to return individuals with disorders to their highest level of adaptive, productive functioning as soon as possible (Caplan, 1964). An example of tertiary prevention would be teaching social skills to a child with attention-deficit/hyperactivity disorder whose excessive motor activity has been managed through stimulant medication.

Two updates regarding this prevention typology are in order. First, the study of primary prevention continues its extreme popularity among human service professionals. For example, Trickett, Dahiyat, and Selby (1994) noted that there were over 1,300 professional papers on primary prevention published from 1983 to 1991. Second, Gordon (1983, 1987) has advanced a new typology for prevention of physical disease containing the terms, *universal, selective,* and *indicated* prevention. These terms bear some resemblance to, though are not the same as, *primary, secondary,* and *tertiary* prevention, respectively. Because the Committee on Prevention of Mental Disorders of the Institute of Medicine has dropped the original public health terms and has adopted instead *universal, selective,* and *indicated* prevention as part of its overall model of intervention, Gordon's terms are likely to be used more often in the future (Mrazek & Haggerty, 1994).

Crisis Model

A crisis is a short period of psychological upset that occurs when a person encounters significant life problems that cannot be escaped and are not easily solved with his or her usual problem-solving strategies (Caplan, 1974). A crisis may be developmental, arising from the physiological and psychological changes that are part of normal growth (cf. Erikson, 1959), or it may be situational, arising from changes in a person's environment, social role, or health status. When a person's customary problem-solving responses do not resolve the crisis, he or she becomes upset and distressed at both the continuation of the stressor and the inability to deal with it successfully. Typical patterns of functioning are disrupted, and negative emotions that can include fear, anxiety, frustration, or guilt are experienced. The upset and tension become an impetus for the person to mobilize internal and external resources. He or she is more likely to seek the help of others, and is more suggestible and receptive to new approaches to solve the problem. If these approaches turn out to be helpful, the tension and upset subside and psychological equilibrium returns. However, if the problem continues, "major disorganization of the individual" (Caplan, 1964, p. 41) results.

How one resolves a crisis has future implications. If, during a crisis, a person learns appropriate and adaptive coping strategies, then these strategies are available for later use. For example, assisting a recently transferred teacher to mobilize new sources of social support, rather than to reinforce her belief that she will be returning shortly to her former school, can help her cope adaptively with the present and leave her better prepared for the future. Conversely, if a person learns and later uses strategies that are ineffective or maladaptive, he or she is left more vulnerable to psychopathology. Every crisis, therefore, "presents both an opportunity for psychological growth and danger of psychological deterioration. It is a way station on a path leading away from or toward mental disorder" (Caplan, 1964, p. 53).

Support Systems Model

The fundamental premise of the support systems model is that social support plays an important health-promoting function and can reduce the risk of both physical and mental illness (Caplan, 1986). Caplan (1974) defined social support as "an enduring pattern of continuous or intermittent ties that play a significant part in maintaining the psychological and physical integrity of the individual over time" (p. 7). Social support, such as that offered by family members, friends, and community institutions, helps the individual to: mobilize psychological resources and master emotional burdens; learn to distinguish safe from dangerous situations; share tasks; and provide various resources such as money, materials, or skills (Caplan, 1974).

The simple premise underlying the support systems model has profound implications. For primary prevention efforts, it suggests that increasing the social supports available to a population can decrease the incidence of physical and psychological disorders. For secondary and tertiary prevention efforts, it suggests that individuals who are provided with social support in stressful situations will be more likely to experience positive outcomes. In other words, high stress in the presence of high social support does not increase susceptibility to mental illness and generally appears to enhance mental health outcomes (Caplan, 1989; Cohen & Wills, 1985).

In our integrated model of school consultation, we find it useful to distinguish between emotional and instrumental support. *Emotional support* refers to "the provision of aid which reflects concern for a person's emotional reactions to an event" (Tardy, 1994, p. 72). Within consultation, emotional support may be evidenced by a consultant serving as an empathetic and active listener, promoting the functioning of natural helpers in an organization, or convening support groups or mutual help groups for consultees facing a common problem (Caplan, 1986). By comparison, *instrumental support* refers to helping another to solve a problem (Sarason & Sarason, 1986). In offering instrumental support, the consultant may provide consultees with feedback, training, and materials that address problem-solving aspects of consultation. Sharing tasks within consultation is another way a consultant can exhibit instrumental support.

Caplan's Model of Mental Health Consultation

Mental health consultation (including Gerald Caplan's specific model) has been hailed as "a major, if not the major technique and focus of community psychology, community psychiatry, and community mental health" (Mannino & Shore, 1971, p. 1). To some degree, all consultation approaches are based on Caplan's mental health model, which is described in detail in Caplan (1963, 1964, 1970) and more recently in Caplan and Caplan (1993/1999) and Erchul (1993a). Interested readers are encouraged to consult these references for a more comprehensive explanation of the model. Here we describe some underlying assumptions of Caplan's model, define his four types of consultation, and examine key issues related to the model's consultee-centeredness.

Fundamental Assumptions

Brown, Pryzwansky, and Schulte (2001) have explicated five major assumptions of Caplan's model. Because the model is sometimes misinterpreted as being narrowly intrapsychic in nature, and these assumptions are not always explicit in Caplan's writings, they are listed here.

1. *Both intrapsychic and environmental factors are important in explaining and changing behavior.* This approach clearly focuses on intrapsychic variables that are important in behavior change to a greater extent than any other model of consultation. However, much less publicized is the fact that Caplan has promoted a strong environmental focus through a major emphasis on making social institutions (such as schools) function more effectively by improving their ability to deal with the mental health problems of their clients. Astor, Pitner, and Duncan (1998) have illustrated clearly the importance of environmental factors within Caplanian consultation with teachers concerning school violence prevention issues.

2. *More than technical expertise is important in designing effective interventions.* A consultee's decision to adopt an intervention technique is not based solely on its effectiveness. It is influenced by many factors, including elements of the consultee's professional role and organizational culture.

3. *Learning and generalization occur when consultees retain responsibility for action.* The direct involvement of a consultant in problem resolution will diminish the consultee's feelings of ownership over problems and solutions generated to resolve them, and thus is not recommended.

4. *Mental health consultation is a supplement to other problem-solving mechanisms within an organization.* There are several ways of addressing client difficulties within an organization and, for many types of problems, procedures other than consultation are more appropriate. For example, skill deficiencies in consultees are handled better through supervision because consultants are unlikely to understand the skills involved in professions except their own.

5. *Consultee attitudes and affect are important in consultation, but cannot be dealt with directly.* Instead of focusing on consultee affect, the Caplanian consultant develops hypotheses about the types of personal issues that are interfering with the consultee's functioning and then intervenes indirectly by using the work problem as a metaphor for the consultee's problem (Brown et al., 2001).

The Four Types of Mental Health Consultation

Caplan (1970; Caplan & Caplan, 1993/1999) has distinguished among four types of consultation based on two major considerations: (1) whether the content focus of consultation is difficulty with a particular client versus an administrative difficulty, and (2) whether the central purpose of consultation is provision of information in the consultant's area of specialty versus improvement of the consultee's problem solving capacity.

Client-centered case consultation is perhaps the most familiar type of consultation performed by mental health professionals. A consultee encounters difficulty with a client for whom he or she has responsibility and seeks a consultant who will evaluate the client, arrive at a diagnosis, and offer recommendations concerning how the consultee might modify his or her treatment of the client. Often, the assessment, diagnosis, and recommendations are summarized in a written report. The consultee then uses the information provided in the report to develop and implement a plan for dealing with the client, with minimal subsequent involvement of the consultant. The primary goal of client-centered case consultation is to develop a plan for dealing with the client's difficulties; education or skill development for the consultee is a secondary focus.

Consultee-centered case consultation is the type of consultation that is most closely associated with Caplan. Consultee-centered case consultation is concerned with difficulties a consultee faces with a particular client for whom he or she has responsibility in the work setting. The primary goal of consultee-centered case consultation is remediation of the "shortcomings in the consultee's professional functioning that are responsible for difficulties with the present case" (Caplan, 1970, p. 125). Client improvement is a secondary goal.

Program-centered administrative consultation is similar to client-centered case consultation. In both types, the consultant is regarded as a specialist who is contracted to study a problem and to provide recommendations for dealing with the problem. In client-centered case consultation, however, the consultant's assessment, diagnosis, and recommendations deal with the problems of a particular client; in program-centered administrative consultation, the consultant considers the problems surrounding the development of a new program or some aspect of organizational functioning.

Consultee-centered administrative consultation is a fourth type of consultation specified by Caplan. Its goal is to improve the professional functioning of members of an administrative staff. Although consultee-centered administrative consultation may assume different forms, it is generally based on a rather broadly conceptualized role for the consultant. For example, the consultant does not limit consultation to problems brought to his or her attention by consultees, but instead takes an active role in identifying and assessing organizational problems. The consultant may work globally to improve the overall health of the organization, perhaps by having consultees consider the development of system-wide policies that promote the mental health of staff members and their clients.

The Consultant–Consultee Relationship

In establishing relationships with consultees, the Caplanian consultant works to establish a *coordinate, nonhierarchical relationship* in which professional issues and concerns can be discussed openly. Ideally, it should be a relationship of mutual respect in which there is no power differential between parties. Consultees must learn to view themselves as active participants who can educate the consultant about their professional role and its constraints so that the consultant may be most helpful. It is also important that the consultant deal directly with confidentiality issues, specifically assuring consultees that their actions will not be discussed with others without their consent. Consultees also must understand that they retain complete freedom to accept or reject the consultant's advice (Caplan, 1970). Also, unlike mental health collaboration, wherein responsibilities for outcomes are shared between parties (Caplan et al., 1994), consultees must understand that they alone retain full responsibility for consultation outcomes.

Sources of Consultee Difficulty

Caplan (1970; Caplan & Caplan, 1993/1999) has identified four major sources of consultee difficulty: lack of knowledge, lack of skill, lack of self-confidence, and lack of objectivity. Although the first three sources mentioned are relatively straightforward, lack of objectivity is more complex in nature. This type of difficulty occurs when consultees lose their usual professional distance when working with clients and then cannot apply their skills effectively to resolve a current work problem. Lack of objectivity may also be regarded as stemming from consultees' faulty perceptions and incorrect attributions surrounding the present situation. Caplan has noted that, when supervisory and administrative mechanisms are functioning well in an organization (and lack of knowledge and lack of skill can be ruled out as explanations), most instances of consultee ineffectiveness will be attributable to a lack of objectivity (Erchul, 1993b).

Caplan has delineated five major types of consultee lack of objectivity: direct personal involvement, simple identification, transference, characterological distortion, and theme interference. Again, somewhat more complex than the rest is the last one mentioned, theme interference. A *theme* is a representation of an unsolved problem or prior defeat that the consultee has experienced that influences his or her expectations regarding a current work difficulty. For example, suppose a teacher unconsciously harbors the theme, "Boys from single-parent homes are always behavior problems in the classroom." This theme may interfere with the teacher's ability to objectively view a new student named Tom, who lives with his mother, a divorced single parent. The teacher may conclude erroneously that Tom either is, or has great potential to become, a disruptive student. The consultant may try to restore the teacher's objectivity by indicating through indirect confrontation that not all boys who live with one parent are behavior problems (Erchul & Conoley, 1991).

Although the preceding example illustrates the method of *theme interference reduction*, consultee themes may be addressed through other verbally mediated psychodynamic techniques, including the verbal focus on the client and the parable. Still other methods are the nonverbal focus on the case and nonverbal focus on the consultation relationship. These techniques can be used alone or in combination to invalidate the interfering theme and thus improve the consultee's objectivity and problem-solving capacity with respect to the present case (Caplan, 1970).

How the Mental Health Consultant Offers Support to Consultees

Because Caplan clearly regards consultation as part of a support system (Erchul, 1993b), it is important to see how the consultant acts as a supporter. The provision of *instrumental support* is apparent in mental health consultation when the consultant supplies information the consultee needs. In instances of consultee lack of skill, the consultant is to support the consultee in understanding the issues involved in the case, and perhaps engage in limited supervision of consultee skill development. Also, guiding the consultee through the problem-solving process of consultation provides evidence of instrumental support.

It is somewhat more difficult to understand how the Caplanian consultant offers *emotional support*, as he or she is not to address consultee affect in a direct manner. Generally speaking, however, the indirect methods associated with Caplan's model provide emotional support to consultees by permitting them to experience and express intense feelings about an issue without the consultant using insight-giving psychotherapy to illuminate their inner conflicts (Caplan, 1993b). In other words, mental health consultation offers a safe, nonjudgmental arena for consultees to discuss their professional problems. Along these lines, we believe the principal vehicle for providing emotional support in mental health consultation is the coordinate, nonhierarchical relationship. Though a challenge for most consultants to establish and maintain (Erchul, 1993c), this relationship of coordinate interdependence is essential for the success of mental health consultation. A final, specific way in which the mental health consultant provides emotional support concerns instances of consultee lack of confidence. Here, the consultant is to provide nonspecific ego support (i.e., basic support and encouragement) until other sources of support can be located within the host organization (Caplan, 1970).

Our presentation thus far has concentrated almost exclusively on issues concerning how the mental health consultant works with consultees, yet another strength of Caplan's model is its emphasis on understanding the organizational context in which consultation occurs and the entry process itself. We shall consider some of these ideas near the end of this chapter.

BEHAVIORAL PSYCHOLOGY AND BEHAVIORAL CONSULTATION BASES

A second set of influences on the practice of school consultation comes from behavioral psychology. As we have seen, the theoretical basis of mental health consultation is psychodynamic and system-based, and draws from traditions of psychiatric practice. In contrast, a behavioral approach to consultation is based on operant and classical conditioning, observational learning/modeling, and, increasingly, behavioral ecology and cognitive-behavioral perspectives (Vernberg & Reppucci, 1986). Drawing from its laboratory research traditions, the approach is known for its emphasis on quantification, specificity, and empirical validation. At the core of behavioral approaches is the assumption that both normal and abnormal behavior is developed and maintained by the same learning principles. In this section we present three important behavioral psychology bases of our integrated model of school consultation: D'Zurilla and Goldfried's (1971) problem-solving model, Tharp and Wetzel's (1969) application of behavior modification in natural settings, and Bergan's (1977; Bergan & Kratochwill, 1990) model of behavioral consultation.

Problem-Solving Model

Although all models of psychological consultation have problem-solving components (Zins & Erchul, 2002), behavioral consultation, more than other models, makes these components explicit to consultees. A classic exposition of problem solving involving the use of behavior modification procedures is found in D'Zurilla and Goldfried (1971). They described problem solving as a process that makes many potentially effective alternatives available to individuals, and increases the probability of selecting the most effective one. D'Zurilla and Goldfried's model assumes that people behave ineffectively because of a learning or skill deficit, and therefore overall effectiveness can be increased by teaching general problem-solving skills that can be applied across situations.

D'Zurilla and Goldfried's (1971) problem-solving model proposes five stages of effective problem solving. First, during *general orientation*, individuals develop attitudes that include: accepting the fact that problems do occur in life, recognizing these problems when they occur, and inhibiting the tendency to act impulsively or to do nothing. Second, in *problem definition and formulation*, individuals define all aspects of the problem in operational terms and identify relevant aspects of the situation. Third, *during generation of alternatives*, individuals attempt "brainstorming" and later combine various alternatives. Fourth, in *decision making*, individuals predict the outcomes likely to be achieved by each available option. Finally, during *verification*, individuals assess the effectiveness of their efforts by comparing actual outcomes to predicted outcomes.

Interestingly, when a consultant subscribes to the notion of consultation as exclusively a problem-solving process, he or she assumes that effective consultants must be process (but not necessarily content) experts. However, with few noteworthy exceptions (e.g., Schein, 1969), the view that a consultant can succeed having only process skills is not prevalent in the consultation literature. In sum, although heuristically useful, D'Zurilla and Goldfried's (1971) model fails to address critical issues a school consultant needs to know. It does not address, for example, the specifics of problem solving, the basis for selecting effective intervention alternatives, or even how one implements the model in the "real world."

Application of Behavior Modification in Natural Settings

Tharp and Wetzel (1969) presented a comprehensive method of applying principles of behavior modification in human service settings such as schools and residential treatment centers. Their method of consultation is a logical extension of the assumptions of a behavioral approach to therapy. Importantly, they formalized the role of direct care providers (such as parents and teachers) as behavior change agents in natural settings.

Tharp and Wetzel (1969) noted three key participants: (1) *consultant*, who is anyone with knowledge and expertise in behavior analysis; (2) *mediator*, who is anyone who controls reinforcers for client behavior and can administer them contingently; and (3) *target*, who is anyone with a problem. Although their triadic models developed independently, we wish to point out the similarities between Caplan's (1964, 1970) use of the terms "consultee" and "client," and Tharp and Wetzel's (1969) terms *mediator* and *target*.

Tharp and Wetzel's pioneering efforts resulted in other attempts to train staff in principles of behavior modification at various institutions (see, for example, Reppucci & Saunders, 1974). Of interest is that the training usually was conducted by university-based teams who were not staff members and who generally left the setting after the demonstration project grant funds expired. Although these highly financed training efforts enjoyed short-term success, their positive effects often faded after the trainers departed.

Regrettably, a direct translation of behavior theory developed in the laboratory to natural settings (as Tharp and Wetzel attempted) cannot be entirely successful because of factors left unaccounted for in the theory. These missing factors include the constraints of the host organization, verbal messages consultants must deliver in order to be effective, ways of handling problems associated with modifying staff behavior, and the limited resources typically available in most schools and agencies. Fortunately, others writing about school consultation have addressed these topics, at least to some degree.

Bergan's Model of Behavioral Consultation

Further refinement of principles advanced by D'Zurilla and Goldfried (1971), Tharp and Wetzel (1969), and others resulted in John R. Bergan's (1977; Bergan & Kratochwill, 1990) model of behavioral consultation. This model combines strategies and tactics of behavior analysis with a structured problem-solving approach, uses behavioral technology to develop intervention plans, and employs the technology of behavior analysis to evaluate treatment outcomes.

Fundamental Assumptions

Bergan (1977) has listed seven key features that underlie his consultation model:

1. The consultee is an active participant in the process in terms of designing the plan to solve the problem, implementing the plan, and evaluating its effectiveness.
2. The model can develop problem-solving skills in the client by having the consultant involve him or her in the same capacity as the consultee. The extent of the client's involvement is dependent upon his or her developmental level, the nature of the problem, and the consultee's views pertaining to how much responsibility the client should assume.
3. The model provides a knowledge link between the consultant and consultee. Consultants supply a medium through which knowledge producers can communicate information to knowledge consumers.

4. Behavioral consultation attempts to link decision-making to empirical evidence. Decisions relating to the course of action to pursue are based on direct observations of the client's behavior and scientific findings regarding behavior change.
5. The model defines problems presented in consultation as residing outside the character of the client. In contrast, the use of a label such as "retarded" or "emotionally disturbed" does not facilitate understanding of the client's current behavior or specify goals that might be attained in consultation.
6. The model stresses the role of environmental factors in controlling behavior. As such, respondent, operant, and modeling procedures are used frequently in behavioral consultation. Research findings indicate that it is possible to bring about marked changes in behavior by altering environmental conditions.
7. Behavioral consultation focuses its evaluation on goal attainment and plan effectiveness rather than on the client's characteristics. This approach emphasizes what has been accomplished in consultation rather than what is wrong with the client (Bergan, 1977).

Bergan's (1977) behavioral consultation model adheres to a four-stage problem-solving process derived from D'Zurilla and Goldfried (1971), a process that maximizes the chance of generating an effective solution. The four stages of the model include three separate interviews, each of which contains specific objectives that the consultant is expected to achieve. Below we summarize the nature of each stage of behavioral consultation: problem identification, problem analysis, plan implementation, and problem evaluation.

Problem Identification

This first stage involves the specification of the problem to be resolved as a result of consultation. Problem identification is accomplished through a *problem identification interview* (PII) between the consultant and consultee. The PII represents a critical point within behavioral consultation because it creates expectations for the use of a behavioral perspective on the client's problems and stresses the role of current environmental events as being mainly responsible for the problem behavior. Specific objectives associated with the PII are:

1. Assess the scope of consultee concerns;
2. Prioritize problem components or identify a target problem area;
3. Define the target problem in overtly observable behavioral terms;

4. Estimate the frequency, intensity, or duration of the problem behavior;
5. Identify tentative goals for change;
6. Tentatively identify environmental conditions surrounding the problem behavior as antecedents, sequences, and consequences;
7. Establish data collection procedures and responsibilities;
8. Schedule the next interview (Bergan, 1977; Bergan & Kratochwill, 1990; Martens, 1993a).

Problem Analysis

During the second stage of behavioral consultation, the problem is examined further and a plan is designed to solve it. The *problem analysis interview* (PAI) has six objectives:

1. Determine the adequacy of baseline (i.e., preintervention) data;
2. Establish goals for change;
3. Analyze environmental conditions surrounding the problem behavior as antecedents, sequences, and consequences;
4. Design and implement an intervention plan;
5. Reaffirm data collection procedures;
6. Schedule the next interview (Bergan, 1977; Bergan & Kratochwill, 1990; Martens, 1993a).

Plan Implementation

This third stage does not involve a formal interview, but instead assumes that the consultant and consultee will meet through a series of brief contacts. During plan implementation, the consultant helps to ensure that the consultee is implementing the intervention plan as agreed and that the probability of the plan succeeding is maximized. There are three objectives associated with plan implementation:

1. Determine whether consultee has requisite skills to implement the intervention plan;
2. Monitor data collection and overall plan operations;
3. Determine need for plan revisions (Bergan, 1977; Bergan & Kratochwill, 1990).

Problem Evaluation

The fourth and final stage of behavior consultation is problem evaluation, which entails the determination of problem solution and plan effectiveness. Problem evaluation is accomplished through the *problem evaluation interview* (PEI), which has four objectives:

1. Determine whether intervention goals were met;
2. Evaluate plan effectiveness;
3. Discuss continuation, modification, or termination of the plan;
4. Terminate consultation or schedule additional meetings to recycle through the problem-solving process (Bergan, 1977; Bergan & Kratochwill, 1990; Martens, 1993a).

Verbal Behavior of the Behavioral Consultant

As Gutkin and Curtis (1982) noted, "At its most basic level, consultation is an interpersonal exchange. As such, the consultant's success is going to hinge largely on his or her communication and relationship skills" (p. 822). Given the many objectives associated with the conduct of behavioral consultation, it is especially important that behavioral consultants communicate clearly and effectively. To evaluate behavioral consultants' interviewing effectiveness, Bergan and Tombari (1975) developed the Consultation Analysis Record (CAR).

Despite its development nearly 30 years ago, the CAR remains the only coding system designed specifically for quantifying verbal interactions occurring during school consultation (see Martens, Erchul & Witt, 1992, for three other systems that have been applied to study school consultation). Coding using the CAR proceeds in two steps. First, transcribed interviews are divided into independent clauses (the basic unit of analysis) that are then numbered consecutively. Second, each independent clause is coded according to four categories:

1. *Message source* refers to whether the consultant or consultee is speaking.
2. *Message content* refers to the topic under discussion, and contains the subcategories of background environment, behavior setting, behavior, individual characteristics, observation, plan, and other.
3. *Message process* refers to the function served by the independent clause, and contains the subcategories of specification, evaluation, inference, summarization, and validation.
4. *Message control* refers to how the speaker influences the verbal behavior of the other through greater use of elicitors (clauses that request information) than emitters (clauses that present information).

Space does not allow for a detailed description of the CAR and its categories and subcategories. Therefore, we suggest consulting Bergan

(1977), Bergan and Tombari (1975, 1976), or Bergan and Kratochwill (1990) for additional information.

Behavioral Consultation Research Using the CAR

Researchers have used the CAR primarily to obtain indices of consultant effectiveness that subsequently are related to indices of consultation outcome (Martens, 1993a). A sampling of important findings from classic research using the CAR includes: the best predictor of problem resolution is the consultant's skill in having the consultee define the problem in behavioral terms (Bergan & Tombari, 1975, 1976); the consultant's use of behavioral cues—as contrasted with medical model cues—leads to higher teacher–consultee expectations with respect to their ability to teach a client who has academic problems (Tombari & Bergan, 1978); and the odds are 14 times higher that a teacher-consultee will identify resources and a means to carry out an intervention plan if the consultant asks instead of tells the consultee (Bergan & Neumann, 1980). Other research on behavior consultation is presented in Chapter 5.

Social Power and Interpersonal Influence Bases

To provide a summary of the social power and interpersonal influence bases of our integrated model of school consultation, we return to some major principles presented in Chapter 2. In many cases, merely supplying needed knowledge to consultees will prove inadequate relative to having them change behaviors and/or solve problems. Therefore, consultants must use their content expertise along with strategic communication and dyadic social influence to establish a cooperative relationship that ultimately will facilitate positive outcomes in consultation. Operationalizing this approach requires an understanding of social influence.

Raven's (1992, 1993) power–interaction model of interpersonal influence provides the foundation for this approach. In applying this model, the consultant must carefully examine his or her available power bases and determine the advisability of their use in a specific instance. Although at one time only expert and referent power were believed to be relevant to the work of the school-based consultant (Martin, 1978), more recently it has been shown that school psychologists and teachers view expert, referent, and informational power bases specifically, and *soft* bases generally, as effective in influencing teachers in consultation (Erchul, Raven & Ray, 2001; Erchul, Raven & Whichard, in press). Other means of influence may be exercised, such as invoking or reducing the power of third parties, selecting an effective mode of influence, or using preparatory devices to set the stage for social influence. When applying principles of interpersonal influence, the consultant must maintain an ethical focus, which is achieved in part by making consultees more powerful and influential.

SUMMARY OF THE BASES OF AN INTEGRATED MODEL OF SCHOOL CONSULTATION

This chapter has presented many bases that underlie the integrated model of school consultation. In summary, these foundational areas are population-oriented prevention, crisis, social support, Caplan's mental health consultation model, problem solving, behavior modification in applied settings, Bergan's behavioral consultation model, social power, and interpersonal influence. As a prelude to Chapter 5, we proceed by explaining what the consultant must typically do to enter the school in order to conduct consultation.

ACHIEVING ENTRY IN SCHOOL CONSULTATION: ENTERING THE SERVICE DELIVERY NETWORK

Although the hypothesized steps in consultation are not generally sharply defined, entry into an organization may be considered a four-step process (Gallessich, 1982). First, an organization's needs are explored and the match between these needs and the consultant's skills are assessed. Second, assuming a good match, the consultant and the host institution proceed to negotiate a contract. As the third step, the consultant makes *physical entry* into the organization. Finally, the consultant interacts directly with consultees and eventually achieves *psychological entry*, signifying that consultees trust and have confidence in the consultant. Others (Brown et al., 2001) have referred to physical entry as *formal entry* and psychological entry as *informal acceptance*.

The reader may recall from Chapter 1 that our integrated model of school consultation is not an organization development model. Notwithstanding, it is necessary that the consultant understand the school as an organization along the lines presented in Chapter 3. Following a brief presentation of selected aspects of assessing a school's functioning, we consider critical issues of contracting and entry within school consultation.

Assessing the School as an Organization: Some General Considerations

Getting to "Know the Territory"

In beginning his work as a school consultant in the early 1960s, community psychologist Ira Iscoe was instructed by one of Gerald Caplan's staff members, Charlotte Owens, to "know the territory" (Iscoe, 1993, p. 92). By this she meant that Iscoe should take the time to study what goes on each day in the school and attempt to understand its organizational atmosphere, as well as to explore the neighborhood in which the school is located. Such study will lead to the uncovering of regular patterns and insights as well as the generation of hypotheses that ultimately will facilitate the consultant's work.

In our experience as school consultants, we have gained an understanding of "the territory" by obtaining answers to questions such as these:

1. What leadership style (e.g., authoritarian, authoritative, democratic, laissez-faire) does the principal exhibit? What are the effects of this style on school staff?
2. How is power displayed in the school, and who wields it? Besides legitimate power by position, who has informal power in the school?
3. Who functions as a "gatekeeper," controlling access to school staff and resources?
4. Where is the school located? What are salient characteristics of the immediate neighborhood?
5. What is the makeup of the students attending the school with respect to socioeconomic status, racial–ethnic composition, percentage of regular education versus special education enrollment, etc.?
6. What is the school's physical layout? How do aspects of the physical structure affect the staff's efficiency and morale as well as students' academic achievement and emotional adjustment?
7. How is the typical school day structured? When do periods begin and end? Do teachers have planning periods during which consultation might occur?
8. What are the school's culture and norms? Are these unusual or different from those of other schools? Do all staff participate in the school's culture and norms? How are those who "deviate" treated by others?
9. What is the school's organizational climate? Are staff members generally satisfied, or is there evidence of widespread professional

burnout? Are staff members' conversations warm, forced, task-oriented, etc.?

10. What are the school's hidden agendas, if any? Is it possible that you will be set up as a scapegoat, to be blamed for others' errors?

11. Are there any taboo or embarrassing topics that you should avoid discussing?

12. What is the history of the school, particularly with respect to its prior use of consultants? Have previous consultants been welcomed and successful in their work?

13. Does the principal understand and completely support your professional mission?

14. What changes does the school anticipate making, and how are they likely to affect your work as a consultant?

In all cases the descriptive information contained in answers to these questions must be carefully analyzed with respect to the implications for the school, administration, staff, students, and, most importantly, your role as consultant.

The careful assessment of any organization can be a lengthy and complex endeavor, and a school presents no exception. Fortunately, some writers, such as Marks (1995), have advanced comprehensive approaches to assessing schools and achieving entry into them. Also, some classic references from the organizational psychology literature include Bennis (1969), Blake and Mouton (1976), French and Bell (1978), and Levinson (1972). The interested school consultant may wish to refer to these sources for further information.

Assessing a School's Readiness for Change

How does one determine whether a school is prepared and receptive to take on a planned change effort, such as an innovative service delivered via consultation? One answer is through the use of the A VICTORY model (Bennett, 1984; Davis & Salasin, 1975; Maher & Bennett, 1984). A VICTORY is an acronym representing Ability, Values, Idea, Circumstances, Timing, Obligation, Resistance, and Yield. The consultant can systematically assess the organizational context of the school by asking key questions related to each A VICTORY factor. The example developed below concerns the introduction of a prereferral intervention program (see Chapter 7), an effort that brings together teachers, students, parents, and the school's support staff to develop accommodations for students before placement in a special education program (e.g., Graden et al., 1985).

Are adequate human, technological, informational, physical, and financial resources available to the school to support the prereferral intervention program (Ability)? Are the values behind the prereferral intervention program consonant with those of the school community (Value)? Does the school community accurately perceive the purposes, goals, and activities associated with the prereferral intervention program (Idea)? What is the nature of factors pressing for or detracting from the integration of this program with other elements already in place in the school (Circumstances)? Does the introduction of the prereferral intervention program synchronize with other important events occurring in the school (Timing)? What is the perceived need on the part of the school community for having a prereferral intervention program (Obligation)? Does anyone demonstrate any overt or covert resistance to the prereferral intervention program (Resistance)? What rewards and benefits are expected by school community as a result of instituting this program (Yield)?

A VICTORY is useful for the consultant in helping a school assess its readiness for implementing contemplated changes. It should be noted, however, that assessment using A VICTORY can lead to the conclusion that bringing about changes through a consultative effort would be ill-advised at the present time. This situation may force the consultant to abandon the effort altogether (cf. Conoley & Conoley, 1992, Chapter 4).

Negotiating the Contract

Assuming that the consultant and the school agree that there is a good fit between the consultant's qualifications and the school's needs, a contract is prepared. A contract is a critical element of consultation, and usually is a written agreement between the consultant and the host institution that specifies the relevant parameters and nature of the consultation (Caplan, 1970). Although agreements of this sort can be verbal, the use of a written agreement is recommended to avoid possible later misunderstandings. If the agreement initially is only verbal, it is advisable that the consultant follow up with a letter that explicitly states what has been agreed to by both parties (Kirby, 1985).

Although the length and coverage of contracts will vary, all consultation contracts or letters of agreement should use precise language and cover the following issues:

1. General goals of consultation;
2. Tentative time frame;
3. Consultant's responsibilities, including services to be provided, methods to be used, time to be committed to the organization, and evaluation of the degree to which goals are achieved;
4. Organization's responsibilities, including nature and extent of staff contributions to consultation, and fees to be paid to consultant;

5. Consultant's boundaries, including: the contact person to whom the consultant is to be responsible; people to whom the consultant is to have (or not have) access; consultant's access to departments, meetings, and documents; conditions for bringing in other consultants or trainees; confidentiality rules regarding all information;

6. Arrangements for periodic review and evaluation of the consultant's work, and explication of either party to terminate the contract if consultation progress is unsatisfactory (Gallessich, 1982, pp. 272–273).

Achieving School-Level (Physical) Entry

After the terms of the contract have been agreed upon, the consultant has official sanction to enter the school and to begin exploring issues of concern. The consultant's assessment of the school may continue along the lines of refining his or her answers to the 14 "know the territory" questions posed earlier as well as A VICTORY. Although it is important for the consultant to proceed in this task-oriented manner, it is equally important for the consultant to develop his or her relationship with the consultee institution and with individual consultees (Caplan, 1970).

Building Relationships with the Host School

Central to the consultant's success in establishing relationships with a host organization is building channels of communication. Caplan (1970) has advocated "finding key members of the communication network who have easy access to significant groups of line workers and also to the authority system, and then building relationships of trust and respect with them so that they will act as communication bridges between the consultant and the staff of the institution" (p. 51). As consultants, we often have involved school counselors and special education lead teachers in this capacity.

There are several predictable obstacles to developing effective communication during entry (Caplan, 1970). First, the consultant can expect ambivalent feelings from school staff who, on one hand, may welcome the consultant's expertise and assistance but who, on the other hand, may feel threatened by the consultant's impending attempts to "change the system." Second, mental health professionals who work as consultants are likely to conjure up anxiety-provoking fantasies in consultees, who believe the consultant will psychoanalyze them, judge them, etc. For both obstacles, Caplan (1970) has instructed consultants to dissipate these inaccurate, stereotypical thoughts principally by interacting with as many people in the setting as possible, and especially with those individuals who are influential in molding the opinions of others. Suspicion of the consultant subsides when all can see that he or she is a person worthy of trust and respect (Caplan, 1970).

Addressing Confidentiality Issues

During formal entry, the consultant's commitment to confidentiality concerns should be made explicit to the head administrator, generally the principal. This administrator needs to understand the limits of what he or she will learn from the consultant about specific staff members. The consultant can share general impressions, organizational issues, or specific problems that seem to be common among the staff. Most administrators accept the limits of what the consultant can report. Perhaps most importantly, the school consultant must tell the principal that he or she is not a "spy" who is there for the benefit of the administration (Conoley & Conoley, 1982; S.B. Sarason, Levine, Goldenberg, Cherlin & Bennett, 1966).

Obtaining the Sanction of the Principal and Other Administrators

It is critical that the school consultant acquire the support of the building principal, keep him or her informed of ongoing activities, and solicit feedback about the nature of services being rendered (Caplan, 1964). Stated alternately, "effective and sustained innovations require sanction and access from the top administrator of the host organization" (Kelly, 1993, p. 77). Within schools, other layers of the bureaucracy to keep informed include vice principal(s) and other educational supervisors (Caplan, 1970). Although this point may be self-evident to seasoned consultants who operate in the private sector, failure to obtain proper sanction has led to the downfall of many change efforts in public education (cf. Sarason, 1982, 1996).

Achieving Classroom-Level (Psychological) Entry

After accomplishing physical entry, the consultant then meets with teachers and other staff members with whom he or she will work directly. Although the consultant may be introduced to the school initially in a large group context, such as a school faculty meeting, eventually the consultant will meet face-to-face with individual consultees. When meeting consultees, the consultant needs to display interpersonal skills expected in many other helping relationships (e.g., active listening, rapport building).

Additionally, the consultant must address aspects of *role structuring* during this stage of consultation.

Role structuring has four major components (Brown et al., 2001). First, the consultant must discuss and/or negotiate the roles that each party will assume. This action models open communication and helps to avoid later misunderstandings. For example, a consultee initially may believe that it is the consultant's job to solve the problem alone, when the consultant thinks that the two will be working together to jointly solve the problem. To avoid misunderstanding, the consultant should indicate to the consultee the general nature of the consulting relationship. This often takes the form of explaining how he or she "usually works" with consultees. For instance, if describing Caplan's (1970) coordinate, nonhierarchical relationship, one could use the terms "egalitarian" or "cooperative partnership," or say, "we will work together." Although the specific elements of roles may be negotiated, the point here is that both parties must understand and agree on the basic parameters of the relationship early on (Zins & Erchul, 2002).

Second, the consultant is to establish an agreement for action. Again, a common consultee misperception is that the consultant will do all the work, including implement the intervention. Assuming that it is consultation rather than mental health collaboration (Caplan et al., 1994) that will take place, however, it is the consultee who will be implementing the intervention. It is extremely important that the consultant convey this point clearly. Third, the consultant is to emphasize the short-term nature of consultation, and prepare the consultee for eventual termination of the process (Brown et al., 2001).

Finally, the consultant is to address confidentiality and its limits (Brown et al., 2001). The consultee must be assured that his or her interactions with the consultant will be completely confidential, or be warned of the limits of confidentiality. Assuming the consultant has previously negotiated this point with the principal, he or she might say to a consultee, "I will regard everything you say as strictly confidential, unless what you say concerns a law that has been, or will be, broken." In school consultation, perhaps the most likely reason for breaking confidence is suspected or documented child abuse or neglect.

To avoid a breach of confidentiality, the consultant should not report even on the consultee's *successes* without permission. However, it is generally safe to comment on shared, public knowledge about a consultee. If a breach of confidence is made unknowingly, it is recommended that the consultant go immediately to the injured party and apologize. It is important to act nondefensively in this situation, should it arise (Conoley & Conoley, 1982).

Beyond the separate components listed above, accomplishing entry in consultation ultimately means having established a safe and comfortable atmosphere in which consultees are free to discuss openly key issues of professional concern. The establishment of this atmosphere is critical to the consultant's success in achieving the problem-solving, social influence, and support and development tasks of consultation. We examine these tasks and the integrated model of school consultation in Chapter 5.

5

Model Description and Application

In Chapter 4 we traced the evolution of two prominent consultation models, mental health consultation and behavioral consultation, and discussed the assumptions and principles underlying each. An approach to strategic communication based on Raven's social power and interpersonal influence models (Erchul & Raven, 1997) was reviewed briefly, followed by a discussion of issues (e.g., the 14 "know the territory" questions, the A VICTORY model) that should be addressed in order to gain successful entry into the service delivery network of schools. In this chapter we discuss research findings that point to the limitations inherent in relying on any one consultation model as a means of delivering comprehensive services in the schools. Based on these limitations, we present an integrated model of school consultation that we believe is particularly appropriate for use by external consultants and that combines the elements of social influence and professional support within a problem-solving context. Each of these elements (problem solving, social influence, professional support) is discussed as a component task of the school consultation process, which begins after the consultant has a basic understanding of schools and classrooms and has successfully entered the service delivery network. The chapter concludes by considering the outcomes of successful school consultation in terms of improving the learning and adjustment of children as clients and improving the professional functioning of teachers as consultees.

A CRITICAL APPRAISAL OF CONSULTATION MODELS

Mental Health Consultation

The concepts and methods of mental health consultation began with Gerald Caplan's efforts during the late 1940s to provide psychological services to large numbers of immigrant children in Israel. Caplan believed that if direct care staff were able to deal more effectively with children's adjustment problems on a daily basis, then more severe disorders could be prevented resulting in fewer institutional placements (Caplan, 1993b). As noted in Chapter 4, this preventive focus became the hallmark of Caplan's mental health consultation model and was instrumental in the widespread establishment of community mental health centers in the United States.

As a prevention model, mental health consultation is based on the assumption that periods of psychological upset or crisis force individuals to mobilize the resources available to them and therefore represent opportunities for personal and professional growth. Support (either emotional or instrumental) provided by community professionals during these times can serve a preventive function by lessening the impact of the crisis and helping the individual resolve their problem. Consistent with this view, Caplan's early efforts were aimed at helping direct care providers (e.g., nurses, clergy, welfare workers) to address the psychological problems of their clients which emerged during their regular professional duties. Because many of these early consultees were highly trained and well-supervised, Caplan found that their need for consultative assistance often resulted from lack of objectivity rather than lack of knowledge or skill (Caplan, 1993b). Given this fact and being true to his psychodynamic training, Caplan's model of mental health consultation has emphasized consultees' perceptions, attributions, and beliefs as barriers to effective functioning.

Although mental health consultation has played a major role in community psychology and psychiatry (Erchul, 1993a; Mannino & Shore, 1971), its contributions to research and practice in school consultation have been more limited. Several reasons likely exist for the lack of emphasis on mental health consultation in the schools. First, as we noted in Chapter 1, the community mental health movement in general and consultation in particular emerged during a time of discontent with traditional approaches to psychotherapy (Hersch, 1968). Included in these criticisms were the disease model of abnormal behavior, the inefficiency of long-term psychotherapy, the unreliability of clinical diagnosis, and the lack of specificity with respect to therapeutic goals, processes, and outcomes (Albee, 1968; Eysenck, 1952; Hobbs, 1964; Szasz, 1960). Because the support strategies of mental health consultation are rooted in a psychodynamic model, in many ways these are inconsistent with the historical antecedents of consultation as a service delivery approach. Second, the processes and outcomes of mental health consultation have not been well operationalized and therefore may be more difficult to teach and implement with integrity (Costenbader et al., 1992). Perhaps related to this issue, mental health consultation enjoys only limited empirical support (Gresham & Kendell, 1987; Gutkin & Curtis, 1990; Medway, 1979). Third, Caplan himself has suggested that in many cases, consultee ineffectiveness is likely to result from lack of knowledge or skill rather than lack of objectivity (Erchul, 1993b), and there is some research to support this observation when consulting with teachers (Gutkin, 1981). Rather than emphasizing psychodynamic techniques such as theme interference reduction, this finding would suggest the importance of enhancing consultee skills through strategies such as modeling, coaching, and performance feedback (e.g., Noell, Witt, Gilbertson, Ranier & Freeland, 1997).

In summary, Caplan's model of mental health consultation has not been used widely in schools because of its psychodynamic approach, lack of specificity, and limited empirical support. As a precursor to all other consultation approaches, however, we believe that mental health consultation holds strong conceptual relevance for school consultants by virtue of (1) the model's preventive focus in which periods of crisis are viewed as opportunities for personal and professional growth when individuals are given the appropriate supports; (2) emphasis on consultee perceptions, attributions, and beliefs when developing intervention plans; and (3) the position that social institutions can serve a preventive function by dealing more successfully with client problems on a day-to-day basis. With respect to the first point, we find it useful to view consultees as individuals who are undergoing crises at the time they seek consultative assistance. The crisis model helps to explain why consultees are likely to seek out others for assistance, be more open to influence, and be more willing to try new behaviors. It also offers a reason to believe that short-term interventions that are developed within a consultative relationship can have significant and long-lasting effects (Caplan, 1964). The essence of the crisis model for school consultation then is that, during times of stress, consultees are receptive to high levels of support and influence to help them overcome presenting problems.

Behavioral Consultation

As discussed in Chapter 4, the historical roots of behavioral consultation include the problem solving approach of D'Zurilla and Goldfried (1971) as well as efforts in the 1960s and early 1970s to apply behavioral treatment principles in human service settings (e.g., Reppucci & Saunders, 1974). A key feature of these early efforts was the involvement of direct care providers as principal change agents in the intervention process. As early as 1969, Tharp and Wetzel described a consultative model for implementing contingency management techniques that required at least three individuals: (1) the behavioral consultant or anyone with knowledge of behavior analysis and intervention; (2) the target client or anyone who exhibited problem behavior; and (3) the mediator or anyone who was in direct contact with the client and was therefore in a position to control reinforcers. During the 1970s, researchers attempted to formalize the behavioral consultation approach by describing a four-stage problem-solving process to be enacted over the course of three interviews, specifying the goals and objectives to be accomplished at each stage, and developing a coding scheme to assess the effectiveness of consultants' interviewing tactics (Bergan, 1977; Bergan & Tombari, 1975).

The behavioral approach continues to enjoy widespread popularity today among school consultation researchers and practitioners. For example, more consultation outcome studies published between 1985 and 1995 were concerned with behavioral consultation than any other model (Sheridan, Welch & Orme, 1996). This model is the most frequently addressed in preservice training programs, and is reported to be the most widely used by practitioners in the schools (Costenbader et al., 1992). Behavioral consultation has also been adopted as a basis for *prereferral intervention programs* or collaborative efforts between teachers, parents, and support personnel to develop accommodations for students before they enter special education (Fuchs, Fuchs & Bahr, 1990; Graden, Casey & Christenson, 1985; McDougal, Clonan & Martens, 2000; Sheridan & Kratochwill, 1992). Although a variety of historical factors have pointed toward a behavioral-ecological approach to school consultation, we believe that two features of the behavioral consultation model itself have contributed to its popularity. First, the goals and strategies of behavioral consultation have been clearly specified, leading to standard interviewing protocols, competency-based training programs, and measures of consultant effectiveness (D. Fuchs & L.S. Fuchs, 1989; Kratochwill, VanSomeren & Sheridan, 1989; McDougall, Reschly & Corkery, 1988). Second, the problem-solving objectives of behavioral consultation are based on the principles of applied behavior analysis (e.g., defining target behaviors, specifying goals, conducting functional assessments, specifying treatment procedures, evaluating outcomes). As discussed in Chapter 6, behavior analytic approaches to instruction and management are effective, empirically validated, and uniquely suited for use by school personnel.

To summarize then, the principal features of behavioral consultation as a service delivery model include: (1) its reliance on a systematic problem-solving process with clearly specified objectives and interviewing tactics; and (2) its use of a behavior analytic approach to intervention, the effectiveness of which has been supported by empirical research. Because it emphasizes problem solving and maintains a strong client-centered focus, behavioral consultation has been viewed as an effective professional practice in the schools (Mannino & Shore, 1975; Medway, 1979; Sheridan et al., 1996). It may seem somewhat paradoxical, therefore, that behavioral consultation services are frequently underutilized by teachers. For example, Martens, Peterson, Witt, and Cirone (1986) found that consultation with a specialist was rated by teachers as being among the least effective and most difficult to use methods of responding to children's learning and adjustment problems. Consistent with these perceptions, Ysseldyke et al. (1983) reported that when generating ideas for ways to accommodate children with special needs, teachers ranked consultation with the school psychologist fifth behind speaking with the principal. When consultation does occur, only half of the intervention plans that consultees agree to implement may actually be completed (Happe, 1982).

We believe that behavioral consultation may be underutilized by teachers for primarily two reasons. First, the model implicitly adopts what is known as an empirical-rational approach for promoting changes in consultee behavior. In order to design and implement school-based interventions, the teacher and consultant must engage in a series of face-to-face meetings or interviews (Gutkin & Curtis, 1982; Witt, 1990). Interventions that are suggested during these interviews typically require some change in teacher behavior as a means of accommodating the student. These changes may require teachers to learn new skills (e.g., momentary time sampling), alter their instructional or managerial practices (e.g., provide student feedback through public posting), or make use of existing resources in different ways (e.g., assign high-achieving students as peer tutors). As noted in Chapter 2, an *empirical-rational approach* to promoting changes in teacher behavior is based on the assumption that if innovative practices can be shown empirically to be superior, then consumers being rational will adopt them because it is in their best interest to do so (Chin & Benne, 1969; Owens, 1981). Although information about a plan's effectiveness can influence teacher perceptions (Von Brock & Elliott, 1987), teachers are not passive recipients of consultant suggestions and often reject these suggestions because they involve too much time, contradict personal beliefs, or reduce personal freedom (Elliott, 1988; Wickstrom & Witt, 1993). Even the manner in which help is offered may influence teachers' decisions to seek assistance and to follow through with suggested interventions (Witt, Moe, Gutkin & Andrews, 1984; Witt & Martens, 1988).

Second, because of its strong client-centered focus, the behavioral consultation model devotes little attention to consultee support and skill development. As noted by Gutkin and Curtis (1990), the goals of any consultation model are twofold; to solve the presenting problem of the client and to increase the consultee's ability to deal effectively with similar problems in the future. Despite the latter goal of enhancing consultee skills, relatively little research has been conducted examining the preventive function of the behavioral consultation process. The available evidence addresses this issue only indirectly by suggesting that teachers perceive their professional skills to have improved following consultation and that fewer children are referred and placed in special education when prereferral intervention programs are in place (Gutkin, 1980, 1986; Gutkin, Henning-Stout & Piersel, 1988; Ponti, Zins & Graden, 1988).

The Consultative Relationship

A widely held assumption in the conceptual literature is that consultation involves a collaborative, nonhierarchical relationship between co-equal professionals (Conoley & Conoley, 1992; Gutkin & Curtis, 1990). Within this collaborative relationship, the consultant and consultee are perceived as having coordinate status and as contributing equally to the problem-solving process. In the absence of empirical support, however, this perspective has been termed by some as the collaborative *myth* of consultation (Witt, 1990). Indeed, several investigations involving relational control (reviewed briefly in Chapter 2) have suggested that consultation may be more accurately described as a cooperative relationship in which the consultant leads and the consultee follows. *Relational control* refers to the manner in which influence is exerted by one person and accepted, rejected, or evaded by another person during a verbal exchange (Erchul, 1987). In an initial study examining the relational control aspects of school consultation, Erchul coded the verbal statements of eight consultant–consultee dyads during problem identification, analysis, and evaluation interviews. Results indicated that consultants made significantly more bids for control during all three interviews, that consultants who had high dominance scores were judged as more effective by consultees, and that consultees who had high domineeringness scores were judged by consultants as less likely to collect baseline data. In a follow-up study, Erchul and Chewning (1990) used the relational coding scheme developed by Folger and Puck (1976) to analyze consultant-consultee interactions in 30 sets of interviews. Within the Folger and Puck scheme, requests are coded as dominant or submissive and affiliative or hostile, whereas responses to these requests are coded as accepted, rejected, or evaded. Results of this study indicated that the number of requests made by consultants far outnumbered that of consultees (more than 6 to 1), and that the majority (94%) of consultee responses involved acceptance of these bids. It was also found that the number of consultant requests decreased during the final problem evaluation interview, whereas requests coded as instructions or orders occurred most frequently during the intermediate problem analysis interview. On the basis of these latter findings, the authors concluded that consultees became more equal in status with the consultant by the time the problem evaluation interview occurred, but that "a mixture of persuasion and negotiation" (p. 15) was used by the consultant during problem analysis to ensure plan implementation.

AN INTEGRATED MODEL OF SCHOOL CONSULTATION

We believe that the client-centered, problem-solving focus of behavioral consultation makes this approach particularly well suited for addressing school-based learning and adjustment problems. Because consultation is an *indirect service model*, however, behavioral consultants typically have limited contact with children and must rely on teachers to carry out recommended intervention plans. This means that achieving the service delivery goals of behavioral consultation (i.e., accommodating special needs students) depends in large measure on the consultant's ability to influence the consultee (Erchul & Martens, 1997; Gutkin & Conoley, 1990). Mental health consultation, with its consultee-centered, preventive focus, is based on the premise that efforts to support and influence consultees during times of stress can lessen the severity of the crisis while expanding the person's resources for dealing with similar problems in the future. Research has suggested that consultees indeed look to consultants to control the relationship, and are likely to follow the consultant's lead during consultative interviews (Erchul, 1987; Erchul, Covington, Hughes & Meyers, 1995; Martens, Erchul & Witt, 1992). However, because the influence strategies of mental health consultation are psychodynamic in origin, there is little documented empirical support for their effectiveness. As discussed in Chapter 2, influence strategies have received considerable attention in social psychological research, and many of these seem applicable to school consultation.

By drawing on the strengths of both the behavioral and mental health consultation models, taking into account the findings from relational communication research (Erchul, 1987; Erchul & Chewning, 1990), and incorporating the principles of social power and influence from the social psychological literature (Chapter 2), we have developed an integrated model of school consultation depicted in Figure 5.1. In our model, school consultation is defined as a process for providing psychological and educational services in which a specialist (consultant) works cooperatively with a caregiver (consultee) to improve the learning and adjustment of a student

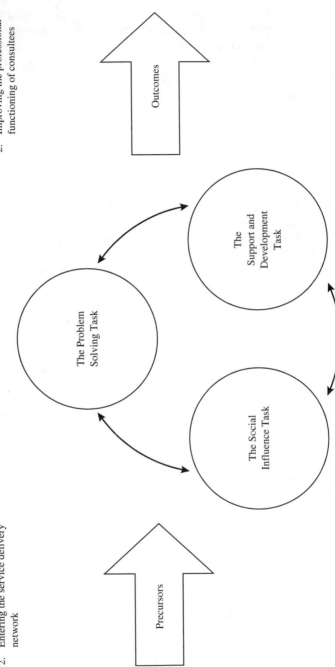

PRECURSORS TO SCHOOL CONSULTATION

1. Understanding schools and classrooms
2. Entering the service delivery network

THE CONSULTATION PROCESS

CONSULTATION OUTCOMES

1. Improving the learning and adjustment of clients
2. Improving the professional functioning of consultees

Figure 5.1. A schematic overview of an integrated school consultation model. Precursors to school consultation are listed on the left. Depicted in the middle portion of the figure are the three interrelated tasks of school consultation which include problem solving, social influence, and consultee support and development. Outcomes of the school consultation process are listed on the right.

(client) or group of students. During face-to-face interactions, the consultant helps the consultee through the mechanisms of systematic problem solving, social influence, and professional support. In turn, the consultee helps the client through selecting and implementing effective school-based interventions. In all cases, school consultation serves a remedial function and has the potential to serve a preventive function (Erchul & Martens, 1997).

As shown in the middle portion of Figure 5.1, the school consultation process is seen as involving three interrelated tasks; problem solving, social influence, and support and development. These tasks are considered to be interrelated because the problem-solving objectives of school consultation can only be accomplished through a social influence process between the consultant and consultee, the goals of which are to assist the consultee in expanding his or her repertoire of professional skills. For example, a school consultant might suggest a cover-copy-compare intervention with progress charting (Skinner, McLaughlin & Logan, 1997) as a means of improving a student's performance in spelling (a problem-solving issue). In the absence of prior experience with these procedures, however, a teacher may be resistant to trying them in his or her classroom. In response to the teacher's resistance, the consultant might offer to assume responsibility for training the student and charting progress initially while the teacher observes in order to: (1) train the teacher in the specifics of the procedure (a support and development issue), and (2) encourage the teacher to take over implementation via the principle of reciprocity (a social influence issue). In another case, a school consultant might use informational power to convince a teacher of the merits of using listening passage preview (e.g., Daly & Martens, 1994) prior to small-group reading instruction (a social influence issue). Due to time constraints, however, the teacher may be reluctant to provide such help. If individual assistance could be provided by a part-time peer tutor (a support and development issue), the teacher might be more willing to implement the agreed upon program (a problem solving issue).

In addition to being interrelated, the three tasks of school consultation must be accomplished within a professional, consultative relationship that can be described by a set of *core characteristics*. These core characteristics derive from the historical antecedents of consultation as a service delivery model, and delineate the boundaries of the consultative relationship. For example, school consultation is intended to be voluntary and work related in focus (Conoley & Conoley, 1992; Gutkin & Curtis, 1982). This means that professional activities that are not voluntary or work related would fall outside the definition of school consultation (e.g., earning continuing education credits to meet employment requirements, seeking counseling for personal adjustment problems). The core characteristics of school consultation are presented in Table 5.1, and components of the integrated model are discussed in turn below.

Precursors to School Consultation

Consultation is only one of a variety of alternative services available to teachers in the school setting. Because of this, we believe that school consultants must have an understanding of schools as organizations and teachers as professionals within that organization before attempting to offer consultation services. Toward this goal, the sequentially coupled and intensive technological aspects of schooling as well as the traditional refer-test-place model of special education were discussed at length in Chapter 3. Chapter 4 discussed several approaches for achieving successful entry into the service delivery network, and the characteristics of teachers as professionals are addressed in Chapter 7.

Perhaps equally important to successful school consultation is being aware of the expectations that teachers bring to the consultative relationship and the problem-solving activities they engage in before seeking assistance from others. The crisis model of mental health consultation suggests that teachers enter into a consultative relationship after attempts to resolve a problem on their own have failed (Caplan, 1963). We believe that the scope and persistence of these problem-solving activities are related to the characteristics of schools in which teachers work as well as the skills which teachers bring to the consultative relationship. For example, the bureaucratic structure of schools often pressures teachers into using special education as their primary means of accommodating students with special needs (Shinn, 1989). In such a climate, school consultation services may be viewed as incompatible with the administration's priorities because these services are more difficult to track for

Table 5.1. Core Characteristics of School Consultation

Triadic alignment between the consultant, consultee, and client
Consultant–consultee relationship characterized by cooperation and teamwork
Voluntary participation by the consultee
Right of the consultee to reject consultant suggestions
Active involvement of the consultee in problem solving and plan implementation
Confidentiality of information shared during the consultative interviews
Focus on professional, work-related issues
Pursuit of problem solving, social influence, and professional development goals
Emphasis on behavior analytic approaches to instruction and management
Systematic evaluation of intervention outcomes

Note. Adapted from Erchul (1993c), Gutkin and Curtis (1990), and Martens (1993a).

purposes of state and federal reimbursement (Piersel & Gutkin, 1983). Support for this position came from a study by Bossard and Gutkin (1983) who assessed the organizational climate and principal leadership style in 10 school buildings. These variables were used to predict the number of consultation contacts that occurred in each building over a 14-week period. Results indicated that consultation services were utilized less in schools with more controlling principals and well defined organizational structures, top-down channels of communication, and standard operating procedures (i.e., a more elaborate bureaucratic structure).

Before seeking consultative assistance, teachers often attempt a number of interventions on their own reflecting their instructional and managerial skills, attributions for classroom behavior problems, and role perceptions as a teacher. Ysseldyke et al. (1983) asked 105 teachers from nine states to describe the interventions attempted and individuals consulted when devising strategies for classroom problems. Results indicated that teachers most often responded to classroom problems by altering their teaching methods (e.g., using small group instruction) or using contingency management procedures (e.g., manipulating reinforcers). Interestingly, most of the interventions reported were implemented for unspecified periods of time and the effects of these procedures were rarely evaluated. Only 13% of the interventions resulted from conferences with other building professionals, suggesting that teachers viewed themselves as assuming primary responsibility for the development of intervention strategies.

In terms of attributions, research has shown that teachers tend to perceive factors within the child or the child's home as the primary causes of classroom behavior problems (e.g., Martens, Kelly & Diskin, 1996). McKee and Witt (1990) have suggested that within-student problem attributions may present barriers to school consultation that is typically aimed at changing some aspect of the instructional environment. Teachers who attribute classroom problems to low student ability may not see the value in significantly altering their own instructional or managerial practices as a means of accommodating a range of student skill levels. Providing feedback about teachers' instructional practices during consultation has been shown to focus attention on these variables, alter teacher attributions, and affect the types of school-based interventions that are selected (Aldrich & Martens, 1993).

The Problem-Solving Task

All psychoeducational services can be viewed as solutions to problems or attempts to reduce the discrepancy between observed and desired student behavior (Reynolds, Gutkin, Elliott & Witt, 1984; Shinn, 1989). In accordance with this view, the first task of school consultation as a service delivery approach is to achieve the problem-solving objectives of behavioral consultation listed in Chapter 4. These objectives are revisited below and research is presented documenting their importance to successful problem resolution.

The Problem Identification Interview (PII)

The primary goals of the PII are threefold: (1) to identify a target behavior and define it in overtly observable terms; (2) to obtain tentative estimates of how often the behavior occurs and under what conditions; and (3) to begin ongoing data collection for use in evaluating treatment outcomes. The importance of successful problem identification in line with the objectives stated above cannot be overestimated. For example, Lambert (1976) found that teachers rarely described children's problems in specific terms and would likely need "considerable support for gathering more precise information about the nature of children's problems before interventions can be considered" (p. 515). McDougall, Reschly, and Corkery (1988) evaluated the effectiveness of a one-day training workshop on consultants' interviewing skills. Participants in the workshop were asked to submit audiotaped interviews before and after training which were subsequently scored for the number of PII objectives met. Consistent with the findings by Lambert (1976), the number of subjects meeting each PII objective at baseline ranged from only 5.9 to 47.1%. After training, between 58.8% and 94.1% of the participants completed the same interviewing objectives. Finally, in the often-cited study by Bergan and Tombari (1976), approximately 60% of the variance in plan implementation was accounted for by merely identifying the problem. Equally as interesting, consultant interviewing tactics were found in the study to have their greatest impact on problem resolution during the initial interview.

The Problem Analysis Interview (PAI)

During the PAI, the consultant and consultee are responsible for (1) using the baseline data that are collected to establish goals for behavior change; (2) conducting a functional assessment and generating hypotheses about why problem behavior is occurring; and (3) designing and implementing an intervention plan. Perhaps the most critical goal of the PAI is to identify factors that contribute to problem behavior as antecedents and consequences by conducting a functional assessment. This goal is typically accomplished by asking the consultee to describe classroom events and conditions that occur before the target behavior (e.g., unstructured free-time, assigning math seatwork), consequences that result from engaging in the target behavior (e.g., attention from peers, being sent to the office), or interventions for the target behavior that were tried previously but failed (e.g., moving the child's location in the classroom, time-out). In addition to questioning the consultee, functional assessment information can also be obtained through more direct methods such as having the teacher complete the Motivation Assessment Scale (Durand & Crimmins, 1988), recording occurrences of problem behavior across different times and instructional conditions, conducting narrative recordings of antecedent-behavior-consequence (ABC) sequences, and reviewing students' work products (Martens & Ardoin, in press). Determining possible reasons why problem behavior is occurring can enable school consultants to develop interventions that teach new skills or that counteract, eliminate, or weaken the consequences supporting problem behavior (Martens, Witt, Daly & Vollmer, 1999).

The Problem Evaluation Interview (PEI)

The primary focus of the PEI is to determine if the goals established during the PAI were met and if the intervention plan was sufficiently effective to warrant its continuation. The former objective (goal attainment) requires that the frequency, intensity, or duration of the target behavior during intervention be compared to the goal established at baseline. Although a variety of statistical methods are available for making this comparison, the most common strategy used in consultation is to display the data in a time-series figure or graph and evaluate the degree of change based on visual inspection (Bergan & Kratochwill, 1990).

Beyond evaluating changes in the target behavior, at least two other issues should be addressed in order to conclude that a plan was effective. First, it must be determined that the plan was implemented by the consultee in the manner intended (i.e., treatment integrity). Second, one must be confident that the plan was responsible for improvements in student behavior before suggesting that the plan be continued or attempted again in the future (i.e., internal validity). Toward this latter goal, several authors have described the design and implementation of school-based interventions as a problem solving process that closely resembles *single-case experimental research* (Barlow, Hayes & Nelson, 1984; Gresham, 1985). Given the logistical similarities between the two activities, we agree with Hayes (1981) that it is desirable to incorporate naturally occurring experimental design elements into consultation casework whenever possible. For example, a teacher and consultant may decide to have two students in a classroom self-monitor the amount of work they complete accurately each day and record this information in a folder. Staggering the procedure's introduction so that the second student begins self-monitoring several days after improvements have been observed in the first student would be consistent with a multiple-baseline-across-subjects design. Implementing the plan in this way would allow one to conclude with greater confidence that self-monitoring rather than some other chance event in the classroom was in fact responsible for improved student performance.

Interviewing Tactics

Bergan and Tombari (1975) originally proposed that consultants should direct the interviewing process by (1) asking questions about children's behavior problems and the conditions surrounding these problems; (2) paraphrasing information provided by the consultee; and (3) soliciting confirmation from the consultee as to the accuracy of these summary statements. Early research by Bergan and Tombari (1976) indicated that consultants who controlled the dialogue with questions, stayed on a topic of conversation that concerned child behavior, and summarized and validated consultee statements engaged in a higher number of initial consultative interviews during an academic year. In a subsequent study, Tombari and Bergan (1978) examined the effects of verbal cues provided by the consultant (i.e., medical model versus behavioral) on consultee behavior. Sixty student–teachers participated in a PII during which they were separated from the consultant by an opaque screen. Results indicated that consultant verbal cues that were classified as behavioral produced significantly more consultee statements about behavior or conditions surrounding behavior, higher expectations for problem resolution, and more behaviorally specific definitions of the child's problem.

Martens, Deery, and Gherardi (1991) compared two types of consultant summarization statements for their effects on consultee verbal behavior during the PII. As part of the study, consultants were instructed to alternate between statements summarizing consultee affect (e.g., "You seem frustrated with Austin") and message content (e.g., "So you estimate that Austin gets out of his seat every five minutes") using a counterbalanced ABCBC design. Consultee agreement was found to occur significantly more often during conditions of reflected content, with consultee statements about themselves and their emotions occurring significantly more often during conditions of reflected affect. Application of lag sequential analysis to the response sequences revealed an immediate dependency between consultee agreement and consultant summarization statements. Findings from these and other studies have suggested that consultants who function as effective problem solvers indeed tend to conduct interviews by asking questions about the child's behavior and surrounding events and by summarizing and expressing agreement with statements made by the consultee (Curtis & Zins, 1988; Martens, Erchul & Witt, 1992; McDougall et al., 1988).

The Social Influence Task

We believe that strategically influencing consultee perceptions in order to promote changes in consultee behavior constitutes the second task of the school consultation process. That is, in addition to problem solving, effective school consultation also involves a social influence task (Erchul, 1993c; Erchul & Raven, 1997; Gutkin & Conoley, 1990; Martens, 1993a; Martens, Kelly & Diskin, 1996). Although social influence has received little attention in the consultation literature, its importance was anticipated by a number of authors. Following attempts to promote the use of behavioral technology in a state institution, Reppucci and Saunders (1974) concluded that the ability to modify staff behavior was ultimately critical to program success. Tharp and Wetzel (1969) anticipated the importance of influencing third-party adults as treatment agents by suggesting that consultee behavior might be controlled by sources of social reinforcement other than the consultant (e.g., supervising teachers, principals). These authors went on to suggest that such individuals might be recruited to promote consultees' adherence to treatment plans (i.e., invoking third-party influence) and that social psychological role theory might be useful in identifying the types of treatment plans which consultees would be likely to implement. Martin (1978) provided one of the first discussions of social power applied to school consultation, suggesting that effective consultants were able to exploit both expert and referent power bases.

Martens, Kelly, and Diskin (1996) examined the effects of two sequential-request strategies, foot-in-the-door (FITD) and door-in-the-face (DITF), on teachers' ratings of treatment acceptability and implementation of a classroom intervention. Both the FITD (Freedman & Fraser, 1966) and DITF (Cialdini, Vincent, Lewis, Catalan, Wheeler & Darby, 1975) techniques represent compliance-gaining strategies in which making an initial request is expected to increase the chances that a person will comply with a second request. In the case of FITD, the initial request is small or trivial, such as answering a question over the phone, and individuals agree to its performance. When asked to comply with a second, larger request (e.g., participating in a 2-hour survey), these individuals are more likely to agree, presumably to maintain consistency in their self-perceptions. In the case of DITF, the initial request is large (e.g., donating 2 hours a week for 2 years), and individuals typically do not agree to its performance. However, when asked to comply with a second, smaller request (e.g., donating 2 hours for a field trip), these individuals are more likely to agree, presumably because a concession has been made and they feel compelled to make a concession also.

In the Martens et al. study, 61 teachers were randomly assigned to one of three experimental conditions in which they complied with a small initial request, failed to comply with a large initial request, or received no initial request. Teachers then rated the acceptability of a classroom intervention (i.e., a fixed-interval schedule of verbal praise) that they were asked to implement for one hour on each of two consecutive school days. Results showed the mean acceptability ratings for the DITF condition to be significantly lower than the Control condition, but neither differed significantly from the FITD condition. Moreover, fewer teachers in the DITF condition implemented the classroom intervention than controls. It was concluded from the study that school consultants should be cautious when attempting to use the DITF procedure because any favorable perceptions that are produced by conceding one's position must overshadow the negative perceptions created from making what may have been an unreasonable request in the first place.

As discussed in Chapter 2, the most comprehensive treatise on social power and influence applied to school consultation can be found in a recent article by Erchul and Raven (1997). These authors expanded on Martin's (1978) argument by describing how all six social power bases, as currently conceptualized (Raven, 1992, 1993), might be applied to the school consultation process. A basic premise of this argument is that the indirect service model of school consultation often requires consultants to alter the attitudes and behaviors of consultees in order to benefit clients (Gutkin & Conoley, 1990). For example, a teacher may be resistant to taking part in a home-based reinforcement program because of the belief that children should not be given special privileges for behavior that is expected of them anyway. Discussing the program as a means of helping the child become more responsible (a trait the teacher values) or as a way to recruit support for schooling at home (a view consistent with the teacher's attributions for student failure) may go far in reducing such resistance.

Because school consultation involves aspects of relational control (Erchul, 1987), we believe changes in consultee behavior can be encouraged in a noncoercive fashion by using the strategic communication approaches described in Chapter 2. Rather than repeat that discussion here, presented in Table 5.2 are examples of how each of French and Raven's social influence tactics is believed to effect behavior change from the perspective of the consultee. A skilled consultant is able to use these tactics as needed during the interview process, thereby accomplishing both problem-solving and social influence goals. As an example, consider the school consultant who, after listening to a teacher's initial description of a child's failure to work independently, summarizes the main points of what was said, and adds, "When I volunteered in a classroom several years ago, I also remember feeling very drained by children who asked

Table 5.2. Examples of Social Influence Strategies from Chapter 2

Influence strategy	Example
Coercive	I will look bad if I didn't do what the CT asked when she checks (Personal and Impersonal)
Reward	I will look good if I did what the CT asked when she checks (Personal and Impersonal)
Legitimate	I feel obligated to do what the CT asks
Position	As a CE, I am expected to do what a CT asks
Reciprocity	The CT has contributed a lot so I should contribute too
Equity	I feel guilty for causing the CT more work and should make up for it
Responsibility	I have a responsibility to help children by doing what the CT asks
Positive expert	The CT knows the best thing to do because she is an expert
Negative expert	The CT is trying to boss me around with her expertise, so I will do what I want
Positive referent	Because the CT and I are alike, it makes sense to do what she asks
Negative referent	Because the CT and I are different, it doesn't make sense to do what she asks
Informational	What the CT suggests really seems like the best thing to do (Direct and Indirect)
Third parties	Mrs. Jones down the hall has done this, so I should do it too
Mode of influence	When the CT uses harsh or threatening language versus friendly or humorous language
Preparatory devices	When the CT emphasizes intimidation to aid coercion, flattery to aid reward, communality to aid referent, self-promotion to aid expert, and CT role and time spent to aid legitimate

Note. CT = consultant; CE = consultee.

for constant attention." Such a statement not only serves the problem-solving function of encouraging additional description from the teacher (Martens, Deery & Gherardi, 1991), but can be instrumental in helping the consultant establish a referent power base. Additional examples of the various and often multiple functions served by consultant statements can be found in the consultation case transcripts presented in Chapter 9.

The Support and Development Task

In keeping with the conceptual underpinnings of Caplan's mental health model, we believe the third task of school consultation is to support consultee efforts in dealing with crises that arise during their normal professional duties while facilitating the development of consultee skills. Although mental health consultation focuses on providing emotional support to consultees, any attempts at supporting teachers' efforts are likely to be viewed as beneficial. Evidence of this was provided in a series of experimental studies that showed individuals who experienced distress from a problem-solving task tended to view messages of emotional and instrumental support as being equally helpful (Tardy, 1994). That is, subjects under stress perceived any support attempt by another as emotionally supportive, even if it was clearly instrumental in nature.

Supporting the consultee's efforts as a teacher and an intervention agent is consistent with what has been termed an empowerment philosophy of helping (Witt & Martens, 1988). An *empowerment philosophy* is based on the assumption that consultees are skilled individuals who can become more capable of resolving their own problems by knowing what resources are available to them and how to make use of these resources (Dunst & Trivette, 1987). For example, our experience in the schools has suggested that many classroom teachers are unaware of the programs and services available in their own building for responding to children's learning and adjustment problems. One of the first assignments for our consultation practicum students, therefore, is to "map out" the various services which are offered in the building in which they are placed. As discussed in Chapter 4, similar organizational mapping activities have been recommended for external consultants in their efforts to gain entry into the service delivery network. Beyond entry, however, sharing this information with teachers through inservice education, team meetings, or even memos distributed in mailboxes can serve a supportive function by promoting their access to existing resources.

Equally important to accomplishing the preventive goals of school consultation is helping consultees develop their professional skills within a problem-solving context. As noted earlier, school consultation typically results in more intensive or direct approaches to instruction (e.g., word list training, classwide peer tutoring) or more structured forms of classroom management (e.g., self-monitoring and charting, time-out) (Martens, Witt, et al., 1999). As such, intervention programs that are developed during consultation require teachers to learn new skills and make what are often significant changes in the way they interact with students.

Noell, Witt, LaFleur, Mortenson, Ranier & LeVelle (2000) observed that school consultants rarely have formal administrative authority over teachers whose behavior they are attempting to change. Thus, the extent to which teachers actually follow through in implementing agreed-upon plans may depend largely on the consultant's interpersonal influence and implementation support skills (Erchul & Martens, 1997). Until recently, however, efforts to promote intervention use by teachers have relied primarily on verbal instruction from the consultant prior to implementation (Bergan & Kratochwill, 1990). Our experiences in the schools suggest that we as consultants typically *underestimate* the amount of training and support that teachers require to successfully change their behavior (Martens & Ardoin, in press). Consistent with this notion, Joyce and Showers (1981) reviewed effective strategies for in-service training and concluded that verbal instruction alone is not likely to promote maintenance of behavior change unless it is followed by demonstration, practice, feedback, and in vivo application. Described below are several strategies identified by Goldstein and Martens (2000) that have been shown to be effective in supporting teachers' use of school-based interventions and developing their intervention skills.

Social Influence

As noted in Chapter 2, social influence strategies that were viewed as most effective by school psychologists included direct informational and positive expert power (Erchul, Raven & Ray, 2001). We believe that several other social influence strategies hold particular promise for school consultants. As professionals-in-training who are external to a school building, our practicum students are often cast in a "one-down" position relative to full-time staff members. At the same time, teachers who spend most of their time during the day talking with children often like to connect and interact professionally with other adults as observed by Sarason (1996). Under these circumstances, our students have realized some success in promoting consultee behavior change by: (1) assuming the bulk of responsibility for material development and plan implementation initially and then gradually reducing their involvement over time (i.e., the legitimate power of reciprocity), (2) praising teachers for participating in meetings and following through with assigned responsibilities (i.e., personal reward power), (3) highlighting similarities with teachers in terms of educational values or past teaching experiences (i.e., positive referent power), and (4) highlighting the successful use of similar interventions by other teaching staff (i.e., invoking the influence of third parties).

Setting Goals for Teacher Behavior

In behavioral consultation, tentative goals for student behavior change are established during the PII to determine if teachers harbor unreasonable expectations, whereas formal goals are set during the PAI to assess treatment outcome (Bergan & Kratochwill, 1990). Interestingly, the same level of goal specificity is not required with respect to changes in teacher behavior which ultimately mediate student improvement. We believe that setting explicit standards for consultee behavior represents an important but largely untapped method for supporting plan implementation. This potential was illustrated in a study by Martens, Hiralall, and Bradley (1997). Baseline observations revealed generally low but variable levels of appropriate behavior by two kindergarten students with emotional disturbance as well as low rates of teacher praise (approximately three times in a 30 minute period). This information was shared with the teacher who established a goal for herself of six praise statements every 30 minutes. Each morning thereafter, the teacher was given a brief feedback note prompting her as to which behaviors to praise in each student and stating whether or not she had met her goal the previous day. As a function of the goal setting plus feedback intervention, the average number of praise statements delivered by the teacher to each student increased to over 14 in a 30 minute period, and mean levels of appropriate student behavior increased to over 80% of the intervals observed.

Modeling, Coaching, and Performance Feedback

Noell and his colleagues (Noell, Witt, LaFleur, Mortenson, Ranier & LeVelle, 2000; Noell, Witt, Gilbertson, Ranier, & Freeland, 1997; Witt, Noell, La Fleur & Mortenson, 1997) conducted a series of investigations examining the effectiveness of performance feedback at increasing intervention use by teachers. Each of the studies employed a similar approach to staggering when feedback began for each teacher, sequence of consultation activities, and method for monitoring teacher implementation. The intervention plan was first described to the teacher, materials needed to implement the plan were provided, and use of the plan was modeled by the consultant who coached the teacher through implementation during one session in the classroom. After this initial training, the teacher implemented the plan independently, received a performance feedback package, and again implemented the plan independently (i.e., a maintenance phase). The performance feedback package consisted of graphs depicting levels of student behavior and teacher implementation (i.e., percentage of steps completed), discussion of implementation errors, and praise for implementing the intervention as planned.

A consistent pattern of findings emerged across the studies. Although teachers initially implemented all intervention steps, implementation dropped considerably within several weeks. Implementation levels increased dramatically with introduction of performance feedback, but maintenance after feedback ended was variable. Because the start of each condition was staggered across teachers, some teachers received performance feedback during a large number of sessions before moving to the maintenance phase. Interestingly, these teachers tended to show greater maintenance, suggesting that performance feedback may have helped them master the skills required for correct implementation and perhaps reinforced their use.

Implementation Protocols

One way to train consultees how to use an intervention plan and promote its use after training has ended is to provide them with checklists or scripts detailing the steps required to carry out the plan. For example, Ehrhardt, Barnett, Lentz, Stollar, and Reifin (1996) developed intervention scripts collaboratively with caregivers for use in responding to behavior problems exhibited by four preschoolers. The scripts detailed in step-by-step fashion what each caregiver was supposed to do in order to implement the intervention and contained a place to indicate when each step had been completed. Results suggested that the scripts were effective at increasing implementation integrity and these levels were maintained at follow-up.

In a similar study, Hiralall and Martens (1998) developed a scripted protocol for use by four teachers in implementing a direct instruction sequence. The protocol was used during a structured art activity and required teachers to engage in a multi-step instructional sequence involving requests for eye contact, instruction, modeling, praise, and redirection. Not only did all four teachers increase their use of instructional statements, modeling, and praise with use of the protocol, but two teachers maintained these levels at one-month follow-up. Implementation protocols appear to be effective at promoting intervention use by teachers, are easy to develop, can be used to monitor treatment integrity, and can be used in conjunction with performance feedback (e.g., Witt et al., 1997).

Outcomes of School Consultation

In order to achieve the goals of school consultation, the consultant and consultee must engage in separate yet complementary activities following each meeting. These activities constitute outcomes of the school consultation process and are depicted in the right-hand portion of Figure 5.1.

Following completion of the PII and PAI, the consultee is expected to assist in the collection of baseline data and assume primary responsibility for implementing the agreed upon plan. As will be discussed in Chapter 6, data-based decision making in conjunction with a behavior analytic approach to instruction and management has been shown to be an effective means of accommodating special needs students. With respect to changing client behavior then, the outcomes of school consultation are likely to involve changes in teachers' instructional practices, the implementation of school-based intervention plans, or the systematic evaluation of alternative educational programs such as peer tutoring (e.g., Aldrich & Martens, 1993; Greenwood, Carta & Hall, 1988).

Whereas the consultee maintains primary responsibility for plan implementation, Gresham (1989) has suggested that consultants should be responsible for monitoring treatment integrity, or the extent to which treatment is implemented in the manner intended. A variety of behavioral assessment methods can be used to monitor treatment integrity, including systematic observation, self-monitoring, and teacher rating scales and checklists. By assessing treatment integrity, consultants can recommend changes in treatment procedures that help consultees incorporate suggested interventions into their professional repertoires. In addition to monitoring treatment integrity, the consultant can also play a principal role in the evaluation of treatment outcome. This role involves helping the consultee determine (1) if the goals established for behavior change were achieved, partially achieved, or not achieved; and (2) if the changes observed in student behavior were a function of the treatment procedure or resulted merely from chance (Gresham & Davis, 1988). Based on these determinations, the decision can be made to continue with an intervention plan or recycle through aspects of the consultation process as necessary. In either event, the consultant is responsible for providing ongoing support to the consultee until a mutual decision is reached to terminate the relationship (Gutkin & Curtis, 1990).

The preventive aspects of school consultation occur when the consultee's professional skills are enhanced as a result of the consultant's support and influence attempts during times of crisis, and when the consultee is able to successfully apply the systematic problem solving process in other situations. With respect to the former issue, Gutkin and Hickman (1988) found that increasing consultees' perceptions of control and self-efficacy over presenting problems resulted in an increased willingness to engage in consultation. Although it is a common belief that consultation serves a primary prevention function (e.g., Meyers et al., 1979), others are skeptical that this in fact is the case (e.g., Gutkin & Curtis, 1982; Trickett, 1993). We and others (e.g., Zins, 1995) believe that today school consultation is more often provided in the service of secondary and tertiary prevention and that data attesting to its primary preventive function are limited. The effectiveness of school-based interventions in ameliorating children's learning and adjustment problems (i.e., tertiary prevention) as well as issues concerning the evaluation of intervention outcomes are discussed in Chapter 6.

6

Selecting and Evaluating School-Based Interventions

A primary goal of school consultation is to help teachers select, implement, and evaluate intervention programs for children's learning and adjustment problems. Accomplishing this goal requires that school consultants go beyond assessment and diagnosis of problems and participate in the treatment process. From our experiences as school consultants and from supervising psychologists-in-training, we realize that being involved in treatment decisions can be both rewarding and challenging. The rewards come from helping a teacher successfully implement an intervention program and seeing dramatic improvements in children's behavior as a result. The challenging aspects of treatment stem from making what are often difficult decisions about program alternatives, tailoring programs to individual case needs, and soliciting judgments of program effectiveness from teachers, parents, and other school personnel.

Although a variety of bases exist for the practice of psychology, we believe that, wherever possible, treatment decisions should be made based on *empirical data* gathered through the *scientific method*. By empirical data, we mean information about treatment effectiveness that is derived from systematic observations of treatment outcome that have been collected across a variety of cases. The scientific method, in turn, refers to the use of strategies for ruling out competing explanations when the effects of treatment are being observed. Together, these principles can minimize the challenging aspects of school-based intervention by (1) increasing one's confidence that a chosen treatment will have the intended effect, and (2) providing a tangible basis for treatment decisions thereby maximizing the accountability of one's professional activities (Martens & Eckert, 2000). Data-based decision making is not only consistent with a scientist-practitioner model of psychological training, but it is in keeping with the Ethical Standards of the American Psychological Association, which state that "psychologists rely on scientifically and professionally derived knowledge when making scientific or professional judgments or when engaging in scholarly or professional endeavors" (Standard 1.06 Basis for Scientific and Professional Judgments, 1992).

This chapter summarizes research concerning the effectiveness of various approaches for addressing children's learning and adjustment problems and discusses the implications of these findings for selecting school-based interventions. Next, four key considerations in designing and implementing any school-based intervention program are discussed, including conceptual relevance, treatment strength, treatment integrity, and treatment acceptability. The chapter concludes with a discussion of systematic formative evaluation as a means of assessing intervention outcomes.

EFFECTIVENESS OF INTERVENTION ALTERNATIVES

Results from Meta-Analytic Reviews

Teachers and educational support personnel are constantly bombarded with new procedures for instruction and management in what some have called "a never ending cycle of fad, excitement, adoption, poor outcome, disenchantment, [and] new fad" (Delmolino & Romanczyk, 1995, p. 27). For example, during the 1990s we witnessed the popularization and subsequent criticism of such approaches as facilitated communication for training individuals with autism and whole language instruction for teaching reading. If we add to this list the literally hundreds of treatment approaches that have appeared in the psychological literature (Lipsey & Wilson, 1993), the potential difficulties in selecting an intervention program for any reported problem become clear. Recent meta-analytic reviews of psychological, educational, and behavioral treatment studies have aided in treatment selection by examining the effectiveness of a wide variety of available procedures (e.g., Kavale, 1990). Consistent with a data-based approach to service delivery, we believe that school consultants should be aware of these findings in order to select intervention programs that have the greatest likelihood of success.

As discussed in Chapter 1, *meta-analysis* is a quantitative approach for summarizing the effects of treatment across large numbers of original research studies (Smith & Glass, 1977). Two meta-analytic reviews have attempted to summarize the effects of a wide range of interventions on educationally relevant outcomes, and therefore seem particularly useful for school consultants (Kavale, 1990; Lipsey & Wilson, 1993). Although a detailed discussion of these reviews would be beyond the scope of the chapter, for comparison purposes the ES statistics for 10 common approaches to school-based intervention are presented in Table 6.1. (The interested reader is referred to the original sources for a description of the sampling procedures and the number of studies included in each calculation.) These approaches were selected because they span the range of interventions being used in schools today, including behavior analysis, psychopharmacology, ability training, diet intervention, and special education placement. As shown in Table 6.1, the first two behavior analytic procedures are extremely effective (ES near 1.0), stimulant medication and peer tutoring are moderately effective (ES near .60), and the two variations of ability training (i.e., modality-based instruction and perceptual-motor training) are patently ineffective (ES approaching 0). What is not obvious from Table 6.1 is that, regardless of the approach taken, most school-based interventions are likely to be more variable in their effects than beneficial (Kavale, 1990). For example, whereas the average ES for special class placement in the review by Kavale was −.12, the standard deviation for this approach was .65! The implications of these data for school consultants should be clear. First, whenever possible we should base our intervention efforts on approaches that have been shown to be effective and avoid those shown to be ineffective. To date, these and other available data have been consistent in arguing for a skill training rather than ability training approach to remediating learning problems as well as a behavior analytic approach to classroom instruction and management (Becker, 1988; R. H. Good, Vollmer, Creek, Katz & Chowdhri, 1993; Martens & Meller, 1990). Generally speaking, skill training approaches

Table 6.1. Effect Sizes of 10 Common Approaches to School-Based
Intervention

Intervention	Mean effect size in standard deviation units
Positive reinforcement procedures	1.17
Instructional cues, student participation, and feedback	.97
Peer tutoring	.59
Stimulant medication	.58
Cognitive behavioral modification	.47
Cooperative learning	.30
Modality-based instruction	.14
Diet intervention	.12
Perceptual–motor training	.08
Special class placement	−.12

focus on behaviors involved in completing actual classroom tasks (e.g., passage reading fluency, phonetic analysis) whereas ability training approaches focus on deficits in inferred mental processes within the child (e.g., sequential processing). Considerations in selecting procedures consistent with both skill training and behavior analytic approaches are discussed below. Second, these findings also suggest that intervention programs need to be tailored to the individual needs of the consultant and consultee, and that the outcomes of these programs should be systematically evaluated because they cannot be predicted with certainty (Ysseldyke & Marston, 1990). Suggestions for accomplishing each of these goals are discussed in turn at the end of the chapter.

Behavior Analytic Approach to School-Based Intervention

Behavior analysis refers to a set of strategies for selecting, implementing, and evaluating intervention programs based on the lawful principles of behavior. A fundamental assumption of behavior analysis applied to school-based intervention is that most teaching and management activities require adult-child interaction, and it is through these interactions that children acquire new skills, are encouraged to engage in certain behaviors, or are discouraged from engaging in other behaviors. The possible ways that teachers can influence children's behavior through their interactions are described by basic behavioral principles (e.g., positive reinforcement), whereas intervention programs designed to invoke these principles refer to behavioral procedures (e.g., point systems for positive reinforcement, overcorrection for punishment, graduated guidance to establish stimulus control). Depending on the type and severity of client problems and consultee skill level, more elaborate or structured programs may be necessary to produce desired changes in student behavior. Finally, because the effects of behavioral procedures in any given case cannot be predicted with certainty, behavior analysis also involves a set of strategies for systematically evaluating intervention outcomes.

We believe that a behavior analytic approach is uniquely suited for use by school consultants for a number of reasons. First, a great deal of research has accumulated over the past 30 years demonstrating the effectiveness of behavioral procedures for teaching new skills and responding to children's learning and adjustment problems (Martens & Meller, 1990; Wolery, Bailey & Sugai, 1988). As noted above, behavioral procedures are associated with larger average effect sizes when compared with alternative approaches to school-based intervention. Second, most behavioral procedures were designed for use by direct-care providers in homes, schools, residential facilities, and other child-related settings. These procedures can be clearly specified and often require little in the way of extra materials or expenditures for implementation. Third, because behavioral procedures promote learning by manipulating events that immediately precede or follow behavior, they are capable of producing relatively rapid changes in performance. This is an important consideration for any school-based intervention program given the limited time available for instruction in a typical school day.

Effective Instructional Procedures

Regardless of the skill or behavior being taught, learning progresses through a series of stages known as the *instructional hierarchy* (Haring, Lovitt, Eaton & Hansen, 1978). Stages of learning in the instructional hierarchy refer to different levels of proficiency in performing a new skill, each being associated with specific instructional procedures that promote mastery at that level (Daly, Lentz & Boyer, 1996). The first stage, *acquisition*, refers to initial attempts to perform a new skill that usually occur with varying degrees of accuracy. The second stage, *fluency*, refers to the proficiency or speed with which an already acquired skill is performed, whereas the third stage, *generalization*, involves the performance of a skill at times or in situations that differ from training. The final stage of the instructional hierarchy is *adaptation*, which involves modifying the performance of a skill to meet the demands of novel situations.

Obviously, classroom teachers are concerned with promoting learning at the stage of acquisition as well as fluency and generalization. The instructional activities that regular education teachers use to accomplish these goals, however, differ primarily from behavior analytic approaches in two ways: (1) behavior analytic approaches call for different instructional procedures for each stage of learning, and (2) behavior analytic approaches call for explicit goal setting, guidance, and support of students' efforts to respond. With respect to strategies at each stage of learning, research has shown that acquisition of any new skill is best accomplished by providing information and assistance in how to perform the behavior through prompting, modeling, and corrective feedback (e.g., Espin & Deno, 1989; Singh, 1990). Fluency, in turn, is best promoted by arranging opportunities for correct practice using high interest materials and providing reinforcement for students' efforts. Generalization can be facilitated in a number of ways, including training a skill in its natural context, teaching skills that are likely to be reinforced by others, and training a skill in more than one situation (Goldstein & Martens, 2000). By identifying the stage of learning at which a student performs a skill, the consultant and consultee can select instructional procedures that are maximally effective and tailored to the individual needs of the student (Daly, Witt, Martens & Dool, 1997).

With respect to supporting students' efforts to respond, providing information about how to perform a behavior, or *prompting*, is recognized as an effective means of promoting the acquisition of a wide range of educationally relevant skills. Prompts refer to any type of assistance provided after a direction is given that increases the likelihood of a correct response. Prompts can vary in their degree of intrusiveness from brief verbal statements or gestures to modeling or pictures to partial or full physical manipulation. The strategic use of prompts is an integral part of errorless learning procedures, the most common of which being prompt and test, prompt and fade, most-to-least prompting, least-to-most prompting, graduated guidance, and time delay prompting (Wolery et al., 1988). The prompt and test procedure requires a series of prompted trials followed by test trials to assess mastery of a skill. The prompt and fade procedure requires teachers to prompt correct behavior on initial trials, then gradually withdraw the prompt until the behavior can be performed independently. Most-to-least and least-to-most prompting both require sequences of progressively less (or more) intrusive prompts to promote independence. Graduated guidance requires that a teacher remain in close proximity to a child and provide assistance as necessary, whereas time delay prompting calls for progressively longer intervals between the initial direction and the prompt. As the interval increases, the child begins to anticipate the correct response and produces it independently before the prompt is given. The errorless learning procedures described above have not only been shown to facilitate acquisition, but they are efficient (i.e., require fewer learning trials), promote positive interactions between teachers and students, reduce the opportunities for students to practice errors, and decrease a child's motivation to escape the learning situation by engaging in disruptive or acting out behaviors (Wolery et al., 1988). Instructional interventions that have been shown to be effective for responding to children's academic problems are listed in Table 6.2 (adapted from Martens, 1996).

Effective Managerial Procedures

Although basic behavioral principles are always operating during teacher-student interactions, teachers are not always aware of the effect their behavior has on that of children. Behavior analytic approaches to classroom management are designed to help teachers achieve greater consistency in encouraging desired or appropriate behavior while discouraging undesired or inappropriate behavior (Martens & Kelly, 1993). As with

Table 6.2. Instructional Interventions for Academic Problems

Matching Instructional Materials to the Student's Skill Level (Instructional Match)

Modeling and Prompting Procedures

Cover-copy-compare
Taped words
Discussion of key words
Listening passage preview
Passage preview

Error Correction

Word supply
Sentence repeat
Word drill
Phrase drill
Phonic drill

Drill and Reinforcement

Response cards
Repeated readings

behavioral approaches to instruction, a variety of procedures can be used to implement any given behavioral principle, and these procedures differ in the degree of structure they place on the nature and frequency of teacher-student interactions. For example, verbal praise and behavioral contracts are both procedures that are designed to invoke the principle of positive reinforcement to increase behavior. Verbal praise requires teachers to reward children whenever possible by stating the desired behavior together with some form of positive evaluation. Behavioral contracts require the teacher and child to specify in writing the desired behavior and its required level of performance as well as any consequences that will be given for failing to meet, meeting, or exceeding the performance criterion. Although both procedures can be effective at increasing desired student behavior, some consultees may require the extra guidance and structure of behavioral contracts in order to successfully change the way they respond to children.

As noted before, a variety of behavioral interventions have been reported in the literature for increasing desired or decreasing undesired behavior (Peterson & Martens, 1995). Although a review of these interventions would be beyond the scope of the chapter, Table 6.3 presents a listing of procedures that have been used successfully in responding to children's classroom behavior problems. (The interested reader is referred to Martens & Meller, 1990, or Wolery et al., 1988, for detailed intervention

Table 6.3. Behavioral Interventions for Classroom Problems

Procedures for Increasing Desired Behavior

Goal setting and feedback
Verbal praise
Self-monitoring (self-reinforcement, self-charting, public posting)
Point systems and token economies
Behavioral contracts
Group contingencies (dependent, independent, interdependent)
Home-based reinforcement

Procedures for Decreasing Undesired Behavior

Verbal reprimands
Ignoring
Response cost
Time-out (contingent observation, exclusionary, isolation)
Overcorrection (positive practice, restitutional)
Differential reinforcement of other behavior (DRO), alternative behavior (DRA), or low rates
    of responding (DRL)

descriptions.) In general, procedures for increasing desired behavior rely on positive reinforcement (presenting something desirable), whereas procedures for decreasing undesired behavior rely on type I punishment (presenting something aversive), type II punishment (withdrawing something positive), or differential reinforcement (increasing time allocated to desired alternative behaviors).

When selecting among the procedures in Table 6.3, it is important to keep the following points in mind. First, whenever possible it is better to select less intrusive, less structured interventions over those that require more time, energy, and resources or that constrain teacher–student interactions. Not only is this practice consistent with IDEA's least restrictive environment mandate, but less complicated procedures can be implemented more quickly and teachers are more likely to use them for extended periods of time. Second, procedures that reinforce appropriate behavior should be emphasized over those that punish inappropriate behavior. Consistently administered reinforcement encourages children to choose certain behaviors over others and these choices extend through time (Martens & Kelly, 1993). Punishment, on the other hand, merely informs children about what not to do, leaving the choice of what to do up to the child's discretion. Third, the overall quality of teacher–student interactions should be taken into consideration before suggesting any school-based intervention. Are the teacher's instructional practices based on an adopted curriculum? Is the difficulty of assigned work appropriate for students' skill levels? Are interactions between the teacher and students generally positive and enjoyable or tense and punitive? Without a foundation of positive teacher–student interactions, many school-based interventions may not have their intended effects or may be too much for teachers to handle given their regular duties (Witt & Martens, 1988). For example, the effectiveness of timeout as a behavior reduction technique is based on a discrepancy between the reinforcing properties of time-in (i.e., time spent in ongoing classroom activities) and time-out (i.e., time spent being excluded from such activities) (Harris, 1985). If students do not find ongoing classroom activities enjoyable, then time away from these activities contingent on misbehavior is not likely to be perceived as aversive.

Limitations of a Behavior Analytic Approach

Despite the effectiveness of behavior analytic approaches on average, their use requires teachers to establish clear goals and objectives for student achievement and to define problem behaviors in operational terms (Kazdin, 1994). Lambert (1976) found that although teachers were sensitive to children's behavior problems, they tended to view those problems in vague or general terms (e.g., the child is lazy or poorly motivated). Other researchers have found that teachers also experience difficulty when writing students' individual educational goals, with such goals frequently stated in terms that are either too vague (e.g., will improve) or too specific (e.g., will make the long-e sound) to allow for systematic progress monitoring (Shinn, 1989).

Behavioral approaches require changes in the frequency and type of teacher–student interactions, and as such are only effective at times and in settings when these changes occur. One implication of this is that, in order to be effective, behavioral interventions must be adopted by teachers and implemented as planned on an ongoing basis. Although issues surrounding program implementation are discussed in the following section, the use of any procedure over time may be difficult if it (1) requires frequent, individual contacts with students; (2) is used in classrooms with high student-to-teacher ratios; or (3) is used by teachers who experience difficulty managing their regular classroom duties. Another implication here is that improvements in behavior that result from intervention are not likely to generalize unless they are explicitly programmed. Generalization programming can be time consuming, and is typically viewed as being less important than initial program implementation. For example, in a review of behavioral treatment studies, Stokes and Baer (1977) found that the most common approach to generalization programming was to implement treatment and *hope* that generalization occurred.

Lundervold and Bourland (1988) reported that only 2% of the treatment studies they reviewed programmed for the generalization of treatment effects.

IMPLEMENTATION ISSUES

A number of factors are likely to influence the effectiveness of any school-based intervention effort. These factors include selecting an intervention that is appropriate for a given problem and which teachers find acceptable, taking steps to maximize treatment strength, and helping teachers implement treatment in the intended fashion. Research in each of these areas is reviewed in the following sections, and suggestions are made for strategically linking the information gathered during problem analysis to plan design.

Conceptual Relevance

According to Yeaton and Sechrest (1981), *conceptual relevance* refers to the appropriateness of treatment for a given problem. In psychology, determinations of conceptual relevance are typically based on a theoretical relationship between the active treatment components and the causes of the problem. For example, if irrational means-end thinking is seen as the cause of poor social relationships, then insight-oriented therapy, which uses confrontation to challenge such thinking, would have conceptual relevance.

A key assumption of the behavior analytic approach is that classroom behavior problems are caused, or at least maintained, by the basic behavioral principles operating during teacher–student interactions. These possible causes for problem behavior are described in Table 6.4 along with the behavioral principle underlying each. Because the active treatment components of behavioral interventions can also be specified in terms of basic behavioral principles, the conceptual relevance of these interventions can be determined empirically by conducting a *functional assessment* (e.g., Ervin, DuPaul, Kern & Friman, 1998). The goal of a functional assessment is to develop hypotheses about why problem behavior is occurring based on a careful examination of the conditions surrounding its occurrence (Martens, Witt et al., 1999). Once these hypotheses are made, interventions can be designed to counteract, eliminate, or weaken the variables believed to be maintaining the problem behavior.

A considerable amount of research over the past 10 years has shown that functional assessment can lead to more effective and non-aversive

Table 6.4. Why Classroom Behavior Problems Occur

Cause	Behavioral Principle
The child has not learned a more appropriate behavior that leads to the same consequence.	Skill deficit
More appropriate behaviors are ignored.	Extinction
More appropriate behaviors lead to undesired consequences.	Punishment
The problem behavior is followed by desired sensory, edible, tangible, social, or activity consequences.	Positive reinforcement
The problem behavior allows the child to stop or avoid undesired situations.	Negative reinforcement
The problem behavior occurs when it is likely to be reinforced.	Stimulus control
The problem behavior occurs when it is initiated by other individuals.	Prompting
The problem behavior occurs because the child observed someone else doing it.	Modeling

interventions (Horner, 1994). As a result, functional assessment became a legal mandate in certain situations with passage of the IDEA 97 amendments. Specifically, a functional assessment *must* be conducted when a student with disabilities has 10 cumulative school days of suspension, is removed in a manner that constitutes a change of placement, or is placed in an interim alternative education setting for a weapons or drug offense (Drasgow & Yell, 2001). These same authors suggest that functional assessments *should* be conducted when problem behavior impedes learning, is dangerous, or when suspensions approach 10 cumulative days.

Martens and Ardoin (in press) identified several methods for gathering information when conducting a functional assessment. As mentioned in Chapter 5, perhaps the most widely used method is to ask the teacher to describe conditions surrounding problem behavior during the PAI. Though teachers can often provide a considerable amount of information during the interview, this will depend on the interviewing skills of the consultant, the teacher's ability to recall prior events, and the extent to which the teacher is aware of or has had the opportunity to observe the child. When additional information is needed, school consultants may have to rely on other, more direct forms of assessment (Martens & Kelly, 1993).

One such method is to have teachers complete the Motivation Assessment Scale or MAS (Durand & Crimmins, 1988). The MAS is a 16-item questionnaire that asks teachers to rate the frequency with which problem behavior seems to occur for various reasons using a seven-point scale (0 = never, 6 = always; Sample item: Does the behavior occur following a request to perform a difficult task?). Items on the MAS are combined into four subscales representing possible sources of reinforcement (sensory stimulation, escape, attention, access to tangibles).

Another approach is to ask teachers to record occurrences of problem behavior across different times of the day (e.g., morning, after lunch), different content areas (e.g., math, reading, social studies), or different instructional arrangements (e.g., independent seatwork, small-group instruction, large-group lecture) (e.g., Axelrod, 1987). These data can help identify when problem behavior is most likely to occur and lead to the development of hypotheses concerning aspects of these situations that are problematic (e.g., assignment of frustrational-level work) (Touchette, MacDonald & Langer, 1985).

Direct observation by the school consultant is a third method of information gathering. This method can help confirm information provided by the teacher and assess whether the child's problem behavior is typically preceded or followed by certain events. One means of collecting this information is to conduct narrative ABC recordings (Bijou, Peterson & Ault, 1968). The observer records the target student's behavior in the center column (B), peer or teacher behavior that precede the student's behavior in the left-hand column (A), and peer or teacher behavior that occurs as a consequence of the student's behavior in the right-hand column (C). Once these narratives are collected, one can calculate the type and frequency of various consequences provided by the teacher for appropriate as well as inappropriate behavior. Based on previous teacher interviews or anecdotal observations, the consultant may already have an idea of the consequences available for behavior (e.g., praise, help from the teacher, removal of work, ignoring). In such cases, simply recording the frequency with which each of these events follows occurrences of behavior can be helpful in identifying what the child might gain from behaving inappropriately (e.g., calling out is regularly followed by assistance from the teacher).

Another method of gathering information is to assess the student's academic skills. Skill assessment can be conducted by reviewing the student's previous work products and/or having the student complete work from his/her curriculum. To determine if students have the skills necessary to engage in appropriate classroom behavior, they can be asked to describe classroom rules and demonstrate examples of appropriate behavior in accordance with those rules. Finally, in some cases it may be useful to conduct a reinforcer preference assessment in order to determine whether rewards that are being used in the classroom are valued by students and what rewards might be used as part of the intervention (Berkowitz & Martens, 2001; Northup, George, Jones, Broussard & Vollmer, 1996).

As an example of a functional assessment sequence, consider a teacher who reports in a PAI that she sends a child out of the room to the hallway for 10 minutes contingent on misbehavior. When asked to completed the MAS, the teacher gives high ratings to items on the "escape" and "attention" subscales. Narrative observations of the child suggest that misbehavior typically occurs after an assignment is made in language arts and that, while in the hallway, the child jokes and plays with children passing by. Examining the child's work samples reveals that assignments are completed sporadically but with near perfect accuracy. Referring to Table 6.4, these data might suggest that the problem behavior is being maintained by negative reinforcement in the form of escape from boring, mastery-level tasks as well as positive reinforcement in the form of social interaction with peers.

When functional assessment data do not provide a clear picture of potential causes for problem behavior, competing hypotheses can be tested by arranging analog conditions or briefly comparing two or more treatment options (Iwata et al., 1982/1994; Martens, Eckert, Bradley & Ardoin, 1999). The strategy of designing analog conditions to test hypothesized causes was pioneered by Iwata and his colleagues in their work with self injurious behavior (SIB). To identify possible reasons for engaging in SIB, Iwata et al. exposed individuals to a series of test conditions in counterbalanced order. Although the specifics of these test conditions varied from case to case, they generally involved brief sessions (i.e., 10–15 minutes) in which different types of reinforcement were made contingent on the problem behavior. Reinforcers that were manipulated included social–positive reinforcement in the form of contingent attention, social–negative reinforcement in the form of removal of task demands, and automatic reinforcement in the form of time alone. The logic of these comparisons is that increases in SIB will be observed when the reinforcer maintaining it is delivered more frequently. As expected, increases in SIB were observed under at least one condition for each individual tested, and intervention programs based on these findings were dramatically effective in decreasing the problem behavior. Within the past several years, analog conditions have also been used to identify the causes of classroom behavior problems with excellent results (Ervin et al., 1998; Kern, Childs, Dunlap, Clarke & Falke, 1994; Lalli, Browder, Mace & Brown, 1993).

In cases where it is impractical or too time consuming to arrange a series of analog conditions, hypotheses about the causes of problem behavior can be tested indirectly by implementing one or more treatment procedures that employ a conceptually relevant behavioral principle (e.g., Martens, Eckert et al., 1999). For example, it was hypothesized earlier that the child's misbehavior was caused either by negative reinforcement in the form of escape from boring work or positive reinforcement in the form of attention from peers. The former hypothesis might be tested by assigning work that is instructionally matched to the student's skill level while observing changes in behavior. The latter hypothesis might be tested by allowing the child to earn time with a peer contingent on periods of appropriate behavior. Alternating these two interventions across days would allow one to determine the most effective option prior to full-scale implementation.

Treatment Strength

Although classroom behavior problems are often maintained by one or more of the principles described in Table 6.4, the research discussed above has shown that these principles operate in ways that are unique to each case. One implication of these findings is that a given treatment procedure will not be universally strong for all children, and that interventions need to be tailored to the individual needs of each case. Yeaton and Sechrest (1981) define *treatment strength* as the likelihood prior to implementation that treatment will have the intended effects. The authors suggest further that the likelihood of producing intended effects increases for interventions that contain larger amounts of the active treatment component. Thus, if the goal of treatment is to promote self-disclosure through questioning, reflection, and support, then treatment approaches that contain relatively more questions, reflective statements, and supportive comments would be considered "stronger." Similarly, if the goal of treatment is to increase desired behavior using a point system, then the intervention program would be strengthened by delivering points on a more frequent schedule or by arranging more desirable backup reinforcers. In general, reinforcement-based procedures can be strengthened by using highly preferred reinforcers, providing reinforcement on a rich schedule, and delivering reinforcement shortly after behavior has occurred (Neef, Mace & Shade, 1993; Northup et al., 1996).

There are several dimensions of treatment strength that can be applied to almost any psychological intervention, and these should also be considered when implementing school-based procedures (Gresham, 1991). First, intervention programs tend to be stronger if they are implemented for longer periods of time or with greater intensity (e.g., continuously throughout the school day versus one hour in the morning). Second, interventions are likely to be stronger if the procedures for their implementation and the responsibilities of participants are clearly specified. Third, treatment programs produce greater effects if they are implemented or assisted by individuals with special expertise and experience in using the procedure. These latter two points are particularly relevant to school consultation because they emphasize the importance of communicating program requirements clearly to teachers and supporting teachers' implementation efforts using the strategies described in Chapter 5.

Treatment Acceptability

Because teachers maintain primary responsibility for implementing school-based intervention programs, whether they agree with these programs in principle or view them as acceptable is likely to influence program success (Reimers, Wacker & Koeppl, 1987; Witt & Elliott, 1985). *Treatment acceptability* refers to judgments by teachers about whether treatment is fair, reasonable, or intrusive, appropriate for a given problem, and consistent with notions of what treatment should be (Kazdin, 1980). Research in this area has demonstrated that both preservice and experienced teachers view treatment acceptability as a multi-factor construct that includes such considerations as appropriateness, potential risk to the target child, time and skill required for implementation, and effects on other children in the classroom (Witt & Martens, 1983). Acceptability has also been shown to differ by virtue of the procedure being recommended, with procedures that reinforce desired behavior being viewed more favorably than those that punish undesired behavior (Witt, Martens & Elliott, 1984). Finally, a number of variables other than type of treatment have been examined for their effects on acceptability ratings including problem severity and type (Elliott, Witt, Galvin & Peterson, 1984; Kazdin, 1980); status of the rater (Witt & Robbins, 1985); the way the intervention is described (Witt, Moe, Gutkin & Andrews, 1984); gender and race of the teacher (Elliott, Turco & Gresham, 1987); student handicapping condition (Epstein, Matson, Repp & Helsel, 1986); and years of teaching experience (Witt, Moe et al., 1984).

These findings provide a number of directions for tailoring suggested intervention alternatives to teachers' preferences. Although teachers' preferences should be taken into consideration during plan development, we do not believe that judgments of acceptability should be used as the sole criterion for program selection. First, treatment acceptability is not an outcome variable in the consultation process but rather a predictor of more important outcomes such as treatment integrity and effectiveness. As a predictor variable, pretreatment ratings of acceptability have been shown to correlate only modestly ($r = 0.30$) with actual plan implementation (Martens, Kelly & Diskin, 1996). Second, a defining feature of the school consultation model presented in this book is that change is difficult and that many of us resist change even when it may be in the best interest of the children for whom we have responsibility. Thus, when faced with consultee resistance to a suggested intervention, one approach is to work together with the consultee to develop an equally suitable but more acceptable intervention program. An alternative approach, which was discussed at length in Chapter 2, is to attempt to reduce consultee resistance by strategically altering teachers' attitudes and perceptions.

Treatment Integrity

Many times, the realities of classroom instruction require teachers to alter an intervention program as discussed during the problem analysis interview. The extent to which a plan is implemented as intended is referred to as *treatment integrity* (Gresham, 1989). Because most behavioral interventions were designed for use by direct care providers rather than expert clinicians, one might expect that adherence to treatment guidelines is routinely assessed, but such has not been the case. In a review of behavioral intervention studies published between 1968 and 1980, L. Peterson, Homer, and Wonderlich (1982) found that only 20% of the studies sampled provided data concerning treatment integrity. In a review of treatment studies addressing behavior problems in children, Gresham, Gansle and Noell (1993) found that only 15.8% of studies between the years 1980 and 1990 reported treatment integrity data.

Although several authors have argued for the need to assess treatment integrity in research, this practice is even more important when treatment plans are being implemented within an indirect service model like school consultation (Gresham, 1989). During consultation, plans are developed primarily through a series of brief, face-to-face meetings between the consultant and consultee. Oftentimes these meetings may be insufficient for communicating clearly the various procedural details of an intervention, particularly if the intervention requires activities with which teachers have had little or no prior experience. Moreover, when teachers knowingly deviate from a plan as discussed, they often do so for good reason. Assessing treatment integrity can help identify those aspects of a plan that were difficult to implement, focus efforts to revise the plan, and ultimately lead to greater acceptance and use of the plan over time.

Treatment integrity can be discussed from two perspectives as it relates to school consultation. On the one hand, it is meaningful to talk about the integrity of the consultation process, or the extent to which the various interviewing objectives are successfully addressed during the PII, PAI, and PEI. In a study by Fuchs and Fuchs (1989), consultation services were provided to 24 teachers of difficult-to-teach students in four schools. Evaluation of consultation integrity revealed that the interviewing process occurred as planned in more than 80% of the cases. This high degree of process integrity, however, was attributed to the consultants' use of standard interviewing protocols. In the absence of such protocols and prior to training in the consultation process, McDougall, Reschly, and Corkery (1988) found that only between 6% and 47% of consultants met any single PII objective. On the other hand, it is also meaningful to talk about the integrity of the intervention process itself. Although minor deviations from treatment protocols are to be expected, there comes a point when changes in the treatment procedure are so extensive that the treatment principle is sacrificed. For example, suppose the decision is made to implement a program whereby a child earns one point for each in-class assignment completed correctly, and these points are to be exchanged for special privileges at the end of each day. After 2 weeks of implementation, you discover that the teacher's busy schedule has precluded time at the end of the day for exchanging points, and that the child is completing less work than ever. Without the opportunity to exchange what are essentially meaningless points for desired privileges, the principle of positive reinforcement never occurred when the teacher deviated from the plan.

EVALUATING INTERVENTION OUTCOMES

A key feature of any school-based intervention program should be efforts to systematically monitor its effects on student performance. Fuchs and Fuchs (1986a) refer to the ongoing evaluation of program outcomes which lead to revisions in program procedures as *systematic formative evaluation*. Systematic formative evaluation is based on the assumption that outcomes of school-based intervention programs cannot be predicted with certainty, but instead represent hypotheses that must be tested empirically (Ysseldyke & Marston, 1990). This view can be contrasted with an ability–training approach in which academic failure is attributed to deficits in one or more inferred mental processes within the child (i.e., student aptitudes). Standardized tests are typically used to diagnose these process deficits, and it is believed on the basis of theory that certain instructional programs can be used to remediate certain underlying deficits (Shinn, 1989). Once the appropriate aptitude X treatment interaction has been identified, program effectiveness is assumed. As noted earlier in the chapter, there is no empirical support for an aptitude X treatment interaction approach to school-based intervention. Reasons for this lack of support include poor psychometric properties of many existing aptitude measures as well as uncertainty over the extent to which various instructional programs actually address the aptitudes being targeted (R. H. Good et al., 1993; Ysseldyke, 1979).

Although federal law requires that IEPs for children receiving special services be reviewed at least annually, monthly or even weekly monitoring of progress has been shown to significantly increase student achievement. For example, Fuchs and Fuchs (1986a) conducted a meta-analysis of the effects of systematic formative evaluation on student achievement. For purposes of the study, evaluation was defined as twice-weekly monitoring of student progress using materials taken from the curriculum, depicting these data in a figure or graph, and using data-evaluation rules to guide decision making. Results indicated that monitoring progress and graphing the data were associated with an average ES of .70 regardless of the instructional procedure used. Using data evaluation rules increased the average ES to .91. These findings indicate that students' achievement test scores improved by nearly one standard deviation over controls simply as a function of how the instructional program was monitored. Fuchs, Fuchs, Hamlett, and Allinder (1991) compared the effects of weekly progress monitoring on students' achievement in spelling. Teachers who monitored student progress, graphed the results, and decided when to change instruction based on explicit rules averaged 2.7 instructional adjustments over an 18-week period. Teachers in the control group averaged only .17 changes in instruction during the same time period. Not surprisingly, the students of teachers who frequently monitored progress learned three times more spelling words by the end of the study.

To be useful in evaluating intervention outcomes, measures of student performance must have certain characteristics. When monitoring academic performance, measures must be directly related to the skills taught, sensitive to short-term improvements, capable of repeated administration, and time and cost efficient in addition to being reliable and valid (Fuchs & Fuchs, 1986b; Martens, Eckert, Bradley & Ardoin, 1999). One assessment method that has these characteristics is known as *curriculum-based measurement* (CBM). CBM probes are brief samples of production-type responses that are obtained using materials from the local curriculum (Shinn, 1989). Administered in standardized format, CBM probes involve 1 minute of passage reading, 2 minutes of spelling from dictation, 2 minutes of math computation, and 3 minutes of writing from a story starter. Different materials are selected at each grade level and scored for fluency, or the number of correct responses in the time allocated (e.g., correctly read words per minute). Not only are these measures psychometrically sound, but they have been used to monitor the effects of a variety of instructional programs including special class placement

(Shinn, 1986), instructional intervention (Daly & Martens, 1994), and stimulant medication (Stoner, Carey, Ikeda & Shinn, 1994).

When monitoring intervention effects on classroom behavior, it is important that the measures selected assess the actual behavior of interest at the actual time and place of its occurrence (Cone, 1978; Hayes, Nelson & Jarrett, 1986). *Direct observation* is one of the few assessment methods that accomplishes this goal, and as a result is commonly used to evaluate the effects of school-based interventions (Alessi, 1980; Lentz, 1988). A variety of approaches have been reported in the literature for collecting direct observational data including continuous event recording, duration recording, discrete categorization, and time sampling (Kazdin, 1994). Continuous event recording simply involves tallying the number of times behavior occurs during an observation session, and is most appropriate for behaviors with brief durations (Saudargas & Lentz, 1986). Duration recording involves the use of a stopwatch to record the cumulative duration of behaviors that extend in time, whereas discrete categorization involves the use of a checklist to record the occurrence of behaviors containing several discrete steps. *Time sampling* refers to a set of procedures for observing behavior in which occurrence or nonoccurrence is recorded during brief, consecutive intervals (e.g., 15 seconds) (Powell, Martindale & Kulp, 1975). Time sampled data are summarized as the percentage of intervals in which behavior occurred during any part of an interval (partial interval time sampling), during an entire interval (whole interval time sampling), or at the end of an interval when the observer looks up (momentary time sampling).

Procedures for monitoring intervention outcomes are typically discussed early in the consultation process prior to plan implementation (i.e., during the PII or PAI). These data are then used to set goals for improvement, monitor treatment integrity, and evaluate treatment effectiveness. Although it may be possible for teachers to assume the primary responsibility for data collection in many cases, this will depend on a variety of factors including when and how frequently the data are to be collected, the observational method used, and competing demands on teacher time. Because these and other issues that are negotiated during consultation are specific to each case, we believe school consultants should have an appreciation for teachers' roles and responsibilities in schools, their reasons for seeking consultative assistance, and their expectations for receiving such assistance. These issues are the focus of Chapter 7.

III

Key Participants in Consultation

7

Teachers as Consultees

Although the school consultant may assist many different consultees—including administrators, counselors, and parents—he or she is most likely to consult with teachers (Costenbader, Swartz & Petrix, 1992). Furthermore, given the fact that most school consultation occurs in elementary schools (Alpert & Yammer, 1983; Gresham & Kendell, 1987), it is reasonable to assume that the consultant's most frequent consultee will be an elementary school teacher. For this reason, in Chapter 7 we shall focus to a large extent on characteristics of teachers who have been assigned to kindergarten through grade 6 classrooms as well as aspects of consultation that occur at these grade levels. Chapter topics that pertain to the general enterprise of teaching are the complexity of classroom teaching; rewards and challenges of teaching; and teacher recruitment and retention issues. Other topics regarding teachers and consultation are: why teachers seek consultation; teacher expectations for consultation; how teachers view and respond to student problems prior to consultation; and characteristics that differentiate teachers who participate in consultation from those who do not. The final section of Chapter 7 presents potential strategies to maximize the effectiveness of consultation with teachers (e.g., adapting consultation methods to fit teachers' daily schedules; working with prereferral intervention teams; and enhancing knowledge and skill transfer back to the classroom). The major point of this chapter is that, although most teachers today are dedicated and want to help students to succeed, often they are not assisted in their efforts to do so. Therefore, it is incumbent upon the school consultant to offer consultative support to teachers so that they may work effectively within the constraints of their role.

PERSPECTIVES ON TEACHERS AND TEACHING

The Complexity of Classroom Teaching

To say the work of a classroom teacher is complex is both accepted fact and gross understatement. Though it is not possible in this chapter to include a detailed description of what goes on in an elementary school classroom (see Good & Brophy, 2000, for examples), consider briefly what a teacher must accommodate on a regular basis:

1. *Multidimensionality.* A multitude of diverse tasks and events happen in the classroom, and a teacher is expected to keep track of them. For example, student work is assigned, monitored, collected, and assessed; records are kept; and schedules are followed. Furthermore, a single teacher behavior can produce very different consequences. For instance, allowing a boy with an articulation disorder the opportunity to give a lengthy oral response may increase his motivation to succeed, but decrease the interest and motivation of the rest of the class.

2. *Simultaneity.* There are many events that occur at the same time in classrooms. During direct instruction, for example, an elementary teacher often simultaneously presents content, monitors student comprehension, and manages student behavior.

3. *Immediacy.* The rate at which classroom events unfold is extremely quick. One indicator of this rapid pace is that an elementary teacher may participate every day in as many as 1000 face-to-face exchanges with students (Jackson, 1968).

4. *Unpredictable and public classroom climate.* Unanticipated events occur regularly in classrooms, often prompting teachers to respond quickly and decisively. Also, how a teacher treats a particular student is usually witnessed by many other students; given this public atmosphere, students often can infer how the teacher feels toward their classmates.

5. *History.* As the school year progresses, a class develops certain norms and common understandings. Occurrences early in the school year also may influence classroom functioning later in the year. For example, a particular boy's severe outbursts of disruptive behavior that occurred when school first began now may cue students to stop whatever they are doing and return to their seats so the teacher can act more swiftly and efficiently to place the boy in time-out (Doyle, 1985).

Good and Brophy (2000) have argued incisively that, because teaching is complex, teachers often lack a full awareness of their behavior and, even if aware of their behavior, they may be unaware of its effects. Major obstacles to greater teacher awareness include the rapid pace of classroom events, preservice training that often fails to equip teachers with specific teaching techniques and skills for analyzing classroom behavior, and lack of a consistent means (e.g., mentoring) to provide teachers with corrective feedback. Unfortunately, many classroom problems can result when teachers lack insight into their professional actions, such as unintentional teacher domination of classroom communication, lowered emphasis on the meaning of concepts presented in instruction, overuse of factual questions, fewer attempts to motivate students, and an overreliance on repetitive seatwork (Good & Brophy, 2000). It would seem that a consultant with an appropriate background could offer valuable assistance with many of these issues.

The Rewards of Teaching

In 1964, Lortie (1975) undertook his classic sociological study of teachers in Dade County, Florida. Using survey and interview methodologies, his major interest was to examine patterns of outlooks and feelings that are unique to teachers and that distinguish the teaching profession from others. In 1984, Cohn and Kottkamp (1993) replicated and expanded on Lortie's original research. This section of the chapter draws on the conceptualizations and findings of these investigators; where relevant, we make comparisons between the two samples.

The rewards associated with the work of teaching may be categorized as extrinsic, ancillary, and intrinsic or psychic (Lortie, 1975). *Extrinsic rewards* relate to the "earnings" associated with teaching, and may be defined more specifically as salary, status, and power or influence over others. In both the 1964 and 1984 samples, only about 14% of teacher respondents indicated that, of all possible extrinsic rewards, they derived the most satisfaction from their earned salary. Extrinsic rewards viewed as much more important to both groups were the respect received from others and the opportunity to wield some influence. Although there were some differences, about one-third of each group endorsed each of these responses as a major basis of their job satisfaction. Interestingly, in a trend that appears to run counter to that observed in the larger U.S. society, almost 28% of the more recent sample claimed they derived *no satisfaction* from any extrinsic rewards associated with teaching (Cohn & Kottkamp, 1993).

Ancillary rewards are objective characteristics of the work situation that some teachers may regard as rewarding but others may not. For example, the rather flexible work schedule of teaching, which includes holidays and summers off, may serve as an ancillary reward for a mother with school-age children but may not be perceived as rewarding by a single male.[1] Across the 20-year period spanning the two research efforts, there was an interesting trend relative to ancillary rewards: whereas in 1964 only 23% of respondents felt that the work schedule of teaching was a significant positive feature, by 1984 over 35% of respondents saw it this way.

Intrinsic or psychic rewards consist of entirely subjective evaluations of the work situation that teachers find rewarding. By far the most common intrinsic reward mentioned by teachers is the satisfaction stemming from the realization that they have successfully instructed a student or group of students. In both samples, 86% of respondents indicated that this outcome was their most satisfying psychic reward. The next most pleasing psychic reward, mentioned by about 7% in both groups, was the opportunity to associate with students and to develop relationships with them.

Across the three types of work rewards, intrinsic or psychic rewards are easily the most important to teachers. In the 1964 sample, about 76% of respondents chose psychic rewards as most important, compared with about 12% each for extrinsic and ancillary. In the more recent sample, the percentage of respondents selecting psychic rewards as most important dropped slightly to about 70%, and ancillary rewards had increased to about 18% (Cohn & Kottkamp, 1993; Lortie, 1975).

Major Challenges Facing Teachers Today

A study of the rewards of teaching, however, necessarily gives way to a presentation of more negative aspects of this occupational role. In addition to problems of the bureaucratic structure of schools and schooling discussed in Chapter 3, we present four other significant challenges for teachers identified by Cohn and Kottkamp (1993).

The Decline and Dearth of Extrinsic Rewards

A teacher's salary may be best viewed as both substance and symbol. Taking salary as substance, it is useful to consider the following:

1. Even after accounting for inflation, teachers' incomes fell from the 1970s through the mid-1980s (Plisko, 1984).
2. The average beginning teacher salary in 1999 was $26,639 compared with $37,194 for all new college graduates. New graduates in engineering and computer science out-earned teachers by $16,000 to $18,000 (Gursky, 2000/2001).
3. The 1999 salary of the modal teacher (someone with about 16 years experience) was $40,574. Engineers with comparable experience earned an average of $68,294; computer systems analysts, $66,782. Thus, the earnings gap that develops over time between teachers and other professionals is huge (Gursky, 2000/2001).

Taking salary as a symbol, it is important to note that salary and social status are tied closely together in contemporary U.S. society.

Unfortunately for teachers, lower salaries suggest lower social status. Interestingly, according to a national Gallup poll in which 12 occupations were ranked, teachers ranked themselves first in making contributions to the overall good of society but last with respect to prestige or status (Elam, 1989).

Students as Less Motivated and More Difficult to Teach

Teachers interviewed by Cohn and Kottkamp expressed great surprise and even shock at students' attitudes toward school and learning. Some teachers had been threatened by students, and others were appalled by the widespread student apathy. Nearly all respondents attributed student motivational problems to changes in the family structure, particularly the aspects related to divorce and single-parenting, as well as the loss of parent-child quality time in dual-earner families. Teachers also believed that student drug use (particularly cocaine) and the materialism inherent in U.S. culture contributed to problems in motivating students.

Updating this list of student-related concerns voiced by Cohn and Kottkamp's teachers, we would add the growing problem of school violence, particularly student-on-teacher assaults (Furlong & Morrison, 1994). Some very telling national statistics in this regard include: (1) 7% of teachers reported having been physically attacked by a student at some point in the past, and 2% reported an assault in the last year; and (2) the lifetime prevalence of a teacher being attacked is more than three times higher (10% vs. 3%) in schools having 41% or more students participating in the free-lunch program than in schools in which 10% or fewer students receive free lunches (Mansfield, Alexander & Farris, 1991).

Parents as Unsupportive

Although some of Cohn and Kottkamp's respondents who taught in suburban school systems praised parents for their support, the majority instead cited parents for their failure to provide it. Teachers apparently view the concept of parental support bimodally, seeing problems with parents who show either too little interest or involvement or, on the other hand, too much interest or involvement. In the first case, teachers noted a lack of support with respect to parents' failures to attend scheduled school meetings, to monitor completion of homework, to take an interest in children's report cards, and to take notice of other critical school events. Parental reactions to teacher telephone calls reporting discipline problems also shocked many teachers; whereas parents previously would have generally "backed up" teachers' disciplinary actions, teachers could no longer count on them to do so. In the second case, teachers characterized many parents who displayed too much interest or involvement as unsupportive. For example, some overinvolved parents were said to make excuses for their children, attempt to get them out of work, or even lie for them. Wealthy parents allegedly were able to exercise their influence to change grades, classes, programs, and school policies.

Increased Vulnerability

In Cohn and Kottkamp's sample of teachers, 93% saw themselves as more vulnerable professionally at that time than in the past. For 51% of the group, this increased vulnerability was connected to the possibility of personal liability in lawsuits over student rights and welfare. Some elementary school teachers, for instance, were fearful of groundless accusations of student molestation and abuse. Another major source of vulnerability, expressed by 57% of respondents, was the school system's expectation that they be held accountable for student acquisition of basic skills as reflected in standardized test scores.

From this discussion, it may be concluded that teachers today tend to view their work to be more difficult and less rewarding than it was previously. In particular, the last three challenges illustrate the decline of psychic rewards for teachers. Knowing that psychic rewards hold the greatest importance for teachers (Cohn & Kottkamp, 1993; Lortie, 1975), this situation is very serious indeed. Facing these challenges without adequate support is likely to increase stress, which can result in burnout, which in turn, may lead one to decide to abandon the teaching profession altogether (Darling-Hammond, 1997).

Attracting and Retaining a Quality and Diverse Teaching Force

The demand for teachers currently is high and shortages are apparent in much of the U.S., and especially in inner cities and rural communities. Teachers trained in subject areas such as mathematics and physical science are particularly in demand. These shortages notwithstanding, between 1998 and 2008, 2 million to 2.5 million individuals will be entering the teaching profession. About half of these professionals will be newly trained teachers and most others will be returning teachers and/or unlicensed personnel. Clearly, recruitment and retention of quality teachers is currently a problem and one that will continue to grow (Darling-Hammond, Berry, Haselkorn & Fideler, 1999). Strategies implemented by school systems to address this problem include: (1) mounting aggressive outreach programs that target university teacher education programs;

(2) offering financial incentives such as signing bonuses, low-interest mortgages, housing allowances, and day care subsidies; and (3) establishing "returnment" policies that allow retired teachers to return to teaching without losing full pension benefits (Supply and Demand: The Teacher Shortage, 2001).

Like other states, North Carolina has encountered difficulties in attracting and keeping good teachers. During 1992–1993, for example, nearly 20% of first-year teachers left the profession. Certain types of teachers (e.g., special education, speech-language, science) are in particularly short supply, and there is an overall shortage of minority group teachers (North Carolina Professional Practices Commission, 1995). In addition to the challenges identified by Cohn and Kottkamp (1993), other reasons for teacher attrition in North Carolina include: (1) many who enter teaching are young and perhaps lack the maturity to understand the demands and realities of teaching, and thus experience "cultural shock"; (2) appropriate, regular mentoring of beginning teachers frequently does not occur; (3) certain education reforms (e.g., proposals to remove teacher tenure) emphasize the supposed inadequacy of teachers; and (4) acceptable teaching resources and physical facilities are frequently lacking. Some reasons for the shortage of minority teachers are a low value placed on education and teaching in some minority communities, an absence of minority teachers to serve as role models, and inadequate financial assistance available to minority students for teacher training (North Carolina Professional Practices Commission, 1995).

Implications for the School Consultant

From these selected perspectives on teachers and teaching, one is led to conclude that many teachers need and deserve support in their professional role beyond that provided already by our nation's school systems. A summary of factors underlying this conclusion includes: teaching is a complex activity, the salary is not sufficient compensation for the demands of the job, the status associated with teaching is lower than that for other occupations requiring similar education, preservice training is said to fall short in providing specific and pragmatic classroom strategies, quality mentoring experiences are not always available, students and parents today appear to be less cooperative and more problematic, teachers perceive themselves as more vulnerable to lawsuits than before, some reforms in education assume that it is teachers who are to blame for lower student achievement and thus must be held accountable, and adequate teaching resources and physical facilities often are unavailable. To this summary we add other factors raised in Chapter 3, including Paradox 2 of school consultation: Most teachers want to be involved in responding to children's learning and adjustment problems, but schools are run in ways that limit this involvement.

Taken together, these factors constrain what teachers are able to accomplish in their professional role. *The experienced school consultant thus recognizes that a realistic goal is to help consultees function better within the constraints of their role rather than to expect that his or her assistance somehow will allow consultees to overcome these constraints.* We advocate this as a realistic goal of school consultation primarily because truly overcoming these constraints would require massive changes in the culture of schools (Sarason, 1982, 1996; Wyner, 1991), the culture of teaching (Ost, 1991), and certain trends in contemporary U.S. culture (e.g., low teacher salaries despite the high importance placed on public education). Attempts at school reform, including those that direct extensive resources to individual schools (e.g., Perry et al., 1996), have demonstrated how changes along these lines can be made. These types of activities, however, are still fairly rare.

PERSPECTIVES ON TEACHERS AND SCHOOL CONSULTATION

Stepping back from these larger, societal issues regarding teachers and teaching, we now examine various aspects of school consultation from the teacher's standpoint.

Three Views on Why Teachers Seek Consultation

Although a teacher may acknowledge a work-related problem in approaching a consultant, the specific reasons why there is a need for assistance may not be apparent "on the surface." Assuming teacher participation in consultation is generally voluntary rather than forced (cf. A. M. Harris & Cancelli, 1991), we offer three different but overlapping perspectives on this issue.

The first view comes from the behavioral approach to consultation, presented in Chapters 4 and 5. The behavioral perspective, very much embedded within a problem-solving tradition (Bergan, 1995), regards consultee difficulties as arising from a lack of knowledge and/or skills. Along these lines, as consultants we have found that teachers may readily acknowledge their current problems as stemming from a failure to understand the classroom situation or an inability to do what it takes to solve the problem at hand. Accordingly, the focus of behavioral consultation often involves the direct, explicit remediation of knowledge or skills deficits in the consultee and/or client. The major approaches to intervention within behavioral consultation thus tend to involve education and skill development for consultees, and these approaches plus a variety of behavioral interventions for clients (Bergan, 1977; Bergan & Kratochwill, 1990; Gallessich, 1982).

A second view regarding why teachers seek consultation takes the behavioral view and adds other possibilities to it. Within his model of mental health consultation, Caplan (1963, 1970; Caplan & Caplan, 1993/1999) has posited four sources of consultee difficulty: lack of knowledge, lack of skill, lack of self-confidence, and lack of objectivity. To the extent that supervisory and administrative mechanisms are functioning poorly in schools, Caplan would agree with the behavioral view and assert that most teacher difficulties probably result from a lack of knowledge and/or skill (Erchul, 1993b). He then would add that a consultee's low self-confidence also may explain impaired work performance under the described organizational conditions. However, when supervision and administration practices are functioning well in an organization, Caplan (1970) has stated that a lack of objectivity is more likely to explain consultees' work difficulties. In contrast to knowledge or skill deficits, highly trained and competent consultees rarely have the insight that lowered objectivity is hindering their effectiveness.

When objectivity is the hypothesized source of the problem, consultees may harbor unconscious themes or irrational assumptions (Caplan, 1963, 1970). While implementing mental health consultation with elementary school teachers, Robinson and Falconer (1972) discovered these irrational assumptions held by their teachers:

1. The teacher who is competent and working to capacity can do the job without help.
2. A good teacher should be able to work with any and every child.
3. The teacher must be friendly at all times.
4. The teacher next year will blame me if the student has not learned all he is supposed to know.
5. If I fail in a particular area, I will be revealed as the failure I always feared I was.

The question of whether teachers display a greater number of problems related to a lack of skills, knowledge, confidence, or objectivity has not been answered satisfactorily, nor do we believe that it is a critical question for most consultants. In the only empirical study, Gutkin (1981) examined daily logs from 10 advanced school psychology graduate student consultants in order to determine the relative distribution of consultation cases into the four categories. In reviewing 171 consultation cases, Gutkin found that 38, 27, 27, and 7% of the cases resulted from a lack of consultee knowledge, skill, confidence, and objectivity, respectively. Although these findings suggest that objectivity rarely is viewed as the source of teachers' difficulties, Gutkin's consultants, trained in behavioral consultation, were more likely to attribute consultee problems to knowledge or skill deficits than to lowered objectivity (Conoley & Wright, 1993). To the individual consultant, then, the relative distribution of cases into the four categories would seem to be less important than an understanding of which reasons are most relevant to the case he or she is handling at the present time. The school consultant also must be alert to the strong possibility that more than one reason may best explain teacher difficulties.

Accepting the validity of the first two perspectives, but also acknowledging the literature on teachers and teaching reviewed earlier, as well as the content of Chapter 3, we present a third perspective. Increasingly, we believe that many teachers approach consultants due to a *lack of support* from the schools and society. This perspective recognizes the value of skills, knowledge, confidence, and objectivity as explanations for individual consultee problems, but it also places this issue into a larger sociological and career path context that directly acknowledges the occupational role of "teacher." As Darling-Hammond et al. (1999) have noted:

> What has been lacking in most districts, states, and at the national level is a framework for policy that creates a coherent infrastructure of recruitment, preparation, and *support programs* [emphasis added] that connect all aspects of the teacher's career continuum into a teacher development system that is linked to national and local education goals. (pp. 184–185)

Also undergirding our third perspective is the characterization of teaching as a lonely profession, with teachers expressing feelings of isolation in their work (Jackson, 1968; Sarason, 1982, 1996). Thus, an elementary teacher who spends most of his or her day interacting with young children may have a strong desire to speak with a caring, supportive adult. Teacher isolation is another indicator of the clear value of supporting teachers through consultation services.

Teacher Expectations for Consultation

In examining teachers' expectations for consultation, we rely on a sampling of research that has documented teacher perceptions of school consultation. Some of this literature was presented in Chapter 2, including investigations by Erchul (1987), Erchul and Chewning (1990), and Witt et al. (1991). Here we present findings of several additional studies relevant to this topic.

Gutkin (1980) surveyed 171 teachers from 12 different schools in order to understand their perceptions of consultation following the provision of consultative services to them by advanced school psychology graduate students over a 14-week period. Important results were: (1) 88% of teachers believed it was desirable to have a psychological consultant available at school, and only 4% viewed it as undesirable; (2) 69% felt consultation services were more effective than traditional assessment services offered by the psychologist, and only 4% indicated consultation was less effective; and (3) 81% of teachers agreed that working with a consultant would result in an improvement of their professional skills, and only 6% disagreed with the likelihood of this outcome. These robust findings indicate clear teacher support for school-based consultation services. Importantly, Gutkin (1980) noted that these results do not vary as a function of the demographic characteristics of the schools or communities from which he sampled teacher opinions.

In a follow-up investigation, Gutkin (1986) polled 191 teachers from 24 schools with respect to their reactions to consultation services that were provided by graduate student consultants. Stepwise regression analyses were conducted to predict teachers' perceptions of several key outcomes, including the utility of the ideas and programs generated as a result of consultation, improvement in their professional skills, and overall consultant effectiveness. The utility of ideas and programs developed in consultation was best predicted by a model comprised of the following entry of variables: consultant knowledge and application of psychological principles, consultant communication skills, consultant interest, and enthusiasm ($R^2 = .48$). The best models for predicting both teachers' improvement in professional skills and consultant effectiveness were composed of variables having the following order of entry: consultant knowledge and application of psychological principles, consultant communication skills, and teacher understanding of the consultation process (R^2s = .52 and .64, respectively).

Using a similar method for data collection, Hughes, Grossman, and Barker (1990) investigated how elementary school teachers' self-efficacy and outcome expectations affect their participation in and evaluation of consultation. *Self-efficacy* refers to a person's confidence that he or she can accomplish a specific task or solve a given problem; *outcome expectancy* refers to an individual's estimate that a particular behavior or activity (e.g., consultation) will lead to certain outcomes (Bandura, 1977). Hughes et al.'s major results were: (1) a significant negative correlation existed between self-efficacy and outcome expectancy ($r = -.37$), suggesting that teachers with higher self-efficacy scores have lower expectations that consultation can really help them; (2) a trend was found between self-efficacy and teacher reported change in their professional performance ($r = -.44$, $p = .11$), suggesting that teachers with high self-efficacy are less likely to report changing their approach to handling classroom problems following consultation; and (3) a significant correlation was found between teacher outcome expectancy and teacher evaluation of consultation ($r = .42$), suggesting that teachers having high positive expectations for consultation perceive the consultant as more effective.

In exploring relationships between processes and outcomes of school consultation, Erchul, Hughes, Meyers, Hickman, and Braden (1992) used an interpersonal perspective in which consultee and consultant perceptions on the same issues were compared and then correlated with several outcome measures. Sixty-one advanced graduate students engaged in problem-solving consultation with one consultee each, after which perceptions of the process were obtained from both parties. Key findings were: (1) a variable based on the extent to which, within a particular dyad, the consultant understood the consultee's role and vice versa was significantly related to consultee perceptions of both the beneficial nature of consultation ($r = .38$) and consultant effectiveness ($r = .45$); and (2) the degree to which consultant and consultee saw themselves as a "team" was significantly related to consultee perceptions of the beneficial nature of consultation ($r = .56$), growth in consultee competence ($r = .42$), client improvement ($r = .34$), and consultant effectiveness ($r = .57$). Given these findings, Erchul et al. reasoned that more favorable outcomes in consultation result from consultants and consultees agreeing on their respective roles and seeing their actions as stemming from teamwork.

Results of these four studies, all based on teacher perceptions of consultation, suggest several conclusions regarding teacher expectations for consultation. In general, teachers look forward to consultation, viewing it as more effective than traditional psychological assessment and capable of enhancing their professional skills. However, teachers who have a high degree of self-efficacy may have lower expectations regarding the beneficial nature of consultation, and may see themselves as not changing their usual approach to solving classroom problems following consultation. Teacher expectations regarding the usefulness of ideas produced in consultation, the probability his or her skills will be upgraded, and the effectiveness of the consultant seem to be linked to a perception of the consultant as a skilled communicator who understands psychological principles and knows how to apply them. Furthermore, the extent to which consultant and teacher see themselves as a team appears to enhance teacher perceptions of similar outcomes in consultation. It should be noted, however, that the univariate correlations reported by Hughes et al. (1990) and Erchul et al. (1992), although statistically significant, are of only modest magnitude and account for only 12% to 33% of variance in outcomes. Thus, caution is urged in their interpretation.

What Teachers Do before Seeking Consultation

This issue may be recast as the question, "How do teachers view and respond to student problems?" Findings from several studies indicate that teachers prefer to take an active role in attempting to resolve problems before a consultant is called for assistance. Most elementary teachers (96%) want to be involved in responding to children's learning and adjustment problems (Gutkin, 1980), and they often attempt two or three types of interventions on their own before asking for help (Ysseldyke et al., 1983). Furthermore, of the interventions that might be implemented in the classroom, teachers rate as highest those that they direct themselves (Algozzine et al., 1983).

Despite elementary teachers' strong interest in intervening, research suggests that they typically do not assess student problems well or intervene in a systematic way on their own. For example, Lambert (1976) asked 47 teachers to specify problems and possible solutions for 246 students who were identified as having chronic learning and behavior difficulties. Lambert found that teachers described individual student problems in vague or general terms (e.g., "poor motivation"), and proposed only about one solution per problem. In studying teacher reactions to actual cases of prereferral intervention, Ysseldyke et al. (1983) noted that teachers tend to use interventions that are not related to the original reasons for referral, implement interventions for an unspecified time period, and employ few evaluation measures that document behavior change. Finally, Algozzine et al. (1983) had 174 elementary teachers rate 40 intervention choices for each of three student problems: immaturity, perceptual difficulties, and unmanageability. One key result was that the type of student problem was unrelated to teachers' choice of intervention, leading Algozzine et al. to two conclusions: (1) detailed assessment data apparently have little value in teachers' intervention planning, and (2) the selection of interventions by teachers may be the result of an unsystematic process.

From this discussion it may be seen that before requesting consultation, a teacher typically has tried several interventions that have been unsuccessful for the various reasons noted. When the teacher then approaches a consultant, he or she is often very frustrated because of the lack of prior success and possibly because the problem has gotten even worse. Though a lack of knowledge or skills may account for the teacher's inability to resolve the problem, his or her rising frustration level may result in a failure to see the problem with reasonable objectivity. A consultant therefore needs to be aware of how the history of a problem may constitute a crisis (Caplan, 1964) for the teacher and perhaps focus initial attention on the support and development task rather than rush into the problem-solving task.

Factors That Distinguish Teachers Who Participate in Consultation from Those Who Do Not

Consultation may be of benefit to many teachers but, in most cases, teachers first need to seek out the service. Along these lines, Stenger, Tollefson, and Fine (1992) sought to determine which variables differentiate elementary teachers who have engaged in consultation from those who have not. Stenger et al. surveyed a randomly selected group of 500 female, predominantly white elementary school teachers and obtained 352 usable questionnaires (a 70% return rate). Of this number, 186 teachers had consulted with a psychologist within the past 10 months, and 166 others had not. A stepwise discriminant function analysis was conducted to determine the variables that offered the greatest degree of discrimination between the two groups. A single discriminant function, correctly classifying 73% of the sample, contained five significant predictor variables.

In order, the variables that distinguished the users of consultation from the nonusers were:

1. The perception that the psychologist offers help on a regular basis at the teacher's school (standardized canonical coefficient = .75).
2. The perception of themselves as having good problem-solving skills (.60).
3. The perception that the psychologist has had training in problem-solving skills (.28).
4. The teachers having fewer years of teaching experience (.20).
5. The perception that the entry-level training required for the psychologist is higher than that required for a teaching position (.12).

These results suggest that teachers will be more likely to engage in consultation with psychologists whom they see as available, knowledgeable, and competent in problem solving. Interestingly, the finding that teachers with good problem-solving skills are more likely to use consultation runs counter to what Hughes et al. (1990; reviewed earlier) found. Stenger et al. (1997) attributed this discrepancy to the different definitions of problem solving used in the two studies, specifically that self-efficacy cannot be equated with problem solving.

INCREASING THE EFFECTIVENESS OF
CONSULTATION WITH TEACHERS

Adapting Consultation to the Teacher's Schedule:
The 15-Minute Consultation

As noted in Chapter 3, another constraint that teachers (and many psychologists) operate under is having limited time for consultation. The school day is tightly structured, suggesting that before school and after school as well as during recess, lunch, and teacher planning periods (if available) are the times that consultation can occur. Unfortunately, these occasions often do not provide extended blocks of time (e.g., 30 or more minutes) that are usually needed to explore problems in a thorough manner. Another drawback to meeting during one of these times is that a teacher may want to be doing something other than consultation.

Assuming that consultation should provide an opportunity for unhurried, systematic reflection (Caplan, Caplan & Erchul, 1995), there is no simple solution to this vexing problem. However, one response to time constraints in schools is the "15-minute consultation," so named because it is assumed that no single contact with a consultee will exceed about 15 minutes (Brown, Pryzwansky & Schulte, 2001). Steps that a consultant would follow in the first meeting are:

1. Help teacher prioritize the issues of concern, and have him or her identify an important issue that could be addressed given the limitation of time.
2. Inform teacher about the advantages and disadvantages of this approach to consultation as well as other consultation models that could be used (see trade-offs below).
3. Determine whether teacher has a hypothesis regarding the problem, and ask what interventions have been tried already.
4. Advance alternative (perhaps competing) hypotheses, and emphasize that different hypotheses usually result in different interventions.
5. Agree on follow-up responsibilities and the time of the next meeting or contact.

After the first session, Brown et al. (2001) have suggested that telephone contacts be used in conjunction with face-to-face meetings, and that a classroom observation take place, particularly if there is a clear reason to do so. Interventions developed over the course of subsequent "15-minute consultations" appear to be devised by the consultant, rather than through the joint efforts of both parties. Evaluation of outcomes remains an important goal, although it may be based on more expedient measures (e.g., brief classroom observations). To illustrate the approach, Brown et al. provide a brief case study in which a psychologist consults with a teacher across six sessions, each ranging in length from 5 to 20 minutes.

Brown et al. (2001) have noted definite trade-offs associated with the 15-minute consultation. On the negative side, a teacher may distort or misrepresent problems that, given the time frame, the consultant is unable to assess or verify further. When a consultant acts on incomplete information and then is wrong in setting the course for consultation, the teacher may find the consultant to be unhelpful and perhaps the consultant's credibility with other potential consultees will suffer. The brief time available also tends to preclude the implementation of a complex intervention, which may be needed. Finally, a quick approach to school consultation unfortunately encourages a view that a consultant is omniscient and thus minimizes the consultee's active participation (Brown et al., 2001).

More positively, the 15-minute consultation tends to fit a teacher's schedule better and thus reduces one predictable source of resistance to consultation. Administrators and school boards may like it because precious classroom instruction time does not have to be sacrificed for the sake of perhaps only one student. In principle, a consultant could work with greater numbers of teachers using this approach as opposed to using a more in-depth consultation model for the same amount of time. Also, it is arguable that brief contacts spread out over an extended period of time may benefit consultees and clients more than would a focused and intense problem-solving period (Brown et al., 2001).

We believe that the 15-minute consultation has merit and deserves further study. At present its greatest strength is its guiding assumption that teachers are extremely busy and do not have the time that consultants usually prefer to devote to consultation. However, instead of leaving important elements out of consultation due to time constraints, we prefer to address them over an extended period, using several brief contacts. For example, a behavioral consultant may consider achieving all of the goals of the Problem Identification Interview (Bergan & Kratochwill, 1990) across two or three short meetings with a teacher rather than in a single, longer session (which may not be an option for either party anyway).

Consulting as Part of a Prereferral Intervention Team

As mentioned in Chapter 3, teachers are now required in many states to implement some type of intervention for students experiencing difficulties in their classroom before referring them for evaluation (Carter & Sugai, 1989; Zins, Kratochwill & Elliott, 1993). In order to comply with this mandate, school districts have developed multidisciplinary groups of consultants in each school building known as *prereferral intervention teams.* As summarized by McDougal, Clonan and Martens (2000):

> Prereferral intervention is a consultation-based approach for provid- ing behavioral and/or instructional support to students experiencing problems before considering their eligibility for special class place- ment.... As such, prereferral intervention services involve consulta- tion between a referring teacher and a team of consultants toward the common goals of specifying the referral problem in behavioral terms, analyzing maintaining variables, and designing, implementing, and evaluating one or more intervention plans. (p. 150)

In New York State, for example, Section 4401-a of the Education Law was amended in 1999 to require a written description of attempts to address a student's learning and adjustment problems prior to referral. School districts, in turn, were required to develop school-wide prereferral intervention programs.

Numerous examples of prereferral intervention programs have been reported in the consultation literature (e.g., Graden, Casey & Christenson, 1985; Gutkin, Henning-Stout & Piersel, 1988; Fuchs, Fuchs and Bahr, 1990; McDougal et al., 2000; Rosenfield, 1992; Rosenfield & Gravois, 1999). Typically, a school-based prereferral intervention team is comprised of the school psychologist, an instructional specialist or special education teacher, one or more support personnel (e.g., a social worker or language specialist), a regular education teacher, and a school administrator. Other common characteristics of prereferral intervention teams are that they: (1) adhere to the four-stage problem-solving process of the behavioral consultation model, (2) have regularly scheduled meetings to discuss cases, (3) make use of some type of recording form, checklist, protocol, or manual to guide team interactions, and (4) use both direct (e.g., classroom observation, cur- riculum-based assessment) and indirect (e.g., teacher report) measures to evaluate the consultation process and intervention outcomes. At an organi- zational level, successful prereferral intervention programs tend to have the active support of key administrators, commitment to provide needed resources (e.g., funds for release time, training by external consultants, part- time aides), a planning team of consultants internal to the district, and a process for conducting formative evaluations (McDougal et al., 2000).

Prereferral intervention programs like those described above have been shown to be effective in responding to children's problems and in decreasing the number of students ultimately referred for special education placement. For example, Fuchs, Fuchs, and Bahr (1990) reported that students referred to their Mainstream Assistance Teams achieved approximately 75% of their identified goals. Only 11% of these students on average were referred to special education at year's end, whereas 50% of students in the control condition were referred. After evaluating their School-Based Intervention Team (SBIT) Project, McDougal et al. (2000) found that: (1) consultation objectives were either met or partially met during 90.5% of observed team meetings, (2) teachers rated children's problems as significantly less severe after participating in the SBIT process, (3) children referred for classroom behavior problems showed a 20% increase in time on-task over baseline following intervention, (4) children referred for reading problems gained an average 3.7 words per week, and (5) referrals to special education decreased by 36%.

As one might suspect, the dynamics of consulting with teachers as part of a team are likely to differ from those of individual case consultation. For one, each team member can expect fewer opportunities to participate in discussion simply as a result of having more people present. Beyond this, however, mandates for team consultation may call into question several of the core characteristics of consultation described in Chapters 1 and 5 (Goldstein & Martens, 2000). First, school consultation was initially conceived of as involving a collaborative relationship between co-equal professionals (Gutkin & Curtis, 1982). Subsequent research on relational control has depicted consultation more as a cooperative relationship in which the consultant leads and the consultee willingly follows toward the mutual goal of intervention design. Second, with mandates for prereferral intervention, consultation has become a stand-alone educational service regulated by state law. One result of such mandates is that all members of the intervention team, including the referring teacher, are held to higher levels of accountability with respect to intervention integrity and outcome. Whereas teachers may have been free to reject consultants' suggestions when consultation was delivered informally, doing so following mandated team consultation may be tantamount to denying children access to an appropriate education. Third, school consultants have historically relied on teacher verbal report as a basis for intervention design (Witt, 1997). Higher levels of accountability and the need to demonstrate beneficial outcomes for children have made it increasingly more common for intervention teams to supplement teacher verbal reports with more direct assessment data (e.g., classroom observation), particularly when conducting a functional assessment as described in Chapter 6.

Increasing Knowledge/Skill Transfer and Maintenance

Despite the best intentions of all involved parties, why do changes in teacher behavior not always generalize beyond the face-to-face meetings with the school consultant? Goldstein and Martens (2000) have suggested three reasons. First, many consultants erroneously assume an *empirical–rational* approach to change will be effective when it generally is not (see discussion in Chapter 2). Second, even in behavioral consultation—the most widely used and researched model of school consultation—often a naive "train and hope" model of generalization (Stokes & Baer, 1977) is relied upon. Third, it is difficult (particularly for external consultants) to adequately understand the contingencies under which consultees operate to harness these contingencies to optimize follow through efforts.

Chapter 5 specified the importance of four components relative to the support and development task of school consultation: social influence; goal setting; modeling, coaching, and performance feedback; and implementation protocols (Goldstein & Martens, 2000). We continue by offering some strategies from the staff development literature.

The school consultant may benefit from knowing what makes staff development activities result in having teachers transfer a high level of knowledge and skill back to the classroom. The research program of Bruce Joyce and Beverly Showers is instructive in this regard (see Showers, 1990). Joyce and Showers have documented the odds of achieving knowledge and skill transfer can be increased through training activities designed to help teachers accomplish these objectives: (1) to understand fully the theoretical basis of the innovation and what it is supposed to accomplish; (2) to observe demonstrations of the innovation through the use of both live and taped models; (3) to take advantage of opportunities to practice new skills in the training setting; and (4) to participate in peer coaching teams in which teachers provide instrumental and expressive support to each other in the implementation of the innovation in the classroom (Showers, 1990).

With respect to the last objective, Joyce and Showers (1988; cited in Showers, 1990) reasoned that teachers' difficulty in transferring technology back to the classroom could be attributed to characteristics of the school setting, particularly the isolation that many teachers face. To combat this isolation and enhance the quality and frequency of teachers' implementation attempts, they organized groups in which teachers coached one another in the use of new classroom strategies through collegial interaction. In these mutual help teams, teachers shared curriculum materials, observed one another using the new strategies, and provided peer-professional feedback. A controlled study of peer coaching study teams showed that, after one year, 80% of the teachers who participated in peer coaching had transferred the new teaching strategies into their active repertoire, compared to only 10% of the teachers who had undergone the same theory–demonstration–practice training sequence but had not participated in peer coaching activities (Showers, 1990).

Taken together, findings from the literatures on the generalization of gain in psychotherapy (Goldstein & Martens, 2000) and staff development (Showers, 1990) present several implications for the effective practice of school consultation. First, within consultation there is a need to set performance goals for consultees just as is commonly done for clients. Establishing explicit performance goals for consultees may enable them to become more effective change agents. Second, in our experience many school consultants do not conduct—or even attempt to conduct—the modeling, coaching, and performance feedback activities deemed critical for knowledge and skill transfer and maintenance. These same consultants then wonder why their teachers have not implemented a classroom intervention with integrity and/or demonstrable results. Finally, the peer coaching activity, seen as integral to the success of staff development efforts, argues convincingly for a goal of consultation to provide a support system for consultees (Erchul, 1993b) as well as for the greater use of group consultation with teachers (Babinski & Rogers, 1998; Caplan & Caplan, 1993/1999).

PROVIDING CONSULTATIVE SUPPORT TO TEACHERS

School consultation usually results in additional teacher responsibilities or demands, which we know are already considerable. Therefore, a major task of the consultant is to offer support and assistance to teachers during the consultation process. As a way of making some of the more abstract concepts of this chapter more concrete, we conclude Chapter 7 by listing a dozen pragmatic ways consultative support may be offered to teachers:

1. Listen attentively to teacher frustrations with classroom problems.
2. Provide a "sounding board" for teacher ideas.
3. Compliment teacher actions when successful.
4. Offer encouragement when teacher efforts are less than successful.
5. Instruct teachers in how to assess classroom problems in a systematic manner.
6. Help identify and, whenever possible, take an active role in recruiting additional resources or seeking alternative solutions that may be available elsewhere in the school.
7. Help teachers help themselves, as in peer coaching.
8. Make school-based consultation available to a greater number of consultees.
9. Inform teachers of the best available treatment technologies.

10. Guide teachers through the problem-solving process of consultation.
11. Assist teachers in systematic treatment implementation and evaluation.
12. Help teachers make assessment information relevant for intervention.

Exactly how the consultant should perform these activities is not firmly established, as specific behavioral markers of the optimal consultant/consultee relationship continue to defy easy identification (e.g., Busse, Kratochwill & Elliott, 1999). Notwithstanding, the transcribed case study presented later in Chapter 9 offers one consultant's attempt to demonstrate some of these actions. Before considering this case, Chapter 8 examines a variety of issues germane to a greater understanding of child and adolescent clients, considered more specifically as students in classrooms.

NOTES

1. Since the time of Cohn and Kottkamp's data collection, the year-round school has grown in popularity. Under this schedule, there are typically 9-week academic sessions alternating with 3-week breaks throughout the 12-month year. Again, some teachers may view this schedule as rewarding and others may not.
2. Due to IDEA 97 mandates, many states now require that teachers implement several classroom interventions designed in consultation with school staff before they refer students for psychoeducational evaluation. In North Carolina, for example, teachers must document at least two intervention attempts prior to referring students suspected of being behaviorally–emotionally disabled, specific learning disabled, or traumatic brain injured (North Carolina State Department of Public Instruction, 2000).

8

Students as Clients

Each September, millions of children across the country return to their classrooms ready to begin another year of public schooling. The majority of these children will be successful in learning the material presented to them, will earn passing marks from their teacher, and will be promoted to the next grade level. For a certain proportion of children, however (approximately 11% nationwide; Reschly, 1988), the year at school will be a markedly different experience. Some of these children will lack the skills needed to tackle grade-level material, and as a result will struggle with even routine classroom assignments. Others will be unaccustomed to waiting patiently for the teacher's attention or working quietly in their seat, and as a result will engage in behavior that disrupts others.

For over 25 years now, American schools have been committed to providing a free, appropriate, public education (FAPE) to those students who find it difficult to succeed in the regular education system (Telzrow, 1999). This commitment has been the direct result of federal legislation mandating services in the schools, and has increased the range of opportunities for school consultants to work alongside teachers in meeting the needs of exceptional students. This chapter begins with an overview of federal legislation governing service delivery in the schools, and identifies the implications of these mandates for school consultation services. Next, educational approaches to classifying students as handicapped are discussed, including the rationale underlying ability grouping, characteristics and examples of state diagnostic criteria, and the relationship of educational classification schemes to the *Diagnostic and Statistical Manual* (*DSM-IV*) of the American Psychiatric Association (1994). In order to highlight the limitations of educational approaches to classification, issues surrounding the identification of children as learning disabled and emotionally disturbed are discussed in detail. Following this presentation, we consider the characteristics of regular education classrooms that limit the degree to which students with special needs can be accommodated in the mainstream. The chapter concludes with a description of variables in the instructional environment that have been shown to influence student achievement, and that therefore represent important considerations for the school consultant.

LEGISLATION GOVERNING SERVICE
DELIVERY IN THE SCHOOLS

Without question, the two pieces of legislation that have had the greatest impact on the types of services delivered to children in schools have been *Public Law (P.L.) 94-142 The Individuals with Disabilities Education Act* (IDEA; formerly the Education for All Handicapped Children Act) and *Section 504 of the Vocational Rehabilitation Act*. IDEA was passed by the 94th Congress and signed into law by President Ford on November 29, 1975. The intent of IDEA was to make law the decisions and mandates that had been reached in a number of court cases heard prior to 1975. The majority of these cases involved class action suits against defendant school districts that were brought on the basis of (1) unequal access to public education by students with disabilities; (2) minority overrepresentation in special classrooms offering inferior educational opportunities; and (3) inappropriate uses of standardized tests to make student placement decisions (e.g., administering intelligence measures in English to Spanish-speaking students). Stemming from the decisions in these cases, IDEA guarantees to all students between ages 3 and 21 a free, appropriate public education, which includes special education and related services needed to meet their unique needs. *Free* means that education is to be provided at public expense and the appropriateness of this education is to be agreed upon and documented in writing by the student's *individualized education program* or IEP.

Beyond guaranteeing the right to a free appropriate education, IDEA contains a number of protections involving the process that is due a student being considered for special education placement. Included in these *due process requirements* is the need to obtain parental consent before evaluating a student for possible classification, the parents' right to obtain an independent evaluation at the school's expense, and the use of evaluation instruments that are reliable and valid for the purposes intended. With respect to the child's IEP, the law mandates that it be developed by a team of qualified professionals which include the child's parent or guardian; that it contain statements about the child's present levels of functioning, annual goals, and criteria for evaluating progress; and that it be reviewed at least annually. Finally, with respect to the services provided, IDEA mandates that school districts make available a continuum of alternative placements and services to meet the needs of students with handicaps. The law states further that students with handicaps receive their education in the *least restrictive environment* and alongside nonhandicapped peers to the maximum extent appropriate.

In the spring of 1997, IDEA was amended by Congress and signed into law by President Clinton on June 4th to reflect a number of changes in the way that students with disabilities were evaluated. Telzrow (1999) summarized these changes which included: (a) elimination of the term "serious" from the category of emotional disturbance, (b) participation by students with disabilities in district-wide assessments with appropriate accommodations, (c) inclusion of parents as evaluation team members, (d) inclusion of a regular education teacher as an evaluation team member for students placed at least part-time in regular education, and (e) use of existing data where appropriate during reevaluations.

In response to increased concern over school violence, the IDEA 97 Amendments also made provisions for students with disabilities who exhibit severe problem behavior or who violate school rules. Specifically, IDEA 97 required that "if a student with disabilities exhibits problem behaviors that impede his or her learning or the learning of others, then the student's IEP team shall consider strategies, including positive behavioral interventions, strategies, and supports to address that behavior" (Drasgow & Yell, 2001, p. 240). Positive behavioral interventions refer to procedures that teach and/or reinforce appropriate behavior instead of relying on punishment to reduce inappropriate behavior. IDEA 97 stipulated further that positive behavioral interventions were to be based on a functional assessment as described in Chapter 6. Functional assessments were also required when a student with a disability accumulated 10 school days of suspension, was removed from school in a manner that constituted a change of placement, or was placed in an interim alternative education setting for a weapons or drug offense (Drasgow & Yell, 2001).

Using somewhat different wording, the right to a FAPE with due process requirements was also guaranteed by Section 504 of the Vocational Rehabilitation Act of 1973. Section 504 is a civil rights statute that states:

> No otherwise qualified handicapped individual in the United States shall, solely by reason of his [sic] handicap, be excluded from the participation in, be denied the benefits of, or be subjected to discrimination under any program or activity receiving Federal financial assistance.

Section 504 in general and IDEA in particular have had far-reaching implications for the delivery of services in the schools. For example, with the mandate for multidisciplinary teams to evaluate students' eligibility for special education, individually administered tests of achievement and intelligence became increasingly popular as diagnostic tools. Because school psychologists often administered these tests, they found themselves cast in the role of gatekeeper for entry into special education with corresponding increases in caseloads. As controversy heightened over the use of intelligence tests to classify children as mentally retarded (particularly children from minority groups), the years following passage of IDEA saw "a veritable epidemic" of students classified with learning disabilities (Reschly, 1988, p. 460).

IDEA also has had important implications for the role of support personnel (e.g., psychologists, psychiatrists, reading specialists, social workers) in configuring educational programs for special needs students. First, by mandating a continuum of services, IDEA introduced the concept of the resource room. A *resource room* is a classroom in which children with handicaps can receive special education services for only a portion of the school day while spending the majority of their instructional time in the regular classroom setting. In contrast to previous policies of "place or not place," children needing special services could now receive those services on a part-time basis. In keeping with the least restrictive environment mandate, two arrangements emerged for providing part-time special education services including the *pull-out program* in which students with mild handicaps received remedial instruction in a resource room and the *push-in program* in which students with more severe handicaps received instruction in a regular classroom. An important implication of these arrangements was that regular classroom teachers who had been trained to teach relatively homogenous groups of typical children were now required by law to accommodate students with special needs for a portion of the school day. Second, in order to help regular education teachers accommodate a more diverse student population, the instructional and managerial strategies used by special education teachers were to be shared with their regular education counterparts. This sharing of instructional technology was to be accomplished through mandated personnel development programs and the delivery of consultative services by special education resource teachers. Thus, IDEA provided an important impetus for school consultation through what has become known as the *teacher consultant model*. In New York State, consultant teacher services refer to "specially designed instruction provided by a special education teacher to a student with a disability" or "consultation provided ... to regular education teachers to assist them in adjusting the learning environment ... or instructional methods of a student with a disability."

EDUCATIONAL APPROACHES TO CLASSIFICATION

As discussed in Chapter 3, in order to receive special education and related services in the schools, students must be deemed eligible by a team of professionals based on a comprehensive psychoeducational evaluation. Completing the evaluation and arranging for appropriate services can take up to 90 days from the time a child is referred and can include, but is not limited to, a physical examination, a psychological evaluation, a social history, and assessments in other areas required to determine the child's need for special education programming. An important outcome of this evaluation that renders children eligible for special services is being classified as handicapped under one or more of the conditions specified in IDEA and interpreted with respect to regulations developed by each state's education agency. Because obtaining a handicapping classification plays such an important role in the types of school-based services children receive, we believe that school consultants should be aware of the rationale behind educational classification systems, the various handicapping conditions and criteria contained in state regulations, and the ways in which school-based practitioners translate these criteria into practice.

Rationale for Classifying Special Needs Students

We began the chapter by observing that children who enter school each year represent a diverse population in terms of skills and behaviors. As with most measured characteristics of individuals, student abilities can be viewed as continuous variables that tend to be normally distributed in the general population. This suggests that student achievement levels will range incrementally from about three standard deviations above the mean to about three standard deviations below the mean, with the majority of children who enter school (i.e., the 68% found between plus/minus one standard deviation from the mean) performing in the average range. This also suggests that children who have adjacent scores on a test of intelligence or achievement are best viewed as differing quantitatively rather than qualitatively with respect to the characteristic being measured (Reschly, 1988).

Just as students are likely to enter school with a range of abilities, teachers also are likely to bring a range of instructional and managerial practices to the classroom. These practices are developed through formal training in teacher preparation programs, and evolve as a function of experience and informal contacts with other faculty. Teachers' instructional and managerial practices are also determined in part by the practical constraints of moving large numbers of students through a basal curriculum. A *basal curriculum* is a hierarchical sequence of academic skills and corresponding instructional materials that are organized by learning objectives. These learning objectives are linked from year to year, with mastery being synonymous with academic achievement and failure having cumulative effects as students advance through the grade levels.

Interestingly, research into the nature of teachers' instructional practices has shown that these practices are consistent across schools, differ little between regular and special education classrooms, and have changed little over time (T.L. Good, 1983; Sirotnik, 1983; Ysseldyke, Christenson, et al., 1989). Together, these findings suggest that the range of teachers' instructional practices are likely to be narrower than the range of student abilities these practices are intended to accommodate. As early as 1977, Steven Apter described this situation as the "One Right Model" of public education. Specifically, Apter suggested that the bureaucratic structure of schools produces a certain rigidity of educational programming in which teachers focus their efforts on the average students in the classroom. Because the majority of children in classrooms are by definition average, this approach enables schools to educate most children most of the time. However, the "One Right Model" model also ensures that some children will not succeed in regular education because their skills and behaviors fall outside the acceptable range of the regular classroom teacher. For these children, a discrepancy exists between their performance and the teacher's performance expectations (Shinn, 1989). Consistent with the belief that it is easier to teach 10 children who are similar than 10 children who are different, special education was developed as the solution of choice for students who failed in regular education. Special education is expensive, however, costing approximately twice as much per pupil as regular education (Reschly, 1988). Some system was required therefore to identify those students most in need of the additional expenditures associated with special education services. This system was mandated by IDEA and translated into the various handicapping conditions and classification criteria specified in state regulations for students with disabilities.

Overview of Handicapping Conditions

The two major approaches for classifying childhood psychopathology in use today are individual state's regulations for students with disabilities and the *Diagnostic and Statistical Manual* (*DSM-IV*) of the American Psychiatric Association (1994). Although similarities exist between the two systems, they were developed to fulfill somewhat different functions. Regulations for students with disabilities were developed by state education agencies primarily to serve an administrative function by (1) assisting in the identification of students who are eligible for special services, placements, or resources; and (2) providing a system for calculating the amount of state and federal aid received by schools from one year to the next. Evidence that these guidelines were designed to meet administrative rather than diagnostic goals can be found in Section 200.6, subsection (g)(3) of New York state's regulations, which declares that, "A special class shall be composed of students with disabilities with similar individual needs." This suggest that a student's educational needs rather than handicapping condition was intended as the basis for determining placement.

Handicapping labels, definitions, and criteria for classification are likely to vary from state to state (e.g., Epstein, Cullinan & Sabatino, 1977), although in all cases the language used must be in accord with IDEA. For comparison purposes, the handicapping conditions specified in the regulations for the states of North Carolina and New York are listed in Table 8.1. Although it would be beyond the scope of the chapter to list the classification criteria under each condition, several common features are noted below, and the definitions for two conditions, Specific Learning Disabled and Emotionally Disturbed, are discussed in detail in subsequent sections.

One common element found in both states' classification criteria is that the language used to describe handicapping conditions often suggests a medical model rather than an ecological view of childhood disabilities (Gresham & Gansle, 1992). For example, *specific learning disabled* is a term used in North Carolina to "denote various processing disorders presumed to be intrinsic to an individual."

Second, the criteria for classifying children as handicapped differ in specificity across conditions, and these differences tend to reflect current standards of practice and training. For some years now, individually administered tests of intelligence and adaptive behavior have been the standards of practice in diagnosing mental retardation (Grossman, 1983; Witt & Martens, 1984). Accordingly, the New York State guidelines define the condition of mentally retarded based on assessment in these two areas. In contrast, the criteria for emotionally disturbed in New York State are much less precise, containing such language as "an inability to build or maintain satisfactory interpersonal relationships" and "inappropriate types of behavior or feelings under normal circumstances." Gresham (1985) observed that psychologists working in the schools are often inadequately trained to assess children's social-emotional functioning, and suggested that this may contribute to the lack of precision in state definitions. Indeed, one-third of psychologists belonging to the National

Table 8.1. Handicapping Conditions Specified in *DSM-IV* and the Regulations for North Carolina and New York State

North Carolina	New York State	*DSM-IV*
Autism	Autism	Autistic disorder or other pervasive developmental disorder
Behaviorally–Emotionally Disabled	Emotional Disturbance	Disruptive behavior disorders; Certain mood disorders
Deaf-Blind	Deafness and Deaf-Blindness	Axis III medical condition
Hearing Impaired	Hearing Impairment	Axis III medical condition
Mentally Disabled	Mental Retardation	Mental retardation
Multihandicapped	Multiple Disabilities	–
Orthopedically Impaired	Orthopedic Impairment	Axis III medical condition
Other Health Impaired	Other Health-Impairment	Axis III medical condition (e.g., ADHD)
Pregnant Students	–	Axis III medical condition
Developmentally Delayed	–	Mental retardation or other delay in development in 3- to 8-year old children
Specific Learning Disabled	Learning Disability	Learning disorders
Speech-Language Impaired	Speech or Language Impairment	Communication disorders
Traumatic Brain Injury	Traumatic Brain Injury	Axis III medical condition
Visually Impaired	Visual Impairment Including Blindness	Axis III medical condition

Association of School Psychologists identified the assessment of emotional disturbance as their greatest training need (Ramage, 1979), and most psychologists surveyed judged their training in this area to be moderately adequate at best (Prout, 1983).

Third, state regulations concerning the identification of students with handicaps often contain exclusionary criteria. Ostensibly, these *exclusionary criteria* were designed to prevent certain groups of children who might be served by other means from entering the special education system (e.g., students for whom English is a second language, children placed as juvenile delinquents by the courts) (Forness & Knitzer, 1992). In actual practice, however, these exclusions imply a hierarchy of causes for certain disorders that may be difficult to tease out during a typical psychoeducational evaluation. For example, students classified as learning disabled in both North Carolina and New York State cannot have learning problems that result primarily from visual, hearing, or motor disabilities, mental retardation, emotional disturbance, or environmental, cultural, or economic influences. Research has shown that children with learning disabilities often exhibit social skill deficits and other problem behaviors (e.g., Gresham & Reschly, 1986). Although a comprehensive assessment could describe a student's current levels of academic and socioemotional functioning, it would be difficult to conclude that a causal relationship existed between the two areas.

With its multiaxial classification approach, the *DSM* system was designed to aid in the diagnosis of psychopathology while organizing a wide range of information about client functioning. Evidence of this can be found in the descriptions of Axis II disorders (personality disorders and mental retardation) that include key diagnostic features, subtypes and/or specifiers, procedures for recording the diagnosis, associated diagnostic features and related disorders, and criteria for rendering a differential diagnosis. *DSM-IV* also provides epidemiological summaries of the various disorder types including prevalence, culture, age, and gender features, course of the disorder, and familial patterns. Together with the requirement by the Joint Council on Accreditation of Hospitals that individuals receive a *DSM* diagnosis upon institutionalization, the *DSM* system serves an administrative function by (1) helping to forecast incidence rates in populations served and (2) creating a system of accountability for third-party reimbursements to health care providers.

DSM-IV classifies handicapping conditions in children under Disorders Usually First Diagnosed in Infancy, Childhood, or Adolescence. Presented in Table 8.1 is a list of childhood disorders contained in this section of *DSM-IV*. As shown in the table, several of the more general disorder labels overlap with the handicapping conditions specified in state regulations. State education agency regulations, however, do not include the subcategories that are listed under each disorder label in the *DSM* taxonomy. Thus, a child classified as autistic according to the North Carolina regulations might be diagnosed in *DSM-IV* with a pervasive developmental disorder (Rett's disorder, childhood disintegrative disorder, Asperger's disorder) or a feeding and eating disorder of infancy or early childhood (Pica, rumination disorder). The lack of specificity evident in state regulations is consistent with their administrative function of determining eligibility for special services rather than providing a comprehensive system of clinical diagnosis as in *DSM-IV*.

The majority of children (up to 90%) who receive special education services in the schools are classified as mildly handicapped (Algozzine & Korinek, 1985). Prevalence rates of children with mild handicaps indicate that classification as specific learning disabled is the most common (4.7% of the student population), followed by speech impaired (2.9%), mildly mentally retarded (1.3%), and emotionally disturbed (1%) (Reschly, 1988). Because school consultants are likely to be involved with students who at some point may be considered for classification as learning disabled or emotionally disturbed, we believe it is important to understand the characteristics of these children and the issues involved in determining their eligibility for special services.

Students Classified as Specific Learning Disabled

The definition of specific learning disabled (SLD) contained in the 2000 North Carolina special education regulations reads as follows:

> Specific learning disability is an inclusive term used to denote various processing disorders presumed to be intrinsic to an individual (e.g., acquisition, organization, retrieval, or expressions of information). For the purpose of special education services, students classified as learning disabled are those who, after receiving instructional intervention in the regular education setting, have a substantial discrepancy between ability and achievement. The disability is manifested by substantial difficulties in the acquisition and use of skills in listening comprehension, oral expression, written expression, basic reading, reading comprehension, mathematics calculation, and mathematics reasoning. A learning disability may occur concomitantly with, but is not the primary result of, other disabilities and/or environmental, cultural, and/or economic influences.

This definition is consistent with that of most states in conceptualizing SLD as a processing deficit that is manifested as a discrepancy between student ability and achievement. In a review of the literature on SLD, Merrell and Shinn (1990) identified five competing views of the SLD construct, including processing deficit models, ability–achievement discrepancy models, low academic achievement models, social policy models, and social skill deficit models. Based on this review, the authors concluded that a lack of consensus presently exists concerning key features of the SLD construct. To identify those variables most predictive of SLD classification, Merrell and Shinn compared children referred and classified as SLD to a matched group of children who were referred but not classified. Results of a discriminant function analysis revealed that the most critical determinant in the decision to classify a child as SLD was low academic achievement in the areas of reading and written language. Surprisingly, only 37.5% of the children in the SLD group actually met the discrepancy criterion for classification in their state.

In practice, children are usually classified as SLD after being administered standardized tests of intelligence and achievement by evaluation team members. The scores on these tests are used to determine if a child is achieving significantly below grade level in relation to same-age peers and whether this level of achievement is discrepant from the child's measured intelligence (e.g., Reynolds, 1981). Although low academic achievement is often predictive of SLD classification, many students who experience failure in the local curriculum are deemed ineligible for special education services. One reason for this inconsistency has to do with the degree of content overlap between the student's curriculum materials and the items contained on standardized achievement tests, or what is known as *curriculum content validity* (Fuchs & Fuchs, 1986b; Jenkins & Pany, 1978). Numerous studies have examined the degree of overlap between standardized, norm-referenced achievement tests and commercially available basal reading curricula (e.g., Armbruster, Stevens & Rosenshine, 1977; Bell, Lentz & Graden, 1992; Good & Salvia, 1988; Jenkins & Pany, 1978; Shapiro & Derr, 1987; Webster, McInnis & Craver, 1986). In the majority of these studies, overlap was assessed by comparing word lists from the basal readers with word lists from the word recognition subtests of standardized instruments. Different numbers of exact word matches were found across tests when compared to a single reading program and across reading programs when compared to a single test, leading to conclusions of curriculum bias.

Jenkins and Pany (1978) concluded that these differences could significantly affect a child's eligibility for special education services depending upon which test was administered in conjunction with what program. Shapiro and Derr (1987) found that the majority of grade equivalent scores obtained by a hypothetical student who had mastered all words taught in a curriculum fell below expected grade levels regardless of the test administered. These results suggest that scores on standardized tests may not accurately reflect what a student has learned. Curriculum bias also appears to exist for standardized measures of reading decoding (Martens, Steele, Massie & Diskin, 1995). These authors compared four basal reading programs to the phonetic analysis subtests of three standardized achievement tests and found that: (1) programs differed in the number and sequence of phonics skills taught; (2) percentile and grade equivalent scores differed across programs at each grade level for a given test; and (3) the proportion of grade equivalent scores falling at or above expected grade levels differed across tests for a given program (range of 29–71%).

Children are classified as learning disabled on the basis of teacher and parent referral, with approximately 73% of all referrals nation-wide resulting in a positive classification decision (Graden, Casey & Christenson, 1985; Rosenfield, 1992). Teachers refer students because of chronic failure in the regular education curriculum relative to same-grade peers and following unsuccessful attempts to accommodate the student in the regular classroom setting. Two key determinants in the decision to classify a child as learning disabled, therefore, are the classroom teacher's success in accommodating the student's needs and the decision to refer a student for evaluation (Merrell & Shinn, 1990). The role of teachers' accommodation efforts in the numbers of children subsequently placed in special education was highlighted in a study by Rosenfield (1992). During the year prior to establishing school-based consultation teams to assist teachers in the development of instructional interventions, 73% of chil-dren who were referred were later placed in special education. This per-centage declined steadily following implementation of the project, with only 6% of children referred to the instructional consultation teams receiv-ing placements in year 4. Acknowledging the importance of prereferral intervention in making classification decisions, the North Carolina State regulations now require "dated and signed documented evidence of at least two interventions attempted within the regular education setting and the effects of each" before a student can be evaluated for a learning disability.

Students Classified as Emotionally Disturbed

According to the New York State regulations, emotional disturbance (ED) is defined as:

> a condition exhibiting one or more of the following characteristics over a long period of time and to a marked degree that adversely affects a student's educational performance: (i) an inability to learn that cannot be explained by intellectual, sensory, or health factors; (ii) an inability to build or maintain satisfactory interpersonal relation-ships with peers and teachers; (iii) inappropriate types of behavior or feelings under normal circumstances; (iv) a generally pervasive mood of unhappiness or depression; or (v) a tendency to develop physical symptoms or fears associated with personal or school problems. The term includes schizophrenia. The term does not apply to students who are socially maladjusted, unless it is determined that they have an emotional disturbance.

The majority of children referred for classification as ED are male (approx-imately 67%), and these children tend to be referred for disruptive, acting-out behaviors. Whereas SLD makes up approximately 48% of all students with mild handicaps, ED constitutes only about 10% (Reschly, 1988), and there is evidence to suggest that students with ED may actually be underidentified in the schools (Brandenburg, Friedman & Silver, 1990; Forness, Bennett & Tose, 1983). Despite the least restrictive environment mandate of P.L. 94-142, students with behavioral or emotional problems tend to be overrepresented in self-contained placements (U.S. Department of Education, 1987), and children classified as ED are particularly at risk for segregated schooling. In fact, residential schools for children with ED are used throughout the nation despite little evidence that these restrictive placements result in demonstrable improvements in behavioral or social functioning (Elmquist, 1989).

Due in part to the imprecise language contained in state definitions, psychologists working in the schools evaluate children for ED classification using a wide range of assessment instruments (Gresham, 1985). For example, best practices in the assessment of children with attention deficit hyperactivity disorder call for a multimethod approach that includes parent and teacher interviews, reviews of school records, behavior rating scales, and systematic classroom observations (DuPaul, 1992). By comparison, when psychologists were asked to identify the instruments they used most commonly with adolescents, between 51 and 84% of respondents reported frequently or almost always using projective measures such as the Rorschach or Human Figure Drawings (Archer, Maruish, Imhof & Piotrowski, 1992). Less than 20% of those surveyed reported using behavior rating scales such as the Conners or Child Behavior Checklist. Similarly, Prout (1983) found that systematic classroom observation was rated only sixth in importance as a method of assessing children for possible ED classification. After reviewing evidence concerning the use of figure drawings, Motta, Little, and Tobin (1993) concluded that "figure drawings should not be used as personality test instruments in that they do not provide valid descriptions of personality, behavior, or social-emotional functioning" (p. 165).

To aid in the identification of children as ED, the Workgroup on Definition of the National Mental Health and Special Education Coalition proposed an alternative definition to that contained in IDEA (Forness & Knitzer, 1992). Children are classified as ED under the alternative definition if their behavior in school differs so much from age-appropriate norms that it adversely affects academic performance. In addition, behavior that is judged to be inappropriate must be more than temporary, exhibited in two different settings, and unresponsive to interventions in the regular education setting. The first requirement, determining if behavior differs significantly from age-appropriate norms, is consistent with

Ullmann and Krasner's (1969) interactional perspective on deviance known as *social labeling*. From a social labeling perspective, behavior is judged to be deviant based on an interaction of behavior, the tolerance level of an observer, and the context in which the behavior occurs. For example, frequent out-of-seat behavior is likely to be viewed as abnormal in a traditionally structured classroom where the teacher demands quiet seatwork. The same behavior, however, may well be within tolerable limits for a teacher who emphasizes cooperative learning and organizes his or her classroom into work stations. Instead of viewing behavioral and emotional problems as being intrinsic to the child, social labeling suggests that behavior is abnormal if it is judged as such by significant adults in the child's environment. Because these judgments are based implicitly or explicitly on comparisons to other children, social labeling argues in favor of using structured informant reports when making decisions about ED classification (Martens, 1993c).

As with learning disabled students, the 2000 North Carolina special education regulations require "dated and signed documentation of at least two interventions to make behavioral and academic achievements possible within the regular educational setting" prior to classification as B-ED (i.e., ED). This requirement is consistent with research showing that fewer children are ultimately placed in special education when prereferral intervention services are available (e.g., McDougal et al., 2000). As noted earlier, state regulations were designed to serve an administrative function by helping to identify and place students who had failed in regular education. If the needs of difficult-to-teach students can be met successfully in regular education classrooms, then there is no need to refer the student for a special education placement. Gresham (1991) made a similar argument by suggesting that decisions about whether to classify students as ED should be based primarily on a criterion of *resistance to intervention*. Resistance to intervention is a notion derived from basic experimental research by Nevin (1988) that suggested the persistence of behavior in the face of changing conditions (e.g., removal of reinforcement) is analogous to the momentum of moving objects acted on by an external force. According to Newton's First Law of Motion, momentum is a function of an object's mass and velocity. Nevin's research showed that, in behavioral terms, momentum is a function of how frequently a behavior occurs (i.e., velocity) and how much reinforcement is associated with the conditions under which it occurs (i.e., mass). Problem behaviors that occur at high rates and are frequently reinforced will have a great deal of momentum. According to Gresham, it is unlikely that such behaviors will respond to prereferral interventions given the practical constraints under which regular education teachers operate. On the other hand, children whose problem behaviors can be addressed by interventions in the regular classroom setting should be precluded from receiving special services, because prereferral intervention efforts can be sufficient to meet their needs.

In the following section, we consider the constraints present in regular education that limit a teachers' ability to accommodate difficult-to-teach students. We then discuss those variables in both regular and special education classrooms that have been shown to influence student achievement.

A CONTEXTUAL MODEL OF STUDENT ACHIEVEMENT

As noted earlier, children fail under the "One Right Model" model of regular education because their behavior or achievement levels are not being adequately addressed by the instructional practices of the class-room teacher. This does not mean that students who fail automatically require special education placements, nor does it mean that classroom teachers are unwilling to assist children with special needs. Rather, this means that the range of instructional and managerial techniques used by the teacher is narrower than the range of skills and behaviors exhibited by the students. For students with behavioral problems, the usual incentives (e.g., teacher approval, written feedback) and disciplinary actions (e.g., stern looks, visits with the principal) may be insufficient to bring about compliance with classroom rules. Appropriate behaviors must be taught more explicitly and encouraged more consistently during daily teacher–student interactions (Gettinger, 1988; Martens & Kelly, 1993). Students with achievement problems may have insufficient opportunities for active responding in curricular materials, inadequate amounts of prompt-ing and feedback, instructional demands that do not promote mastery of curricular objectives, or grade-level material that is too difficult (Daly, Witt, Martens & Dool, 1997). Teachers must provide more elaborate help in the form of prompts and models, more opportunities to respond in the form of drill and reinforcement, or curriculum materials that are matched to the student's skill level (Martens, Witt et al., 1999). In both of these cases, efforts to accommodate students' needs are synonymous with more explicit practices for promoting learning. Prereferral intervention prior to classification as ED suggests that these more explicit practices can and should take place in the regular classroom setting for many students with mild handicaps. *When working with classroom teachers to develop and imple-ment intervention programs, we believe that school consultants should be aware of the variables that constrain a teacher's ability to accommodate diverse learners.*

These constraints are inherent in regular education classrooms, and success-ful accommodation efforts may require that they be partially overcome through the infusion of additional resources or the introduction of new knowledge and skills.

Variables Limiting Individualized Instruction

It is probably the case that all students could benefit from individual-ized instruction. Why is it then that individualized education programs are reserved for special education students and regular classroom teachers find it so difficult to accommodate special needs students? One way to answer these questions might be to consider for a moment the characteris-tics of a typical regular education classroom and the ways in which these constrain teachers' instructional and managerial activities. First, regular education teachers must conform to daily or weekly schedules of content instruction, lunch and recess, and special activities such as music, art, and gym. For example, during a 6-hour school day, students may be scheduled to spend an hour at lunch, 30 minutes at recess, and an hour each at both music and gym. This leaves approximately 3 1/2 hours of *allocated time* for instruction in the basic content areas (e.g., reading, arithmetic), not taking into account time spent preparing materials or transitioning from one task to the next (e.g., Gettinger, 1986; Ysseldyke et al., 1989). The same periods of allocated time are scheduled for all students in the classroom regardless of skill level, and teachers usually have little freedom to alter the schedule by, for example, doubling the amount of time spent on reading at the expense of math. This can pose a problem for students who may be doing well in one subject, but are struggling and therefore could benefit from increased instructional time in another subject.

Second, regular education teachers are required to adopt a basal cur-riculum which is consistent with the school district's *scope and sequence charts*. School district scope and sequence charts specify the grade level at which various learning objectives are to be introduced, instructed, and mastered in each content area. Because these learning objectives are linked from year to year, it is important for students to master the cur-riculum material in the correct sequence and at the specified rate. This means that regardless of a given student's ability, teachers must focus the majority of their efforts on material contained in the curriculum and must limit the time spent on each lesson so students can be instructed in most or all of the objectives at their grade level. Because of the need to move students along in the curriculum, teachers may be limited in the amount of time they can spend helping low achievers acquire the skills introduced in one unit before moving on to the next unit.

Third, it is not uncommon to encounter student to teacher ratios of 30:1 or higher in many regular education classrooms. As the number of students in a classroom increases, it becomes more difficult for teachers to set ambitious goals for classwide achievement, to actively engage each student in the learning process, and to monitor student progress and adjust instruction accordingly. Research in both psychology and education has shown that an effective sequence of academic instruction involves gaining students' attention, specifying the goals of what you want them to do, providing them with enough assistance until they can do it correctly, having them do it correctly a number of times while providing feedback, and reinforcing effort (e.g., Wolery et al., 1988; Gettinger, 1986; Martens & Kelly, 1993; Wyne & Stuck, 1982). In order to effectively manage large classrooms, however, teachers must often rely on group instructional techniques (Gettinger, 1988). Although many components of effective instruction can be implemented at a group level, students with different abilities will require differing amounts of alerting, assistance, feedback, and reinforcement to maximize learning.

Variables Related to Student Achievement

Given that regular education teachers are often constrained in their attempts to individualize instruction, school-based interventions must involve effective and efficient educational practices. Interestingly, research in this area has shown that the same set of variables leads to increased student achievement in both regular and special education classrooms (e.g., Ysseldyke, Christenson & Thurlow, 1987). This research has also called into question the traditionally held assumption that achievement is primarily a function of within-student characteristics (Ysseldyke & Marston, 1990). After reviewing the literature, Christenson and Ysseldyke (1989) argued that an *ecological perspective* which acknowledges a variety of influences on student achievement (both intrinsic and situational) is necessary to design effective school-based interventions. Key assumptions of this ecological perspective, known as the Student Learning in Context (SLIC) model, are that (1) learning involves an interaction between student skills, the instructional environment, and the demands of the curriculum; (2) instructional interventions are subordinate to the curriculum and must facilitate movement through the curriculum; (3) changes to instruction are best viewed as hypotheses that must be tested empirically; and (4) the effects of these changes should be evaluated as frequently as possible on the basis of student performance on actual curriculum materials.

With respect to the first assumption, a number of teacher variables has been shown to influence student achievement including clearly communicated goals and expectations for student progress, detailed lesson plans and briskly paced instructional presentations, rules for behavior that are consistently reinforced and trained at the beginning of the school year, and procedures for evaluating student performance that are sensitive to short-term gains (Brophy, 1983; Christenson & Ysseldyke, 1989; Fuchs & Fuchs, 1986a; Gettinger, 1988). Also related to student achievement is the degree of correspondence between the difficulty level of the curriculum materials and the student's skill level, or what is referred to as *instructional match*. In order to benefit from instruction, students must be able to complete assigned tasks with a high degree of accuracy and minimal errors (Haring & Eaton, 1978; Wolery et al., 1988; Gettinger, 1986). When modifying students' instructional programs, it may be necessary to adjust their placement in the curriculum sequence downward until they consistently exhibit a high proportion of correct responses (e.g., 80% or above) (Shinn, Rosenfield & Knutson, 1989).

With respect to the second assumption, the majority of low achieving and mildly handicapped students are capable of pursuing the same curriculum as their regular achieving peers (Reschly, 1988; Shinn, 1989). What distinguishes these groups of students, however, is the level at which they are placed in the curriculum and their rate of progress as a function of programming effectiveness. For example, Shinn (1986) assessed the reading performance of 505 students with mild handicaps between the grades of 1 through 6 who had been placed in special education. The students were tested at three points during the school year using passages sampled from their curriculum materials. Similar data were collected on approximately 9,000 regular education students at the same intervals. Although the number of words read correctly by the students in special education increased significantly at each time of testing, their performance became significantly more discrepant from regular education peers as the year progressed. These findings indicated that while the students in special education were improving in reading, their counterparts in regular education were improving at a much higher rate. Given that many of the constraints present in typical classrooms are relaxed in special education, one has to wonder why special education programming is not more effective. Kavale (1990) suggested that special education students may not achieve at higher rates because their teachers do not set ambitious goals and expectations for learning. In the absence of ambitious goals, special education may ultimately serve a maintenance rather than a remediation function.

Finally, as discussed in Chapter 6, the available evidence suggests that school-based interventions are likely to be extremely variable in their effects on children, and that we cannot predict the outcomes of these interventions with certainty (Kavale, 1990; Ysseldyke & Marston, 1990).

This means that decisions about intervention effectiveness can only be made by systematically evaluating program outcomes. This also means that one cannot predict with certainty whether a student with special needs will require a special education placement until prereferral interventions are tried and evaluated in the regular classroom setting.

In the following chapter we consider many of the issues and concepts presented thus far in this book via a case study example. The transcribed consultation sessions comprising the case as well as our retrospective analysis represent attempts to demonstrate the integrated model of consultation "in action."

9

Consultation Case Study

From our earlier chapters, one can see that the school consultant's effectiveness depends a great deal on his or her strategic interpersonal communication (Daly & Wiemann, 1994). We therefore consider the study of messages that are exchanged in consultation to be an extremely important means for learning how to consult. The strength of this belief leads us to devote an entire chapter to a single example of school consultation. Seeing many of the concepts discussed thus far actually carried out may enable readers to incorporate more readily the integrated model of school consultation into their daily work.

Chapter 9 contains a set of three interviews between a psychologist-consultant and a second grade teacher-consultee who discuss a 7-year-old boy who displays aggressive behaviors. The case described is a composite of several cases handled by the first author in his experience as a school psychologist and supervisor of psychologists who consult in schools. Colleagues graciously provided other elements of this case, in part to make it more representative of the issues faced by school consultants. The dialogue is also representative of the first author's overall style, in that the majority of the consultant's messages were taken directly from transcribed audiotapes.

Following each interview, we provide an analysis of the consultant's approach. The content of these analyses may serve as a reminder that, despite empirical advances, consultation remains to a great extent an "artful science" (Idol & West, 1987; Rosenfield, 2000). Borrowing from Caplan's (1970, p. 192) suggestion, the reader initially may wish to read all three transcripts together in order to gain a perspective on the entire consultation. Interviews then may be reread separately, this time incorporating the analyses.

FIRST INTERVIEW: TUESDAY, SEPTEMBER 21

CONSULTANT: (1) Hi, Karen, it's good to see you. How are you doing?

TEACHER: Hi, it's good to see you too. I'm pretty good.

CONSULTANT: (2) I received your note saying you've got some concerns about a child in your classroom. Why don't you tell me about it?

TEACHER: We have one boy in our classroom who is quite aggressive, always bothering others. It makes it hard for me to instruct the class and difficult for my students.

CONSULTANT: (3) Oh, that must be annoying to you and distracting to your students. Tell me what things he does.

TEACHER: Well, he gets into fights with other boys. He wants what he wants and if things aren't going his way, he just bullies. He's also stubborn. If he doesn't want to do something I tell him to do, he just doesn't do it. He complains that it isn't fair.

CONSULTANT: (4) It's right for you to be concerned about these behaviors. Aggressiveness and bullying are serious problems that need to be addressed.

Since this is the first time you and I have really worked together, I thought we'd start by talking about how I see us going about this, and then see if you have some comments or suggestions. We'll be getting together three or four times over the next month or so to address this issue.

Every classroom is unique, so I may not have any ready answers for you, but I'm hoping that we can work together to develop a clearer definition of the problem and explore it more. We'll be working together, but when it comes time to actually implement the plan that we devise, that'll be your job, because I'm here only a day each week, and you're in the classroom every day. I think it works out better from that standpoint. But certainly I'll try to assist you as best I can.

The other thing I wanted to mention is that I've cleared it with your principal that everything you talk about will be held in confidence unless I learn that some law has been or will be broken. And sometimes, it happens that there are reports of child abuse that have to be followed up on, but those are relatively rare. But that could come up, and I just wanted to let you know. So that's the way I thought we'd work together. Does that sound reasonable to you?

TEACHER: Yes, I'm just looking for ideas. (laughs)

CONSULTANT: (5) OK. Well, why don't we then start back and have you tell me more about your student. What is his name?

TEACHER: Kenneth.

CONSULTANT: (6) OK. And about how old is Kenneth?

TEACHER: He's seven.

CONSULTANT: (7) OK. Tell me a little bit about your classroom, so I have a picture of what's going on here.

TEACHER: OK. It's a very creative classroom. We do a lot of work in small groups. As you can see, the desks are arranged in groups of four and there are seven teams that work together. Kenneth is in the Panthers group. Our schedule is posted on the wall. We begin with a group meeting, then have language arts with writing centers, then math. We go to lunch and have art and other specials right after that. The rest of our subjects are in the afternoon. This is a pretty good class, except for Kenneth. He sets off a couple of the other kids. When Kenneth is absent, the whole day goes better.

CONSULTANT: (8) OK. Forgive me for writing, but we deal with a lot of information, so it's helpful to me if we write this out. All right, you say Kenneth presents your biggest challenge. Tell me about the last time he got in trouble.

TEACHER: We had an incident this morning on the playground. Kenneth had his turn at the tether ball and you get to hit the ball three times. Well, he's not very good, so his turn is up really quick. He didn't want to give up his turn, and when the next child, Rashon, said it was his turn, Kenneth hit him. I didn't even know about this 'til one of the other kids told me later.

CONSULTANT: (9) How did you handle it then?

TEACHER: I told him he'd violated a playground rule and I was really disappointed in him. He was sent to the office to talk to the assistant principal. But that doesn't seem to do any good, as this is about the tenth time I've sent him.

CONSULTANT: (10) That was on the playground. I assume he's also misbehaving in the classroom.

TEACHER: That's right.

CONSULTANT: (11) Tell me about one of those incidents.

TEACHER: Yesterday, I told the children to put away their writing journals, get out their math materials, and move into their math groups. A boy bumped Kenneth and Kenneth tripped him. I made Kenneth stay in for recess.

CONSULTANT: (12) So problems occur on the playground, and during transitions. Are there any other times?

TEACHER: He seems to do OK when we're in a small group and I'm right there or my assistant, Laura, is. Independent work time is also a problem. He'll get up and wander around the classroom.

CONSULTANT: (13) OK, so far you've given me examples that are pretty much physical aggression. Is that the major problem, or are there others?

TEACHER: Well, like I said, he's verbally aggressive too. He'll refuse to do things I tell him to. He also teases kids and tries to get others to join him. He also daydreams a lot and fails to complete work. He's a little bit behind in math, but on grade level in reading. He also talks to himself a lot.

CONSULTANT: (14) Well, that's quite a list! What's your biggest concern? What should we work on?

TEACHER: The aggression, I think.

CONSULTANT: (15) Both the physical and verbal?

TEACHER: Yes.

CONSULTANT: (16) OK. Let's try to understand the specifics of the aggression better, then. By aggression, you mean hitting others, teasing, name-calling, and talking back to you or the teaching assistant.

TEACHER: Yes. All of those, but not just hitting. He's also tripped others.

CONSULTANT: (17) OK. So any behavior that's intended to hurt others, like hitting, tripping, spitting and throwing things at people.

TEACHER: Right.

CONSULTANT: (18) Yeah. How many incidents of verbal or physical aggression do you think occur on a typical day?

TEACHER: Oh, boy. A good day is probably one or two. A bad day, a really bad day, could be as high as eight.

CONSULTANT: (19) Eight!

TEACHER: Well, not eight incidents of physical aggression. I mean that I have to redirect him from teasing, bothering others, and him saying "No" when I tell him to do something.

CONSULTANT: (20) Let's look at the problem systematically to see if we can detect any things that are happening regularly, either before or after an incident of aggression. From your description so far, less structured times like transitions, the playground, and seatwork seem to bring on the problem, and behavior is better in more structured settings.

TEACHER: I guess I never thought about it that way, but yes.

CONSULTANT: (21) Do you see a pattern in the days? Is it more frequent before the weekend, after the weekend, anything like that?

TEACHER: Hmm. That's an interesting question. I probably would say that there's more aggression on a Monday, and less of it on a Friday.

CONSULTANT: (22) That's helpful in terms of identifying times and situations where verbal or physical aggression is likely to occur.
I'm interested in how you and your assistant respond, and how students respond to Kenneth's aggression.

TEACHER: Well, as I've said before, we send him to the assistant principal's office. They have a little talk, but that's not really helping at all. I've kept him in at recess, which he really doesn't like, but that just makes the problem worse. He needs to be running around outside. He's a wiggly boy. I've sent notes home to his parents; they seem concerned but overwhelmed with other things. They both work, Kenneth's older brother is giving them problems, and one of the grandparents is sick.

CONSULTANT: (23) Some of your descriptions of Kenneth, like he's a wiggly boy and he wanders around the classroom, as well as his bothering others, are triggering some concerns in me. I know this is early in the school year and you haven't worked with Kenneth that long, but do you know if he's been evaluated for attention-deficit/hyperactivity disorder (ADHD)?

TEACHER: Yes. I thought of that, too. I talked to his last year's teacher. She encouraged the parents to talk to their pediatrician, but the parents were adamant that there was nothing wrong with their son. I think that the older brother is having some drug problems and the idea of medication brought out all sorts of issues for them. Besides, I don't want to just jump to that type of solution if there's something I can do in the classroom.

CONSULTANT: (24) Great. I'm sorry to digress, but I just wanted a more complete understanding of the situation. Let's go back to your actions in response to his misbehavior. You've tried notes home, visits to the assistant principal, and losing recess time. But they haven't worked consistently.

TEACHER: Right.

CONSULTANT: (25) What is his reaction to being reprimanded?

TEACHER: He pouts. It seems he can get himself into a cycle where if he gets in trouble for one thing, then it's another thing, and he has a really bad day. It makes me hesitate to reprimand him. We just get into this negative cycle.

CONSULTANT: (26) Kind of puts you in a bind, doesn't it? You don't want him to get away with hurting or teasing others, but reprimands escalate the problem.

TEACHER: It's kind of a no-win situation. That's why I called you in (laughs).

CONSULTANT: (27) Well, you've got a point there (laughs). How do the other students in the classroom react?

TEACHER: He doesn't have a lot of friends. Kids go out of the way to avoid him, so he gets his way most of the time. Sometimes when he teases, the other children laugh. Like I said, there's also a couple of other children whom he sets off.

CONSULTANT: (28) OK. So he gets some peer attention for his teasing, and sometimes his aggression toward kids works—he gets his way. In some ways, he gets his way with you too, because he makes it more difficult for you if you reprimand him. You can see yourself getting into this cycle with him.

TEACHER: Yeah, he takes a lot of my energy.

CONSULTANT: (29) I can see that. These are some of the hardest problems to address, because the responses that you use with other children escalate the problem and aggressive responses get Kenneth what he wants. Not to mention you have 27 other students for whom you're responsible. So, what's a goal that you'd like to see us reach as a part of this consultation?

TEACHER: I think, at this point, that we would just like him not to hit others. Or not tease or bother others. I'd like him to be able to work independently so that we can get him into work situations where he won't be distracting other people; he will be able to stay on-task. I'd like him to get along with others.

CONSULTANT: (30) OK. That's about six goals!

TEACHER: (laughs)

CONSULTANT: (31) But your goals seem to center on two things, getting along with others and staying on task. And a key to getting along with others is decreasing the aggression.

TEACHER: Yes.

CONSULTANT: (32) Right now, I think it would be better to stay with the one goal—reducing aggressive behavior. Once we've got a handle on that, we can look at on-task behavior. Before we go on, let's be sure we're both in agreement on what we mean by aggressive behavior. What is your understanding?

TEACHER: Well … it's verbal aggression like teasing and name-calling and talking back to me or Laura. Physical aggression would be hurting or trying to hurt others. Nagging or bothering others, too.

CONSULTANT: (33) That seems like a very complete list of aggressive behaviors, as I see it. It covers everything you've told me about. Before we get into a plan, we need to have some idea of the level of the problem now. That will let us see if we've made a difference. How do you think we should measure his aggressive behavior?

TEACHER: I could write down when it happens.

CONSULTANT: (34) Great! Will that be easy for you?

TEACHER: It would be easier if I made some sort of grid where I could check off things each day.

CONSULTANT: (35) How about a grid that lists behavior, what was happening in the classroom when it occurred, and what happened afterward? Not real wordy, just a few notes to remind yourself. What do you think of this grid? (Consultant sketches a three-column grid and shows it to teacher.) For example, if Kenneth taps somebody on the head with his pencil during seatwork, and you take the pencil away, you'd write "hitting child with pencil," "reading seatwork," and "took pencil away" in the columns on the grid. We'd have a grid like this for each day.

TEACHER: So I'd do this every day? For how long?

CONSULTANT: (36) Can you handle this for 5 days? I know it's just one more thing, but a realistic estimate of how often this is occurring is very important.

TEACHER: OK, do I reprimand him like I've done before during this week?

CONSULTANT: (37) Just do what you've been doing all along.

TEACHER: OK.

CONSULTANT: (38) Please let your assistant, Laura, know what we are doing. Maybe she can write some of the incidents in so it's not always you. I'll make up a grid and put five copies in your box later today. Another thing I'd like to do is to stop by and observe in order to get a better sense of Kenneth's behavior.

TEACHER: That would be great, and you could see the problems it's causing me!

CONSULTANT: (39) Right. I'll plan to do that, and when we get back together next week we can look at the new information. Perhaps then we'll be in a better position to address this issue and make life in the classroom better for both you and Kenneth. I'll see you then.

Consultant's Analysis of the First Interview

3. My initial reaction to the stated problem acknowledged both the consultee's emotional state as well as the probable impact of the problem on the rest of the students. This early statement was an attempt to convey my expectation that our consultation would potentially consider both consultee-centered and client-centered aspects.

4. After validating the consultee's concerns, I presented a rather standard role-structuring statement. A consultant should not allow the first session to advance too far before raising these important contracting issues. Introducing these issues at this time and in this manner is an effective way for the consultant to establish interview control and thereby address the social influence task.

7, 8, 11. In these messages I used the imperative *tell* to elicit information from the consultee. Imperatives and commands present useful alternatives to direct questions and serve to establish and maintain interview control.

8. The need to take notes during consultation will depend on a variety of factors, including one's current caseload and the complexity of issues addressed in interviews. When beginning a consultation, I tend to

draw the consultee's attention directly to the notetaking so that it will not be distracting later on. In this message, I tried to use the technique of "onedownsmanship" (Caplan, 1970, pp. 96–97) as well as to develop some referent power (Erchul & Raven, 1997) by using the word *we*.

8, 11. Having the consultee recall concrete, specific instances rather than a set of generalizations is a useful strategy in the initial interview. The danger of this approach, however, is that the instance described may not be a representative account of the problem.

13. In the initial consultative interview, there is the ever-present danger of prematurely narrowing the focus of problem solving. With this question I tried to avoid (or at least temporarily delay) this pitfall.

7, 12–14, 16, 18, 20–22, 29, 32–33. These selected statements contain either my comments on, or my modeling of, the problem-solving process. As such, the statements exemplify the development portion of the support and development task.

4, 28–29, 31, 35, 38. A consultant needs to be perceived as an expert, and these messages may have increased the consultee's estimation of my expert power (Erchul & Raven, 1997). The information provided also may have had implications for the consultee's professional development.

14, 19, 26, 29, 34, 39. These statements of encouragement and understanding of the consultee's situation illustrate the support aspect of the support and development task.

14, 20, 29, 38–39. My use of the words *we* and *us* was an attempt to develop both rapport and referent power.

9, 24. I do not tend to spend much time in first interviews going over prior interventions and why they were not as successful as they might have been. To do so often reinforces the consultee's previous failure experience and prematurely focuses the content of the interview on solutions to problems that may have not been adequately defined as yet.

20–22, 24–28. Here I conducted a brief functional analysis, a key topic found in Chapter 6. Though not comprising an extensive portion of the interview, these questions and statements illustrate the typical topics covered in a functional analysis. In addition to the techniques presented in Chapter 6, I have found the *VAIL Functional Assessment Model* (Witt, Daly & Noell, 2000) to be helpful.

23. If the consultee had expressed greater concerns about the client's ADHD symptomatology and its possible treatment through medication, I would have followed up on these topics more intently. Because the client's parents were aware of the situation and the consultee did not wish to pursue stimulant medication for the client, I decided to maintain the focus on a classroom-based intervention. Knowing that this situation could change, though, I continued to monitor it throughout the consultation.

30. Drawing attention to the six goals generated by the consultee was an attempt to use the personal form of reward power (Erchul & Raven, 1997) and perhaps some humor.

32. Consultant and consultee agreement on important aspects of the process (e.g., definition of the target behavior) has been linked to important outcomes in consultation (Bergan & Tombari, 1976; Erchul et al., 1992).

38. Although the target behavior was understood, I wanted to see the client in the classroom. Therefore I made arrangements to observe him. The consultee may have perceived my offer to observe as serving a supportive function, knowing that I would be sharing some insights at our next meeting.

39. Similar to message 3, I closed with a statement that suggested both consultee and client issues might be considered as a part of this consultation.

SECOND INTERVIEW: TUESDAY, SEPTEMBER 28

CONSULTANT: (1) Hi, Karen, how are you doing?

TEACHER: Good! How are you doing?

CONSULTANT: (2) Fine. How has your week been?

TEACHER: It's been pretty good overall. But we haven't seen any drastic changes in Kenneth's behavior, of course.

CONSULTANT: (3) Well, let's look at the baseline data. Were you able to complete the grids?

TEACHER: Pretty much. Sometimes I had to wait 'til I had a free minute to fill it out, but it's pretty accurate.

CONSULTANT: (4) That's great! Let's take a look.

TEACHER: Here you go.

CONSULTANT: (5) Hmmm. Well, Kenneth certainly does keep you busy, doesn't he? Monday seemed to be his hardest day, like you predicted. Do you think these 5 days were typical?

TEACHER: Yeah, I do. You can kind of see what I mean about some days seeming to escalate. Monday he came into the room in a bad mood, got in trouble before class started, and it was downhill for the rest of the day. Monday was the day he had the most physical aggression—he hit two kids. That's when I finally sent him out of the room to the assistant principal.

CONSULTANT: (6) Well, you said last week that you had problems with him about one to eight times a day, and the grid basically supports that. You had four incidents on Wednesday and Thursday, three on Friday, eight on Monday, and five today. You must have been really glad when Monday ended. Is there any pattern to the settings in which these aggressive behaviors occur?

TEACHER: Well, you can see that they're mostly during transitions or unstructured time.

CONSULTANT: (7) You're right. There's only one time that he acted out during actual instruction, this one here, right?

TEACHER: Yeah, it's pretty striking when you see it in black and white.

CONSULTANT: (8) Why do you think Friday was his best day?

TEACHER: On Friday, his group gets to spend a lot of time on the computers. This seems to hold his attention well. Anything with computers and he's very focused and interested.

CONSULTANT: (9) Now Thursday was when I was here to observe. It was one of his better days, but I did see a few things, and wanted to share some of my reactions. First, it struck me that anytime manipulatives like your math blocks were involved, he was more attentive and involved. You might want to consider that in planning instruction. Second, he seemed to respond to attention, any kind of attention, from you or his peers. There were even a few times he was making funny faces to try to get the other kids going.

TEACHER: Oh, I missed that.

CONSULTANT: (10) He was pretty subtle about it. He made sure you were otherwise occupied. Did you also notice the way he sought out Laura to show her his work when he finished it? His wanting and responding to attention is something we may want to take into consideration in our plan. I also noticed that both you and Laura have to work really hard at times to manage him. It's more than I expected given your description last week. I had the feeling that if it wasn't for your management style, he'd be having even more problems.

TEACHER: Right, he's constantly demanding some part of our attention.

CONSULTANT: (11) Well, hopefully we can start moving toward some solutions today. But before we look in that direction, I have a few other questions. Could you tell me about some of Kenneth's strengths, such as things he does well, or things that people like him for?

TEACHER: He likes reading and is a pretty good reader. He also likes to draw and will sometimes spend a lot of his work time drawing pictures of superheroes. Usually they're doing something violent to save the world (laughs). The kids like his drawings.

CONSULTANT: (12) That's interesting. Any other strengths?

TEACHER: When you can get him to focus, he can do math. He can do basic addition, and subtraction as well or better than anyone in the class, but only when he applies himself.

CONSULTANT: (13) Good. What are things that he works for or likes to do?

TEACHER: The computer, definitely. He's glued to the screen once he gets there. Drawing, like I said, is a real motivator. I'd guess recess is also a highlight for him.

CONSULTANT: (14) OK, that's helpful. Let me summarize where we are now. We have looked at the baseline data and it's clear that Kenneth is physically and verbally aggressive four to eight times each day during the week. These incidents generally take the form of teasing or verbal bullying, or talking back to you, but there are also incidents of physical aggression such as hitting and tripping. The behaviors are most frequent in unstructured situations. When you reprimand him or he gets in trouble, this can escalate his problem behaviors and he gets even harder to handle. We really saw this Monday. This pattern makes you hesitant to intervene.

TEACHER: Right.

CONSULTANT: (15) So we've got a pretty good picture of the situation. Are there any other things that happen before or after the aggressive behaviors that we haven't mentioned yet?

TEACHER: Not that I can think of.

CONSULTANT: (16) OK. That's a fair answer. My observation really didn't show anything beyond what we've already talked about, except that he does respond to attention, both positive and negative.

TEACHER: Right.

CONSULTANT: (17) OK. Well, we've gone over a lot of information, both last week and today. I have been trying to integrate a lot of this information, so that I understand the problem and have the same appreciation for it as you. And maybe I'm at that point.

TEACHER: OK.

CONSULTANT: (18) As we look at various approaches that have been tried, such as reprimands from you and the assistant principal, as well as loss of activities such as recess, I sense that you want to move on from these techniques because their effectiveness has been limited.

TEACHER: Right.

CONSULTANT: (19) In thinking about a plan, let's go back to some of the things we know about Kenneth. He likes attention, he likes computers, and he likes recess. It's also easy to get in a negative cycle with him. Can we use any of this knowledge in a plan?

TEACHER: I don't know. It would be good to somehow have his participation in activities he likes depend on his behavior.

CONSULTANT: (20) Good idea. How do you think we could link something like access to the computer to his good behavior?

TEACHER: Well, right now his group only gets computer time for an extended period once a week, so it would be hard to do anything with that.

CONSULTANT: (21) Is there any other way to use computer time as a reward?

TEACHER: I don't know. They do have a 20-minute silent reading time in the afternoon. Since he's doing OK in reading, maybe he could earn computer time during this silent reading time.

CONSULTANT: (22) I think that's a good idea. Could we have some standard he has to meet to earn the computer time? The standard should be set at an easily achievable level to start. The average number of times he's aggressive now is about five times a day.

TEACHER: Well, maybe if he has no more than four incidents he gets to go to the computer during silent reading time.

CONSULTANT: (23) That sounds like a good goal to start with. How would you keep track? Would the grid work?

TEACHER: The grid was OK for a week, but I couldn't manage it over the long term.

CONSULTANT: (24) Is there any other way to keep track of Kenneth's aggressive behavior that would also communicate to Kenneth how he's doing? I've seen teachers place a jar on a student's desk with straws in it. Each time the student misbehaves, he or she loses a straw. We could use this with Kenneth and put five straws in his jar each day. If he has any straws left at the end of the day, he could have the computer time.

TEACHER: Kenneth would just play with the straws. But I could put a card on his desk with five happy faces and mark one out each time he misbehaves. If he has any happy faces at the end of the day, he gets computer time that day.

CONSULTANT: (25) What a great idea. I think it would work better than straws.

TEACHER: I think I could manage it.

CONSULTANT: (26) Good. I'd also like to have another component to this plan and set a goal that we "catch Kenneth being good" four times for every time he is caught misbehaving. I think this will help us get at that negative cycle issue we talked about.

TEACHER: What do you mean?

CONSULTANT: (27) Kenneth has a pretty high rate of negative behavior. When we strike off happy faces, we're still reprimanding him. Even though reprimands are necessary, you've seen that they set up a negative cycle. We need to break this cycle and we can do this by being sure positive comments outweigh negative comments.

TEACHER: I guess that makes sense. It is pretty easy to just ignore Kenneth when he's doing something right. You know, the saying, "Let sleeping dogs lie." But when we do that it means we're only interacting with him around negative incidents, and no one responds very well to that.

CONSULTANT: (28) Right. And where I'd like to see many of the instances of "catching him being good" focused is on behaviors that are alternatives to the ones we're trying to change. What positive behaviors can replace his aggressive behaviors?

TEACHER: Taking turns on the playground would be a big one. So would helping others or saying something nice to them instead of teasing or bothering them. Also, working hard instead of wandering around the room getting in trouble.

CONSULTANT: (29) Great. So the plan is to set a standard of four aggressive incidents a day and have a card on Kenneth's desk with five happy faces on it. Every time he teases, bullies, hits, or hurts another, he loses a happy face. If he has any happy faces left, he earns computer time during your silent reading time at the end of the day. Is that right?

TEACHER: Right. Also, Laura and I are going to be sure that we pay attention to Kenneth when he does the behaviors we want.

CONSULTANT: (30) Yes. And you're aiming for four positives for every negative.

TEACHER: That will be a challenge, but if it prevents these negative cycles where the whole day goes bad, it will be worth it.

CONSULTANT: (31) There's one more point I want to be sure we think about in our work with Kenneth. Verbal and physical aggression are hard problems to deal with because they have some immediate payoff for the child. Right now, Kenneth gets reinforced for his aggressive behaviors. They help him get what he wants on the playground, like when he got the extra turn on the tetherball. The behaviors get attention from his peers and from you and Laura.

TEACHER: OK.

CONSULTANT: (32) The payoff of aggressive behaviors is a real problem, because it tends to cause them to escalate. For example, you said that you sometimes let some of Kenneth's behaviors go by because you know he's just going to get worse, right?

TEACHER: Right.

CONSULTANT: (33) So Kenneth is learning that if he makes it hard enough for you, you'll back off. He's getting another reward for being aggressive.

TEACHER: Sometimes that happens.

CONSULTANT: (34) It's a pretty common phenomenon. I'm just pointing this out because I want to emphasize the importance of you and Laura being very consistent in applying negative consequences and not letting Kenneth control the situation. That means that Kenneth shouldn't be allowed to get his way with you or other children by being aggressive. When he escalates his negative behaviors, you still need to enforce consequences.

TEACHER: That makes sense.

CONSULTANT: (35) I think it will be easier to be consistent on the negative consequences if you're also making a point of finding times that Kenneth is being good, so you don't feel that all you're doing is reprimanding him.

TEACHER: OK. Is that the whole plan?

CONSULTANT: (36) That's it. Why don't you walk me through our plan so we can be sure we're both seeing it the same way?

TEACHER: OK, I'll try. Each morning, I'll put a card on Kenneth's desk with five happy faces on it, and every time he teases, bullies, hits, or hurts another, I'll cross out a happy face. If he has any happy faces left, he earns computer time during the silent reading time for that day.

CONSULTANT: (37) Right.

TEACHER: Then, Laura and I are going to be sure that we pay attention to Kenneth when he does the behaviors we want, like when he takes turns on the playground. Like you said, we'll try to find four positives for every negative.

CONSULTANT: (38) Great. What else?

TEACHER: Just the part about being consistent, not backing down when Kenneth gets upset with us.

CONSULTANT: (39) Right, that's a very important piece of the plan. We seem to have the same view of things. Any questions?

TEACHER: Do you want me to still keep collecting data on the grids, like I did last week?

CONSULTANT: (40) No, you won't need to do that because we now have the happy faces.

TEACHER: Right, but how will we keep track of his behavior over time?

CONSULTANT: (41) That's a good question. How do you think that should be handled?

TEACHER: Maybe during the silent reading period I could write down the number of happy faces that weren't crossed out that day.

CONSULTANT: (42) I like that idea a lot. That way we'll have a record of Kenneth's daily and weekly progress. I'd like to switch gears for a minute. This is a very good and interest-ing plan, but all plans can have flaws. Let's look at this one objectively for a minute. Can you think of something that could go wrong with our plan, something that we could possibly prevent?

TEACHER: Well, the one thing that I might be worried about is whether Kenneth will really know what we're doing. He might have trouble, at least initially, knowing that earning computer time at the end of the day depends on his behavior all day long.

CONSULTANT: (43) What could you do to increase the odds that he will understand things from the very beginning—meaning tomorrow?

TEACHER: I guess I could make sure that I explain things very clearly before school begins, and then give him some reminders during the day.

CONSULTANT: (44) That makes sense. How about for now, that you pretend I'm Kenneth. It's tomorrow morning and I've just sat down at my desk. What would you say to me?

TEACHER: Ooh, that's hard! Maybe something like, "Kenneth, starting today Mrs. Smith and I have something new for you. We know how much you like to play on the computer, so we want you to be able to do it more. Do you know our class rule about not hitting or bothering others?"

CONSULTANT: (45) "Yes, but sometimes I forget."

TEACHER: "Well, yes. We know that you try very hard but sometimes you forget. Mrs. Smith and I want to help you to remember it better. Every morning I'm going to put five happy faces on your desk. But every time you hit or bother others or talk back to us, we're gonna cross out one of the happy faces. If you have any faces left, you've earned the privilege to play on the computer when everyone else is reading silently." How was that?

CONSULTANT: (46) That was very good! I have two minor suggestions. Rather than emphasize crossing out faces, you might want to say, "Kenneth, you'll have four chances to earn the privilege to play on the computer in the afternoon." This would put things in a more positive light. Another thing I might add is to ask Kenneth to repeat the basic plan back to me to see if he's really understanding it.

TEACHER: Sure, I can do both of those.

CONSULTANT: (47) One final point. What evidence would there need to be for you to decide that this plan is working or not? How many times would this have to occur before you'd think, "Well, he's mastered that, maybe we can decrease the number of happy faces he's allowed to lose to get computer time"?

TEACHER: Probably more important than him being able to do it consistently each day, is him being able to carry it over, day after day. So, if he got his reward, maybe for five consecutive days, that he would probably ... I don't know, do you think that's too much?

CONSULTANT: (48) We can give it a try. I defer to you on that point, because I think you can judge better whether or not it's likely. But, assuming that he can meet this goal of having at least one happy face remain each day for five consecutive days, how do you think that would change your standards?

TEACHER: Well, I'd probably want to have him start the day with four faces rather than five.

CONSULTANT: (49) OK. We can certainly talk more about that later on, when the picture is clearer. Overall, I think our plan will come across very well.

TEACHER: It's certainly worth trying.

CONSULTANT: (50) Great! I'll check in with you next week to see how things are going. Maybe next month we can sit down and really evaluate our plan. There might be some fine-tuning needed but, at the same time, I think it has a reasonable chance of succeeding. So, let's see how it works.

TEACHER: Great. It sounds good to me.

Consultant's Analysis of the Second Interview

3–4. I began by reviewing baseline data collection procedures. This led to a discussion of the data gathered over the past week.

5–6, 10, 20, 22–23, 25, 29, 38, 41–42, 46, 50. These messages serve a supportive function (i.e., support and development task of consultation), as they generally offer encouragement and acknowledge the difficulties faced by the consultee and her assistant on a daily basis in working with the client.

6, 8, 11, 13–15, 19–26, 29, 36, 42–48. These statements reflect either my comments on, or my modeling of, the problem-solving process.

9–10, 22, 24, 26–27, 31–35. These messages offer information and thus may have enhanced both the consultant's expert power and the consultee's professional development (i.e., support and development task).

11–12. A consultant always should inquire about a client's strengths, if only to build up expectations for the prospect of positive change occurring.

14. I provided a brief summary of information obtained in the initial interview before returning to other elements of the functional analysis.

17. This message marks a clear transition point between assessment and intervention phases of consultation. Also, the indication that I understood the problem perhaps as well as the consultee did was an attempt to develop greater referent power.

19–24. Here I asked the consultee seven questions that led directly to her active involvement in generating the intervention plan (cf. Bergan & Neumann, 1980). This was the key influence attempt that occurred during the second interview. By my serving as a "sounding board" rather than an expert, the consultee appeared to retain responsibility for the problem *and* its solution. Some evidence for the consultee's assuming responsibility may be found in her response to message 24, in which she rejected my suggestion for data collection and advanced her own.

22. Here we used the baseline data to determine an initial manageable goal for the client. Without this information we may well have set our expectations either too high or too low.

26–28. These comments illustrate that the school consultant must possess content expertise in addition to knowledge of the problem-solving process of consultation. The suggestion to acknowledge the client's positive behavior four times for every instance of negative behavior comes from *School-Based Assessments and Interventions for ADD Students* (Swanson, 1992).

41. Reverse questioning, when used infrequently, can be very effective. Having a consultee try to answer the question he or she has just asked reinforces an active, problem-solving role as well as the expectation of problem and solution ownership. When reverse questioning is used often, however, the consultant's credibility and expert power are likely to decline.

42. After an intervention plan has been devised, I usually engage the consultee in a troubleshooting analysis such as this one. Although this type of analysis can reduce a consultee's enthusiasm or optimism for the plan, I have found that it is valuable to add a perspective of realism or greater objectivity prior to plan implementation. The use of *our* and *we* in the last sentence suggests further development of referent power.

44–46. Using role-play in consultation offers an opportunity to observe the consultee's level of skill and to provide corrective feedback if needed. It also elevates consultation from a "train and hope" approach to a coaching-feedback approach (e.g., Noell et al., 1997; Showers, 1990), which can result in better treatment integrity, client gains, and generalization.

47–48. Through these "what-if"-type questions, I attempted to clarify the consultee's anticipated standards for client performance.

48. This was another attempt at "onedownsmanship" (Caplan, 1970), which was intended to support the consultee by deferring to her greater knowledge of the client and the classroom environment.

50. This final statement lets the consultee know the probable course of events to come as well as sends the message that the consultant retains control of the process.

THIRD INTERVIEW: TUESDAY, OCTOBER 19

After exchanging greetings, the consultant and teacher discuss the data that have been collected over the past 3 weeks. Although we have chosen to omit the transcript of this first portion of the interview, the data are presented in Figure 9.1.

CONSULTANT: (1) So, it sounds like we've seen some progress here. Given your earlier goal of reducing Kenneth's aggressive behavior, do you think that this intervention has helped?

TEACHER: It's definitely helped better than anything we've tried before. I think we're going to stick with this plan and continue to see what happens.

CONSULTANT: (2) OK, and that reminds me of something you mentioned about wanting him to achieve 5 days in a row where he got computer time before you'd consider changing your standards.

TEACHER: Right.

CONSULTANT: (3) It looks like he's gotten four consecutive days twice now, but never 5. He's come real close.

TEACHER: No, he's never made it. Monday still seems to be the problem day, although even that's getting better. I bet that within 2 weeks we'll see him get 5 days in a row. Then I'll probably start each day with four happy faces instead of five.

CONSULTANT: (4) It sounds like you're on the right track with this.

TEACHER: Yeah, I'm pleased with it.

CONSULTANT: (5) I don't know how many students you've come across who have had aggressive behaviors like Kenneth's, but do you think that this intervention would work with a student with similar problems?

TEACHER: If the student were interested in computers, then probably pretty well. I think one good thing about using computer time as a reward is

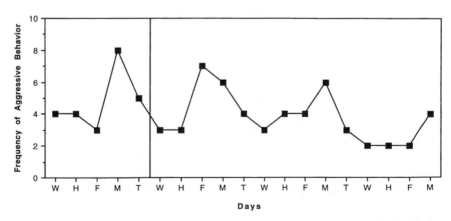

Figure 9.1. Data collected daily on frequency of Kenneth's aggressive behavior during baseline (days 1–5) and treatment (days 6–19) periods.

that there are a lot of software options, so it's a different experience almost every time you sit down. Kids like that novelty, it keeps things rewarding over time. So, for other students like Kenneth, I think the plan could be modified so it could work.

CONSULTANT: (6) Good. Do you think you can attribute the results of this intervention to our plan?

TEACHER: Oh, I definitely think so. I even talked to his mother about it, and she's thrilled that we're finding something that seems to work. And she doesn't believe there have been any changes at home that might account for the behavior change. We both believe that it is this classroom intervention we've tried.

CONSULTANT: (7) That's good information. Have you and Laura been able to point out to Kenneth the times that he has been good? I remember that you were going to try to acknowledge his positive behavior about four times as often as his negative behavior.

TEACHER: Right. This was hard at first, like on the Friday 2-1/2 weeks ago when he was aggressive seven times. There's no way we could find 28 times that he was good that day! But I have to admit that it has gotten easier, especially during the middle of the week.

CONSULTANT: (8) I thought Fridays were generally good days for him. What happened that day?

TEACHER: This was interesting. Kenneth had earned computer time on that Wednesday and Thursday and really enjoyed it. But Friday morning is when his group, the Panthers, gets about 40 minutes on the computer. Well, Kenneth couldn't handle having to wait his turn, share materials, and so on, and he just blew up. He hit one boy and shouted at another. It was clear that he wanted the computer all to himself.

CONSULTANT: (9) That's quite a story. How did you handle that situation?

TEACHER: Well, one thing I've learned here is to stand my ground with Kenneth. I did just that, and sent him to time out. Afterward, we had a talk and, as you can see, the last two Fridays have gone much more smoothly—for both of us.

CONSULTANT: (10) Yes, the data you collected certainly show that. Let's get back to the plan. What do you see as its future?

TEACHER: It's been working, and I think improvement is likely to continue. Like I said, maybe within 2 weeks I'll be changing my standard for his earning computer time. Overall, I'm probably going to keep the plan in place as long as it seems to have a positive effect on him.

CONSULTANT: (11) That sounds like a good way to proceed. Down the line, you may want to think about the possibility of withdrawing the plan and see how he does without its structure. But I don't think we're at that point yet.

TEACHER: No, I don't think so either.

CONSULTANT: (12) Maybe we can look toward that in the future. Something else I'm interested in too is, if you had an opportunity to do this plan over again, what would you do differently?

TEACHER: Hmmm. I don't know. So far it's been working well. I don't know if there's anything I can think of that I would do differently.

CONSULTANT: (13) It has been successful to this point, and that is to your credit. Well, I think you have matters well in hand here. I'll still be at Sloane on Tuesdays and I'll stop by occasionally to see how you and Kenneth are doing. But if you have other students that you'd like to talk about, or wish to continue to talk about Kenneth, I'd be happy to discuss them with you, OK?

TEACHER: Well, I appreciate all the help you've given me.

CONSULTANT: (14) You're quite welcome.

Consultant's Analysis of the Third Interview

1. This message addressed the extent to which the consultee viewed the intervention as effective, which may or may not correspond to what the data indicate.

5. This question concerned the issue of external validity. One can easily see how this issue relates to the likelihood of the consultee preventing similar problems in the future without the consultant's assistance.

6. Similarly, this question addressed internal validity. A client's behavior may improve or worsen for reasons other than the intervention plan, so it is always advisable to check for alternative explanations.

8. I raised this question to address the discrepancy between the frequency of the client's aggressive behavior displayed during the baseline phase versus the treatment phase.

10–11. Here I encouraged the consultee to examine the future of the plan, including possible modifications.

12. Before ending the interview, I asked the consultee to engage in some retrospective troubleshooting. As in message 5, the purpose of my question was to have her think how this intervention (perhaps with alteration) could be applied to future situations.

13. Here I provided the consultee with additional professional support, letting her know that the observed success was due to her efforts. I then brought the consultation to a structured close by indicating my continuing availability, as well as suggesting that the consultee may wish to consider moving on to other issues and clients.

10

Epilogue:
The Effective Practice
of School Consultation

First implemented in 1977, P.L. 94-142/IDEA mandated that prior to classification and placement, a child was to be assessed in all areas related to his or her suspected disability. This assessment was to be conducted by a multidisciplinary team of professionals and include an individual psychological evaluation. The resulting information was to be used for determining eligibility for special education services and for making recommendations about instructional programming to be reflected in the student's IEP. The law also required that following the initial evaluation, students' instructional needs and continued eligibility for special services were to be reexamined at least every three years by appropriate, qualified professionals, usually meaning a psychologist or special education representative. Although P.L. 94-142/IDEA had a broad impact on the delivery of special education services, the evaluation team mandate virtually guaranteed that psychologists employed by school districts or contracted with externally would be needed to diagnose children's learning and adjustment problems. Consistent with this role, survey data suggest that school psychologists spend over 50% of their time conducting psychoeducational assessments (Reschly & Wilson, 1995); about half of these have been mandatory reevaluations (Smith, 1984).

THE LIMITED UTILITY OF
PSYCHOEDUCATIONAL EVALUATION

Special education has been estimated to cost approximately twice as much per pupil as regular education, and a significant portion of this money pays for multidisciplinary team evaluations (Reschly, 1988). Is the money well spent? As discussed in Chapter 3, historically these evaluations have been geared toward addressing the questions of (1) whether a student is eligible for special education services designed and implemented by another professional, and (2) what are the most likely causes of student failure. To answer these questions, psychologists often administer a battery of standardized, norm-referenced tests that lead them to attribute student failure to deficits in one or more underlying psychological processes (e.g., low intelligence) (Ysseldyke & Marston, 1990). The evaluation results are summarized in a report that presumably is used by the special education teacher with whom the child is placed to assist in designing an appropriate instructional program.

The perceived usefulness of standardized test information in designing students' instructional programs was examined in a survey of 200 psychologists and special educators by Thurlow and Ysseldyke (1982). Whereas standardized tests of intelligence and achievement were rated as helpful by psychologists (72% and 80%, respectively), these tests were judged to be instructionally relevant by only 30% and 10% of the resource teachers in the sample. As discussed in Chapter 8, there are several reasons why the information obtained from standardized tests has little relevance for instructional programming: these tests often show little content overlap with commercially available reading programs and their student-centered focus neglects important, controllable, and causal influences on classroom learning (e.g., Christenson & Ysseldyke, 1989; Martens, Steele et al., 1995).

THE EMERGENCE OF SCHOOL-BASED
CONSULTATION TEAMS

Diminishing federal and state funding for education has forced everyone in the schools to "do more with less." Without the money to hire additional teachers, many school districts are reserving self-contained classrooms for the most difficult to teach students and attempting to educate a greater proportion of students with mild handicaps in the mainstream (Fuchs & Fuchs, 1989; Schulte, Osborne & Erchul, 1998). In order to help educators accommodate a wider range of student ability, teacher preparation programs have begun to expand their base of training (e.g., Syracuse University offers an Inclusive Elementary and Special Education Training Program that leads to dual certification). Although graduates of such programs will be better prepared to meet the needs of a diverse student population, many teachers are facing additional numbers of special-needs students in their classrooms today. These teachers require substantial support and assistance in order to develop effective instructional programs, and school-based consultation teams have emerged as the primary vehicle through which this support is provided. School-based consultation teams involve a cooperative effort between regular and special educators, and psychologists trained in consultation are often asked to get these teams up and running or to assume a leadership role in team functioning (Rosenfield & Gravois, 1999).

CHANGES TO IDEA

The 1997 reauthorization of IDEA (IDEA 97) contains features that emphasize consultation and intervention activities and perhaps de-emphasize formal assessment activities (Fagan & Wise, 2000; Hoff & Zirkel, 1999). First, the law's definition of "psychological services" has been expanded to include offering assistance in developing positive behavioral intervention strategies. *This provision legitimizes a consultant role, specifically for creating and implementing positive behavioral supports and behavior intervention plans for students.* Second, triennial psychoeducational reevaluations, formerly required, now may be based on existing information and previous evaluations if deemed appropriate by school personnel and parents. This decrease in formal assessment activities in the service of eligibility determination may create opportunities for psychologists to engage in more consultation and intervention activities (Drasgow & Yell, Ford, 2000). Third, IDEA mandates functional assessment for certain student problems and recommends it for others. One advantage of functional assessment is that it links a problem's definition more directly to its solution, which has clear implications for school consultation and intervention activities.

Psychologists who narrowly view eligibility determination as their primary function in the schools stand to lose a great deal of professional territory given the consultation- and intervention-based aspects of IDEA 97. For psychologists trained in consultation, however, the law may represent an opportunity to redefine their role as service providers. Are we prepared to devote more professional time to school-based consultation and intervention efforts and relinquish our status as special education gatekeepers? Results of a recent survey indicate that for many of us the answer may be "no," and these findings argue in favor of reconceptualizing school consultation along the lines suggested in previous chapters.

RECONCEPTUALIZING SCHOOL CONSULTATION

The Adequacy of Current Training Models

Constenbader, Swartz, and Petrix (1992) examined three aspects of school consultation training from the perspective of consultants, including the adequacy of preservice training, models used in current practice, and self-evaluation of consultation skills. In their study, a 30-item survey was mailed to 1,020 members of the National Association of School Psychologists, the largest professional organization for school psychologists in the country. A total of 333 surveys were returned, and respondents were distributed across 46 states representing all geographic regions.

With respect to preservice training, results of the survey showed that 61% of all respondents had received no formal training or less than one semester of training in consultation. Although all of the psychologists sampled judged consultation training to be important to their professional functioning, 53% rated their quality of training as being less than adequate. Of the models presented in training, behavioral consultation was the most popular (53% of the sample), followed by process and mental health consultation (34 and 32%, respectively). Interestingly, a full 26% of respondents indicated that they had been trained in no particular model at all!

Regarding the use of consultation training in their professional practice, teachers were consulted with most frequently (42%) followed by families (20%), and administrators (18%). Insufficient time was cited as the greatest barrier to consultation in the schools by 50% of the respondents. Perhaps most telling, however, were the percentages of respondents who reported actually using the various models of consultation in which they were trained. Whereas 53% of the sample was trained in behavioral consultation, only 38% reported using this model. More psychologists reported using no particular model at all (26%) than reported using mental health consultation (9%).

Clearly, these findings suggest that many school psychologists are not adequately trained to provide school consultation services. Given the paucity of consultation courses in other specialty areas within psychology, the situation is probably worse for clinical or counseling psychologists who enter the schools as external consultants. Results of the survey also indicate that psychologists are likely to receive training in a variety of consultation models or even no model at all. Unfortunately, relatively few individuals report actually using any of these models in practice suggesting that: (1) any single model is probably inadequate as a basis for delivering consultation services in the schools; (2) although each model has the potential to contribute to the practice of school consultation, this contribution is not fully recognized; and (3) training may be too brief to impart the level of skill mastery required for subsequent application. The integrated model of school consultation that was presented in this book represents an attempt to address these perceived shortcomings by combining the most useful and empirically validated principles from two existing consultation approaches (i.e., mental health and behavioral) with practices shown to be effective in contemporary consultation research (i.e., behavior analysis, social influence, professional support). In so doing, we describe for the first-time consultant when and how to apply these principles in response to a wide range of consultee and client needs, and we offer a thorough discussion of the realities inherent in providing services within a school organizational context.

Key Elements of Our Integrated Model

As discussed in Chapter 5, we believe that effective school consultation involves the completion of three interrelated tasks—problem solving, social influence, and support and development. We consider these tasks to be interrelated because the problem-solving objectives of school consultation can only be accomplished through a social influence process between the consultant and teacher, the goals of which are to support changes in teacher behavior as a means of serving children, given the constraints of his or her professional role. Throughout this volume, we have attempted to describe how existing consultation models and recent research concerning the consultative relationship provide conceptual and empirical bases for each of these tasks. In addition, we have attempted to provide the reader with a "working knowledge" of schools as organizations, teachers as consultees, and students as clients in order to facilitate their entry into the culture of educational service delivery.

With respect to the first issue of the development of an integrated model of school consultation, behavioral consultation was adopted as a basis for the problem-solving task because: (1) it articulates a systematic problem solving process with clearly specified objectives and interviewing tactics; and (2) it relies on an effective technology of classroom instruction and management, namely behavior analysis. Despite these strengths, behavioral consultation as it is typically practiced in the schools represents a somewhat naive approach to service delivery because it assumes that teachers will change their own behavior because it is in the best interest of children to do so, and it offers little guidance for supporting teachers in their attempts to implement agreed-upon intervention plans.

Mental health consultation was adopted as a basis for the support and development task because of its: (1) preventive focus in which periods of crisis are viewed as opportunities for personal and professional growth; and (2) recognition of the importance of consultee perceptions, attributions, and beliefs when attempting to change consultee behavior. These views help to explain why teachers seek out consultative assistance and suggest that during times of crisis these individuals may be more open to influence and more willing to attempt new behaviors. By virtue of its preventive focus, the mental health consultation model suggests that interventions developed within a consultative relationship can also have significant and lasting effects on the consultee. Although conceptually relevant to the practice of school consultation, the processes and outcomes of mental health consultation have not been well operationalized and therefore are difficult to train. Moreover, techniques of mental health consultation, such as theme interference reduction, have very little empirical support (Gresham & Kendell, 1987), and less-than-optimal supervisory and administrative mechanisms in most schools suggest that lack of knowledge or skill rather than objectivity may account for most teachers' difficulties (Erchul, 1993b). Although this latter point suggests the importance of enhancing consultee skills through modeling, coaching, and feedback, these activities have only begun to receive attention in the consultation literature (e.g., Martens, Witt et al., 1999; Noell, Witt et al., 1997; Noell, Witt et al., 2000; Witt et al., 1997).

Finally, research dispelling the collaborative myth of school consultation (Erchul, 1987; Erchul & Chewning, 1990; Fuchs et al., 1990; Martens, Erchul & Witt, 1992; Witt, 1990) was adopted as a basis for the social influence task. These studies suggest rather clearly that school consultation rarely involves a collaborative, nonhierarchical relationship between coequal professionals but is more accurately described as a cooperative relationship in which the consultant leads by directing the process and the consultee, in turn, follows. This being the case, we believe that the bases of social power and influence discussed by J.R.P. French and Raven (1959) and Erchul and Raven (1997) are relevant to the practice of school consultation. Specifically, in order to benefit children within an indirect service delivery model, the consultant must effect changes in consultee behavior. Because school consultation involves aspects of relational control, it should be possible to change consultee behavior in a noncoercive fashion using strategic communication to create a dyadic influence process. Although these strategies have received empirical support in other contexts, they are just beginning to receive attention in the school consultation literature (Erchul, Raven & Ray, 2001; Erchul, Raven & Whichard, in press).

With respect to the second issue of the culture of schools and schooling, we believe that consultants need to be aware of several factors that are likely to influence the success of their service delivery efforts. First, special education placement and the refer-test-place model continue to dominate as the solutions of choice for the problem of student failure. These approaches place few additional burdens on the regular education teacher making a referral, and are easy to justify from an administrative perspective by counting the numbers of students who are referred, classified, and placed within the district (Piersel & Gutkin, 1983). As an alternative approach to service delivery, school consultation must often compete with the status quo. In order to compete effectively, it must be recognized that not all students who fail in regular education can receive special class placements, special education is costly, and its effectiveness is questionable (e.g., Kavale, 1990). In contrast, school consultation services can complement special education by reducing the number of children who are referred, it has the potential to increase teacher skills, and it has been shown to be effective (e.g., Rosenfield, 1992).

Second, because academic achievement can be viewed as a continuous variable that is normally distributed, students can be expected to show varying degrees of failure in the regular classroom. This suggests that students who are classified as mildly handicapped are likely to differ from their regular education peers by a matter of degree, not kind (Reschly, 1988). Although educational classification schemes tend to promote the view that children with special needs are "disabled," referral and placement in special education involves an interaction between the child's behavior, the teacher's expectations and skills, and the availability of alternative services (Shinn, 1989). For many of these students, performance can be improved by encouraging teachers to engage in more explicit instructional and managerial practices as described in Chapter 6.

Third, research has shown that teachers' instructional and managerial practices tend to be consistent across schools, are similar in regular and special education classrooms, and have changed little over time (Ysseldyke, Christenson, Thurlow & Bakewell, 1989). This situation can be attributed to the bureaucratic structure of schools that constrains teachers' efforts to individualize instruction (Apter, 1977). Although this "One Right

Model" model of public education is effective for most children, it suggests that teachers will be unable to successfully accommodate students with special needs in regular classrooms unless they are provided with substantial assistance and support at the building level to do so. In the absence of such support, building teams may be asking teachers to do even more with less.

Contributing to the Future of School Consultation

Researchers in school consultation have made a number of advances over the past few decades. From our perspective, these advances include but are not limited to: (1) comparisons showing that explicit and direct instructional practices are most effective when addressing student skill deficits (Gersten, Woodward & Darch, 1986; Kavale, 1990; Lipsey & Wilson, 1993; Reid, 1986); (2) attempts to develop a technology of interpersonal communication that enhances consultative problem solving (e.g., Erchul, 1987; Martens, Deery & Gherardi, 1991; Martens, Lewandowski & Houk, 1989; Benes, Gutkin, & Kramer, 1995); (3) efforts to incorporate home-school collaboration in the development of consultative interventions (e.g., Christenson & Sheridan, 2001; Sheridan, Kratochwill & Bergan, 1996); and (4) demonstrations that district-wide prereferral intervention programs can be effective and feasible approaches to service delivery (e.g., Fuchs & Fuchs, 1989; Graden, Casey & Christenson, 1985; Ponti, Zins & Graden, 1988; Rosenfield, 1992).

School consultants, both researchers and practitioners alike, will undoubtedly face new challenges in the years to come. We believe that these challenges will fall primarily into three separate areas that in many ways are related to the advances noted above.

A Technology of Instructional Decision Making

Although research suggests that we have an effective educational technology at our disposal and have for some time, this technology has not been widely adopted in the schools (Axelrod, 1993; Wolery et al., 1988). Moreover, many interventions that are developed during consultation rely on aspects of this technology. To the extent that teachers continue to rely on ineffective educational practices, these interventions will be perceived as involving extra work at best or irrelevant to student learning at worst. For example, it has been shown that explicit goal setting and feedback about student performance improves academic achievement (Fuchs & Fuchs, 1986a; Miller & Kelley, 1994; Martens, Hiralall & Bradley,

1997). Although data should be collected during consultation to evaluate intervention effects, these data often differ from the measures typically used by teachers (e.g., curriculum-based measurement probes). The consultant's task would be easier if teachers used these measures routinely when making instructional decisions. We believe that examining ways of promoting effective educational technology in the schools will be critical to consultation success in the future.

A Science of Consultee Behavior Change

As suggested in this volume, the success or failure of school consultation hinges largely on the consultant's ability to promote changes in *teacher behavior*. Toward this goal, we believe that translating the science of social influence into a technology of teacher behavior change will be an important task for consultation researchers in the future. An alternative perspective may be to approach teacher behavior change in the same fashion as we approach child behavior change, namely by analyzing and arranging conditions that promote desired activities (Lentz & Daly, 1996; Noell & Witt, 1996). Recent emphasis on the integrity with which interventions are implemented during consultation, and efforts to systematically teach appropriate implementation behavior appear to hold promise in this area (Noell & Witt, 1996, 1999) as do further explorations of relational communication (Erchul, Sheridan, et al., 1999) and social power in school consultation (Erchul et al., 2001).

A Policy of Implementation Support

In this age of retrenchment in education, teachers are being asked to manage larger classes with fewer resources. From content presented in Chapters 3 and 7, we believe it naive to assume in such a context that regular class teachers will be able to individualize instruction for increasing numbers of special needs students without substantial support. In order for school consultation to stand as a viable alternative to special class placement, we believe that schools must adopt a policy of implementation support. Specifically, the resources needed to successfully implement a procedure should be identified as part of the consultation process (e.g., peer tutors, progress monitors, volunteer assistants), and teachers should be provided these resources to the greatest extent possible. As it stands, teachers are often rewarded for making a referral by having a difficult child removed from their classroom and punished for seeking consultative assistance by being asked to assume additional responsibilities. Although previous research has shown that school consultation is an effective practice for consultants, a goal in the future will be to determine how school consultation can be made a rewarding practice for teachers.

As discussed throughout this volume, the practice of school consultation has made significant strides over the past several decades. At the same time, teachers, support personnel, and parents have become increasingly vocal about the need for educational reform, and policymakers have responded with calls for effective and efficient alternatives to special education services (e.g., the Regular Education Initiative). School consultation stands poised as perhaps the most viable of these service delivery options. As noted in Chapter 1, we have attempted in this book to provide school consultants with information, skills, and perspectives that represent the culmination of our collective experiences as consultation trainers and practitioners and, wherever possible, the very latest advances in consultation research. Although there are many lessons yet to be learned, we hope the information presented will help the reader meet the challenges of school-based intervention today and in the future.

References

Albee, G. W. (1959). *Mental health and manpower trends*. New York: Basic Books.

Albee, G. W. (1968). Conceptual models and manpower requirements in psychology. *American Psychologist, 23,* 317–320.

Aldrich, S. F., & Martens, B. K. (1993). The effects of behavioral problem analysis versus instructional environment information on teachers' perceptions. *School Psychology Quarterly, 8,* 110–124.

Alessi, G. J. (1980). Behavioral observation for the school psychologist: Responsive–discrepancy model. *School Psychology Review, 9,* 31–45.

Algozzine, B., & Korinek, L. (1985). Where is special education for students with high prevalence handicaps going? *Exceptional Children, 51,* 388–394.

Algozzine, B., Ysseldyke, J. E., Christenson, S., & Thurlow, M. L. (1983). A factor analysis of teachers' intervention choices for dealing with students' behavior and learning problems. *The Elementary School Journal, 84,* 189–197.

Allington, R. L. (1980). Teacher interruption behaviors during primary-grade oral reading. *Journal of Educational Psychology, 72,* 371–377.

Alpert, J., & Silverstein, J. (1985). Mental health consultation: Historical, present, and future perspectives. In J. R. Bergan (Ed.), *School psychology in contemporary society: An introduction* (pp. 281–315). Columbus, OH: Merrill.

Alpert, J. L., & Yammer, D. M. (1983). Research in school consultation: A content analysis of selected journals. *Professional Psychology, 14,* 604–612.

American Psychiatric Association. (1994). *Diagnostic and statistical manual of mental disorders* (4th ed., rev.). Washington, DC: Author.

American Psychological Association. (1992). Ethical principles of psychologists and code of conduct. *American Psychologist, 47,* 1597–1611.

Apter, S. J. (1977). The public schools. In B. Blatt, D. Biklen, & R. Bogdon (Eds.), *An alternative textbook in special education*. Denver, CO: Love Publishing.

Archer, R. P., Maruish, M., Imhof, E. A., & Piotrowski, C. (1992). Psychological test usage with adolescent clients: 1990 survey findings. *Professional Psychology: Research & Practice, 22,* 247–252.

Armbruster, B. B., Stevens, R. J., & Rosenshine, B. (1977). *Analyzing content coverage and emphasis: A study of three curricula and two tests.* (Technical Report No. 26) Urbana, IL: University of Illinois.

Astor, R. A., Pitner, R. O., & Duncan, B. B. (1998). Ecological approaches to mental health consultation with teachers on issues related to youth and school violence. *Journal of Negro Education, 65,* 336–355.

Axelrod, S. (1987). Functional and structural analyses of behavior: Approaches leading to reduced use of punishment procedures? *Research in Developmental Disabilities, 8*, 165–178.

Axelrod, S. (1993). Integrating behavioral technology into public schools. *School Psychology Quarterly, 8*, 1–9.

Babinski, L. M., & Rogers, D. L. (1998). Supporting new teachers through consultee-centered group consultation. *Journal of Educational and Psychological Consultation, 9*, 285–308.

Bandura, A. (1977). *Social learning theory.* Englewood Cliffs, NJ: Prentice-Hall.

Barlow, D. H., Hayes, S. C., & Nelson, R. O. (1984). *The scientist practitioner* (pp. 3–37). New York: Pergamon.

Barone, S. G. (1995). The egalitarian virus. *Education Weekly*, March 1, p. 35.

Barry, B., & Watson, M. R. (1996). Communication aspects of dyadic social influence in organizations: A review and integration of conceptual and empirical developments. In B. R. Burleson (Ed.), *Communication yearbook 19* (pp. 269–317). Thousand Oaks, CA: Sage.

Bass, B. M. (1981). *Stodgill's handbook of leadership* (rev. ed.) New York: Free Press.

Baxter, L. A. (1984). An investigation of compliance-gaining as politeness. *Human Communications Research, 10*, 427–456.

Becker, W. C. (1988). Direct instruction: Special issue. *Education and Treatment of Children, 11*, 297–402.

Bell, P. F., Lentz, F. E., & Graden, J. L. (1992). Effects of curriculum-test overlap on standardized achievement test scores: Identifying systematic confounds in educational decision making. *School Psychology Review, 21*, 644–655.

Benes, K. M., Gutkin, T. B., & Kramer, J. J. (1995). Lag sequential analysis: Taking consultation communication research methodology to the movies. *School Psychology Review, 24*, 694–708.

Bennett, R. E. (1984). Information management in educational service delivery. In C. A. Maher, R. J. Illback, & J. E. Zins (Eds.), *Organizational psychology in the schools: A handbook for professionals* (pp. 385–401). Springfield, IL: Thomas.

Bennis, W. G. (1969). *Organization development: Its nature, origins, and prospects.* Reading, MA: Addison-Wesley.

Bergan, J. R. (1977). *Behavioral consultation.* Columbus, OH: Merrill.

Bergan, J. R. (1995). Evolution of a problem-solving model of consultation. *Journal of Educational and Psychological Consultation, 6*, 111–123.

Bergan, J. R., & Kratochwill, T. R. (1990). *Behavioral consultation and therapy.* New York: Plenum.

Bergan, J. R., & Neumann, A. J. (1980). The identification of resources and constraints influencing plan design in consultation. *Journal of School Psychology, 18*, 317–323.

Bergan, J. R., & Tombari, M. L. (1975). The analysis of verbal interactions occurring during consultation. *Journal of School Psychology, 13*, 209–226.

Bergan, J. R., & Tombari, M. L. (1976). Consultant skill and efficiency and the implementation and outcomes of consultation. *Journal of School Psychology, 14*, 3–14.

Berkowitz, L., & Daniels, L. R. (1963). Responsibility and dependence. *Journal of Abnormal Psychology, 66*, 429–436.

Berkowitz, M. J., & Martens, B. K. (2001). Assessing teachers' and students' preferences for school-based reinforcers: Agreement across methods and different effort requirements. *Journal of Developmental and Physical Disabilities, 13*, 373–387.

Bijou, S. W., Peterson, R. F., & Ault, M. H. (1968). A method to integrate descriptive and experimental field studies at the level of data and empirical concepts. *Journal of Applied Behavior Analysis, 1*, 175–191.

Blake, R. R., & Mouton, J. S. (1976). *Consultation.* Reading, MA: Addison-Wesley.

Bossard, M. D., & Gutkin, T. B. (1983). The relationship of consultant skill and school organizational characteristics with teacher use of school based consultation services. *School Psychology Review, 12*, 50–56.

Brandenburg, N. A., Friedman, R. M., & Silver, S. E. (1990). The epidemiology of childhood psychiatric disorders: Recent prevalence findings and methodologic issues. *Journal of the American Academy of Child and Adolescent Psychiatry, 29,* 76–83.

Brehm, J. W. (1966). *A theory of psychological reactance.* New York: Academic Press.

Brophy, J. E. (1983). Classroom organization and management. *The Elementary School Journal, 83,* 265–285.

Brown, D., Pryzwansky, W. B., & Schulte, A. C. (2001). *Psychological consultation: Introduction to theory and practice* (5th ed.). Boston: Allyn & Bacon.

Busse, R. T., Kratochwill, T. R., & Elliott, S. N. (1995). Meta-analysis for single-case outcomes: Applications to research and practice. *Journal of School Psychology, 33,* 269–285.

Busse, R. T., Kratochwill, T. R., & Elliott, S. N. (1999). Influences of verbal interactions during behavioral consultations on treatment outcomes. *Journal of School Psychology, 37,* 117–143.

Caplan, G. (1961). *An approach to community mental health.* New York: Grune & Stratton.

Caplan, G. (1963). Types of mental health consultation. *American Journal of Orthopsychiatry, 3,* 470–481.

Caplan, G. (1964). *Principles of preventive psychiatry.* New York: Basic Books.

Caplan, G. (1970). *The theory and practice of mental health consultation.* New York: Basic Books.

Caplan, G. (1974). *Support systems and community mental health.* New York: Behavioral Publications.

Caplan, G. (1986). Recent developments in crisis intervention and in the promotion of support services. In M. Kessler & S. E. Goldston (Eds.), *A decade of progress in primary prevention* (pp. 235–260). Hanover, NH: University Press of New England.

Caplan, G. (1989). *Population-oriented psychiatry.* New York: Plenum.

Caplan, G. (1993a). Epilogue. In W. P. Erchul (Ed.), *Consultation in community, school, and organizational practice: Gerald Caplan's contributions to professional psychology* (pp. 205–213). Washington, DC: Taylor & Francis.

Caplan, G. (1993b). Mental health consultation, community mental health, and population-oriented psychiatry. In W. P. Erchul (Ed.), *Consultation in community school, and organizational practice: Gerald Caplan's contributions to professional psychology* (pp. 41–55). Washington, DC: Taylor & Francis.

Caplan, G., & Bowlby, J. (1948, April). The aims and methods of child guidance. *Health Education Journal, 6,* 1–8.

Caplan, G., & Caplan, R. B. (1980). *Arab and Jew in Jerusalem: Explorations in community mental health.* Cambridge, MA: Harvard University Press.

Caplan, G., & Caplan, R. B. (1999). *Mental health consultation and collaboration.* Prospect Heights, IL: Waveland Press, Inc. (Original work published 1993)

Caplan, G., Caplan, R. B., & Erchul, W. P. (1994). Caplanian mental health consultation: Historical background and current status. *Consulting Psychology Journal: Practice and Research, 46*(4), 2–12.

Caplan, G., Caplan, R. B., & Erchul, W. P. (1995). A contemporary view of mental health consultation: Comments on "Types of mental health consultation" by Gerald Caplan (1963). *Journal of Educational and Psychological Consultation, 6,* 23–30.

Caplan, G., & Killilea, M. (1976). *Support systems and mutual help: Multidisciplinary explorations.* New York: Grune & Stratton.

Carkhuff, R. R. (1969). *Helping and human relations Vol. 1: Selection and training.* New York: Holt, Rinehart & Winston.

Carter, J., & Sugai, G. (1989). Survey of prereferral practices: Responses from state departments of education. *Exceptional Children, 55,* 298–302.

Chin, R., & Benne, K. D. (1969). General strategies for effecting change in human systems. In W. G. Bennis, K. D. Benne, & R. Chin (Eds.), *The planning of change* (2nd ed.). New York: Holt, Rinehart & Winston.

Christenson, S. L., & Conoley, J. C. (Eds.). (1992). *Home-school collaboration: Enhancing children's academic and social competence.* Silver Spring, MD: National Association of School Psychologists.

Christenson, S. L., & Sheridan, S. M. (Eds.) (2001). *Schools and families: Creating essential connections for learning.* New York: Guilford.

Christenson, S. L., & Ysseldyke, J. E. (1989). Assessing student performance: An important change is needed. *Journal of School Psychology, 27,* 409–425.

Cialdini, R. B., Vincent, J. B., Lewis, S. K., Catalan, J., Wheeler, D., & Darby, B. L. (1975). Reciprocal concessions procedure for inducing compliance: The door-in-the-face technique. *Journal of Personality and Social Psychology, 31,* 206–215.

Cienki, J. A. (1982). Teachers' perception of consultation as a function of consultants' use of expert and referent power. *Dissertation Abstracts International, 43,* (3-A), 725.

Clark, E. G., & Leavell, H. R. (1958). Levels of application of preventive medicine. In H. R. Leavell & E. G. Clark (Eds.), *Preventive medicine for the doctor in his community: An epidemiologic approach* (2nd ed., pp. 13–39). New York: McGraw-Hill.

Cleven, C. A., & Gutkin, T. B. (1988). Cognitive modeling of consultation processes: A means for improving consultees' problem definition skills. *Journal of School Psychology, 26,* 379–389.

Cohen, M. D., March, J. G., & Olsen, J. P. (1972). A garbage can model of organizational choice. *Administrative Science Quarterly, 17,* 1.

Cohen, S., & Wills, T. A. (1985). Stress, social support, and the buffering hypothesis. *Psychological Bulletin, 98,* 310–357.

Cohn, M. M., & Kottkamp, R. B. (1993). Teachers: *The missing voice in education.* Albany, NY: State University of New York Press.

Cone, J. D. (1978). The behavioral assessment grid (BAG): A conceptual framework and a taxomony. *Behavior Therapy, 9,* 882–888.

Conoley, J. C. (1981a). Advocacy consultation: Promises and problems. In J. C. Conoley (Ed.), *Consultation in schools: Theory, research, procedures* (pp. 157–178). New York: Academic Press.

Conoley, J. C. (1981b). The process of change: The agent of change. In J. C. Conoley (Ed.), *Consultation in schools: Theory, research, procedures* (pp. 1–10). New York: Academic Press.

Conoley, J. C., & Conoley, C. W. (1982). *School consultation: A guide to practice and training.* New York: Pergamon.

Conoley, J. C., & Conoley, C. W. (1992). *School consultation: Practice and training* (2nd ed.). Boston: Allyn & Bacon.

Conoley, J. C., & Gutkin, T. B. (1986). School psychology: A reconceptualization of service delivery realities. In S. N. Elliott & J. C. Witt (Eds.), *The delivery of psychological services in schools: Concepts, processes and issues* (pp. 393–424). Hillsdale, NJ: Erlbaum.

Conoley, J. C., & Wright, C. (1993). Caplan's ideas and the future of psychology in the schools. In W. P. Erchul (Ed.), *Consultation in community, school, and organizational practice: Gerald Caplan's contributions to professional psychology* (pp. 177–192). Washington, DC: Taylor & Francis.

Costenbader, V., Swartz, J., & Petrix, L. (1992). Consultation in the schools: The relationship between preservice training, perception of consultative skills, and actual time spent in consultation. *School Psychology Review, 21,* 95–108.

Cowen, E., & Hightower, A. D. (1990). The Primary Mental Health Project: Alternative approaches in school-based preventive services. In T. B. Gutkin & C. R. Reynolds (Eds.), *The handbook of school psychology* (2nd ed., pp. 775–795). New York: Wiley.

Cowen, E. L., Trost, M. A., Lorion, R. P., Dorr, D., Izzo, L. D., & Isaacson, R. V. (1975). *New ways in school mental health: Early detection and prevention of school maladaptation.* New York: Human Sciences Press.

Crowe, D. S. (1982). Effects of expert and referent power in the consultation process (Doctoral dissertation, University of Georgia, 1982). *Dissertation Abstracts International, 43*, 1887A.

Cubberley, E. P. (1916). *Public school administration: A statement of the fundamental principles underlying the organization and administration of public education.* Boston, MA: Houghton Mifflin.

Curtis, M. J., & Zins, J. E. (1988). Effects of training in consultation and instructor feedback on acquisition of consultation skills. *Journal of School Psychology, 26*, 185–190.

Daly, E. J., Lentz, F. E., & Boyer, J. (1996). The instructional hierarchy: A conceptual model for understanding the effective components of reading interventions. *School Psychology Quarterly, 11*, 369–386.

Daly, E. J., & Martens, B. K. (1994). A comparison of three interventions for increasing oral reading performance: Application of the Instructional Hierarchy. *Journal of Applied Behavior Analysis, 27*, 459–469.

Daly, E. J., Witt, J. C., Martens, B. K., & Dool, E. J. (1997). A model for conducting a functional analysis of academic performance problems. *School Psychology Review, 26*, 554–574.

Daly, J. A., & Wiemann, J. M. (Eds.). (1994). *Strategic interpersonal communication.* Hillsdale, NJ: Erlbaum.

Darling-Hammond, L. (1997). *Doing what matters most: Investing in quality teaching.* New York: National Commission on Teaching and America's Future.

Darling-Hammond, L., Berry, B. T., Haselkorn, D., & Fideler, E. (1999). Teacher recruitment, selection, and induction: Policy influences on the supply and quality of teachers. In L. Darling-Hammond & G. Sykes (Eds.), *Teaching as the learning profession: Handbook of policy and practice* (pp. 183–232). San Francisco: Jossey-Bass.

Davis, H., & Salasin, S. (1975). Utilization of evaluation. In M. Guttentag and E. Struening (Eds.), *Handbook of evaluation research* (Vol. 1, pp. 621–666). Beverly Hills: Sage.

Davis, J. M., & Sandoval, J. (1992). A pragmatic framework for systems-oriented consultation. *Journal of Educational and Psychological Consultation, 2*, 201–216.

Delmolino, L. M., & Romanczyk, R. G. (1995). Facilitated communication: A critical review. *The Behavior Therapist*, Feb., 27–30.

deVoss, G. G. (1979). The structure of major lessons and collective student activity. *Elementary School Journal, 80*, 8–18.

Dillard, J. M., & Reilly, R. R. (1988). *Systematic interviewing: Communication skills for professional effectiveness.* Columbus, OH: Merrill.

Dougherty, A. M. (2000). *Psychological consultation and collaboration in school and community settings* (3rd ed.). Belmont, CA: Brooks/Cole.

Doyle, W. (1985). Recent research on classroom management: Implications for teacher preparation. *Journal of Teacher Education, 36*, 31–35.

Drasgow, E. & Yell, M. (2001). Functional behavioral assessments: Legal requirements and challenges. *School Psychology Review, 30*, 239–251.

Dunst, C. J., & Trivette, C. M. (1987). Enabling and empowering families: Conceptual and intervention issues. *School Psychology Review, 16*, 443–456.

DuPaul, G. D. (1992). How to assess attention-deficit hyperactivity disorder within school settings. *School Psychology Quarterly, 7*, 60–74.

Durand, V. M., & Crimmins, D. B. (1988) Identifying the variables maintaining self-injurious behavior. *Journal of Autism and Developmental Disorders, 18*, 99–117.

Dwyer, K. (1995). Congress drafts changes in IDEA. *Communique, 24*, 1.

D'Zurilla, T. J., & Goldfried, M. R. (1971). Problem solving and behavior modification. *Journal of Abnormal Psychology, 78*, 107–126.

Egan, G. (1994). *The skilled helper: A problem-management approach to helping* (5th ed.). Pacific Grove, CA: Brooks/Cole.

Ehrhardt, K. E., Barnett, D. W., Lentz, F. E., Stollar, S. A., & Reifin, L. H. (1996). Innovative methodology in ecological consultation: Use of scripts to promote treatment acceptability and integrity. *School Psychology Quarterly, 11,* 149–168.

Elam, S. M. (1989). The second Gallup Poll of teachers' attitudes toward the public schools. *Phi Delta Kappan, 71,* 785–798.

Elliott, S. N. (1988). Acceptability of behavioral treatments: Review of variables that influence treatment selection. *Professional Psychology: Research and Practice, 19,* 68–80.

Elliott, S. N., Turco, T., & Gresham, F. M. (1987). Consumers' and clients' pretreatment acceptability ratings of classroom group contingencies. *Journal of School Psychology, 25,* 145–154.

Elliott, S. N., Witt, J. C., Galvin, G., & Peterson, R. (1984). Acceptability of positive and reductive interventions: Factors that influence teachers' decisions. *Journal of School Psychology, 22,* 353–360.

Elmquist, D. L. (1989). *Features of effectiveness of residential treatment centers for adolescents with behavior disorders: Literative review.* Logan, UT: Utah State University Department of Special Education.

Epstein, M., Cullinan, D., & Sabatino, D. (1977). State definitions of behavior disorders. *Journal of Special Education, 11,* 417–425.

Epstein, M. H., Matson, J. L., Repp, A., & Helsel, W. J. (1986). Acceptability of treatment alternatives as a function of teacher status and student level. *School Psychology Review, 15,* 84–90.

Erchul, W. P. (1987). A relational communication analysis of control in school consultation. *Professional School Psychology, 2,* 113–124.

Erchul, W. P. (1992a). On dominance, cooperation, teamwork, and collaboration in school-based consultation. *Journal of Educational and Psychological Consultation, 3,* 363–366.

Erchul, W. P. (1992b). Social psychological perspectives on the school psychologist's involvement with parents. In F. J. Medway & T. P. Cafferty (Eds.), *School psychology: A social psychological perspective* (pp. 425–448). Hillsdale, NJ: Erlbaum.

Erchul, W. P. (Ed.) (1993a). *Consultation in community, school, and organizational practice: Gerald Caplan's contributions to professional psychology.* Washington, DC: Taylor & Francis.

Erchul, W. P. (1993b). Reflections on mental health consultation: An interview with Gerald Caplan. In W. P. Erchul (Ed.), *Consultation in community, school and organizational practice: Gerald Caplan's contributions to professional psychology* (pp.57–72). Washington, DC: Taylor & Francis.

Erchul, W. P. (1993c). Selected interpersonal perspectives in consultation research. *School Psychology Quarterly, 8,* 38–49.

Erchul, W. P. (1999). Two steps forward, one step back: Collaboration in school-based consultation. *Journal of School Psychology, 37,* 191–203.

Erchul, W. P., & Chewning, T. G. (1990). Behavioral consultation from a request-centered relational communication perspective. *School Psychology Quarterly, 5,* 1–20.

Erchul, W. P., & Conoley, C. W (1991). Helpful theories to guide counselors' practice of school-based consultation. *Elementary School Guidance & Counseling, 25,* 204–211.

Erchul, W. P., Covington, C. G., Hughes, J. N., & Meyers, J. (1995). Further explorations of request-centered relational communication within school consultation. *School Psychology Review, 24,* 621–632.

Erchul, W. P., Hughes, J. N., Meyers, J., Hickman, J. A., & Braden, J. P. (1992). Dyadic agreement concerning the consultation process and its relationship to outcome. *Journal of Educational and Psychological Consultation, 3,* 119–132.

Erchul, W. P., & Martens, B. K. (1997). *School consultation: Conceptual and empirical bases of practice.* New York: Plenum.

Erchul, W. P., & Raven, B. H. (1997). Social power in school consultation: A contemporary view of French and Raven's bases of power model. *Journal of School Psychology, 35,* 137–171.

Erchul, W. P., Raven, B. H., & Ray, A. G. (2001). School psychologists' perceptions of social power bases in teacher consultation. *Journal of Educational and Psychological Consultation, 12*, 1–23.

Erchul, W. P., Raven, B. H., & Whichard, S. M. (in press). School psychologist and teacher perceptions of social power in consultation. *Journal of School Psychology.*

Erchul, W. P., & Schulte, A. C. (1993). Gerald Caplan's contributions to professional psychology: Conceptual underpinnings. In W. P. Erchul (Ed.), *Consultation in community, school, and organizational practice: Gerald Caplan's contributions to professional psychology* (pp. 3–40). Washington, DC: Taylor & Francis.

Erchul, W. P., Sheridan, S. M., Ryan, D. A., Grissom, P. F., Killough, C. E., Mettler, D. W. (1999). Patterns of relational communication in conjoint behavioral consultation. *School Psychology Quarterly, 14*, 121–147.

Erikson, E. H. (1959). Identity and the life cycle: Selected papers by Erik H. Erikson. *Psychological Issues Monograph, 1*(1), 18–166. New York: International Universities Press.

Ervin, R. A., DuPaul, G. J., Kern, L., & Friman, P. C. (1998). Classroom-based functional and adjunctive assessments: Proactive approaches to intervention selection for adolescents with attention deficit hyperactivity disorder. *Journal of Applied Behavior Analysis, 31*(1), 65–78.

Espin, C. A., & Deno, S. L. (1989). The effects of modeling and prompting feedback strategies on sight word reading of students labeled learning disabled. *Education and Treatment of Children, 12*, 219–231.

Eysenck, H. J. (1952). The effects of psychotherapy: An evaluation. *Journal of Consulting Psychology, 16*, 319–324.

Fagan, T. K., & Wise, P. S. (2000). *School psychology: Past present and future* (2nd ed.). Bethesda, MD: National Association of School Psychologists.

Falbo, T. & Peplau, L. A. (1980). Power strategies in intimate relationships. *Journal of Personality and Social Psychology, 38*, 618–628.

Flugum, K. R., & Reschly, D. J. (1994). Prereferral interventions: Quality indices and outcomes. *Journal of School Psychology, 32*, 1–14.

Folger, J. P., & Puck, S. (1976, April). *Coding relational communication: A question approach.* Paper presented at the meeting of the International Communication Association, Portland, OR.

Ford, J. B., & Zelditch, M., Jr. (1988). A test of the law of anticipated reactions. *Social Psychology Quarterly, 51*, 164–171.

Forness, S., Bennett, L., & Tose, J. (1983). Academic deficits in emotionally disturbed children revisited. *Journal of the American Academy of Child Psychiatry, 22*, 140–144.

Forness, S. R., & Knitzer, J. (1992). A new proposed definition and terminology to replace "Serious Emotional Disturbance" in individuals with disabilities education act. *School Psychology Review, 21*, 12–20.

Freedman, J. L., & Fraser, S. C. (1966). Compliance without pressure: The foot-in-the-door technique. *Journal of Personality and Social Psychology, 4*, 195–202.

French, J. R. P., Jr., & Raven, B. H. (1959). The bases of social power. In D. Cartwright (Ed.) *Studies in social power* (pp. 150–167). Ann Arbor, MI: Institute for Social Research.

French, W., & Bell, C. H. (1978). *Organization development* (2nd ed.). Englewood Cliffs, NJ: Prentice-Hall.

Friedrich, J., & Douglass, D. (1998). Ethics and the persuasive enterprise of teaching psychology. *American Psychologist, 53*, 549–562.

Friend, M., & Cook, L. (1992). *Interactions: Collaboration skills for school professionals.* New York: Longman.

Fuchs, D., & Fuchs, L. S. (1989). Exploring effective and efficient prereferral interventions: A component analysis of behavioral consultation. *School Psychology Review, 18*, 260–279.

Fuchs, D. Fuchs, L. S., & Bahr, M. W. (1990). Mainstream assistance teams: A scientific basis for the art of consultation. *Exceptional Children, 57*, 128–139.

Fuchs, D., Fuchs, L. S., Bahr, M. W., Fernstrom, P., & Stecker, P. M. (1990). Prereferral intervention: A prescriptive approach. *Exceptional Children, 56*, 493–513.

Fuchs, D., Fuchs, L. S., Dulan, J., Roberts, H., & Fernstrom, P. (1992). Where is the research on consultation effectiveness? *Journal of Educational and Psychological Consultation, 3*, 151–174.

Fuchs, L. S., & Fuchs, D. (1986a). Effects of systematic formative evaluation: A meta-analysis. *Exceptional Children, 53*, 199–208.

Fuchs, L. S., & Fuchs, D. (1986b). Linking assessment to instructional intervention: An overview. *School Psychology Review, 15*, 318–323.

Fuchs, L. S., Fuchs, D., Hamlett, C. L., & Allinder, R. M. (1991). Effects of expert system advice within curriculum-based measurement on teacher planning and student achievement in spelling. *School Psychology Review, 20*, 49–66.

Furlong, M., & Morrison, G. (Eds.). (1994). School violence. [Special issue]. *School Psychology Review, 23*(2).

Furlong, M., Morrison, G., & Pavelski, R. (2000). Trends in school psychology for the 21st century: Influences of school violence on professional change. *Psychology in the Schools, 37*, 81–90.

Gallessich, J. (1982). *The profession and practice of consultation*. San Francisco: Jossey-Bass.

Gelzheiser, L. M., Meyers, J., & Prusek, R. M. (1992). Effects of pull-in and pull-out approaches to reading instruction for special education and remedial reading students. *Journal of Educational and Psychological Consultation, 3*, 133–149.

Gersten, R., Woodward, J., & Darch, C. (1986). Direct-instruction: A research-based approach to curriculum design and teaching. *Exceptional Children, 53*, 17–31.

Gettinger, M. (1986). Issues and trends in academic engaged time of students. *Special Services in the Schools, 2*, 1–17.

Gettinger, M. (1988). Methods of proactive classroom management. *School Psychology Review, 17*, 227–242.

Giangreco, M. F. (1989). *Making related service decisions for students with severe handicaps in public schools: Roles, criteria, and authority*. Unpublished doctoral dissertation, Syracuse University.

Gillat, A., & Sulzer-Azaroff, B. (1994). Promoting principals' managerial involvement in instructional improvement. *Journal of Applied Behavior Analysis, 27*, 115–129.

Gilliam, J. E. (1979). Contributions and status rankings of educational planning committee participants. *Exceptional Children, 45*, 466–468.

Goffman, E. (1967). *Interaction ritual: Essays on face to face behavior*. Garden City, NY: Anchor.

Goldbaum, J., & Rucker, C. N. (1977). Assessment data and the child study team. In J. A. C. Vautour & C.N. Rucker (Eds.), *Child study team training program: Book of readings*. Austin, TX: Special Education Associates.

Goldstein, A. P., & Higginbotham, H. N. (1991). Relationship-enhancement methods. In F. H. Kanfer & A. P. Goldstein (Eds.), *Helping people change: A textbook of methods* (4th ed., pp. 20–69). New York: Pergamon.

Goldstein, A. P., & Martens, B. K. (2000). *Lasting change: Methods for enhancing generalization of gain*. Champaign, IL: Research Press.

Goldstein, S., Strickland, B., Turnbull, A. P., & Curry, L. (1980). An observational analysis of the IEP conference. *Exceptional Children, 46*, 278–286.

Good, R. H. & Salvia, J. (1988). Curriculum bias in published, norm-referenced reading tests: Demonstrable effects. *School Psychology Review, 17*, 51–60.

Good, R. H., Vollmer, M., Creek, R. J., Katz, L., & Chowdhri, S. (1993). Treatment utility of the Kaufman Assessment Battery for Children: Effects of matching instruction and student processing strength. *School Psychology Review, 22*, 8–26.

Good, T. L. (1983). Classroom research: A decade of progress. *Educational Psychologist, 18,* 137–144.

Good, T. L., & Brophy, J. E. (2000). *Looking in classrooms* (8th ed.). New York: Longman.

Gopaul-McNicol, S. (Ed.) (1992). Understanding and meeting the psychological and educational needs of African-American and Spanish-speaking students [Special issue]. *School Psychology Review, 21*(4).

Gordon, R. (1983). An operational classification of disease prevention. *Public Health Reports, 98,* 107–109.

Gordon, R. (1987). An operational classification of disease prevention. In J. A. Steinberg & M. M. Silverman (Eds.), *Preventing mental disorders* (pp. 20–26). Rockville, MD: U.S. Department of Health and Human Services.

Gouldner, A. W. (1960). The norm of reciprocity: A preliminary statement. *American Sociological Review, 35,* 161–178.

Graden, J. L., Casey, A., & Bonstrom, O. (1985). Implementing a prereferral intervention system: Part II. The data. *Exceptional Children, 51,* 487–496.

Graden, J. L., Casey, A., & Christenson, S. L. (1985). Implementing a prereferral intervention system: I. The model. *Exceptional Children, 51,* 377–384.

Grant, W. V., & Snyder, T. D. (1986). *Digest of education statistics 1985–1986.* Washington, DC: Government Printing Office

Greenwood, C. R., Carta, J. J., & Hall, R. V. (1988). The use of peer tutoring strategies in classroom management and educational instruction. *School Psychology Review, 17,* 258–275.

Gresham, F. M. (1985). Behavior disorder assessment: Conceptual, definitional, and practical considerations. *School Psychology Review, 14,* 495–509.

Gresham, F. M. (1989). Assessment of treatment integrity in school consultation and prereferral intervention. *School Psychology Review, 18,* 37–50.

Gresham, F. M. (1991). Conceptualizing behavior disorders in terms of resistance to intervention. *School Psychology Review, 20,* 23–36.

Gresham, F. M., & Davis, C. J. (1988). Behavioral interviews with teachers and parents. In E. S. Shapiro & T. R. Kratochwill (Eds.), *Behavioral assessment in schools: Conceptual foundations and practical applications* (455–493). New York: Guilford.

Gresham, F. M., & Gansle, K. A. (1992). Misguided assumptions of *DSM-III-R*: Implications for school psychological practice. *School Psychology Quarterly, 7,* 79–95.

Gresham, F. M., Gansle, K. A., & Noell, G.H. (1993). Treatment integrity in applied behavior analysis with children. *Journal of Applied Behavior Analysis, 26,* 257–263.

Gresham, F. M., & Kendell, G. K. (1987). School consultation research: Methodological critique and future research directions. *School Psychology Review, 16,* 306–316.

Gresham, F. M., & Noell, G. H. (1993). Documenting the effectiveness of consultation outcomes. In J. E. Zins, T. R. Kratochwill, & S. N. Elliott (Eds.), *Handbook of consultation services for children: Applications in educational and clinical settings* (pp. 249–273). San Francisco: Jossey-Bass.

Gresham, F.M., & Reschly, D. J. (1986). Social skills deficits and low peer acceptance of mainstreamed learning disabled children. *Learning Disability Quarterly, 9,* 23–32.

Gresham, F. M., Reschly, D. J., & Carey, M. P. (1987). Teachers as "tests": Classification accuracy and concurrent validation in the identification of learning disabled children. *School Psychology Review, 16,* 543–553.

Grossman, H. J. (1983). *Classification in mental retardation.* Washington, DC: American Association on Mental Deficiency.

Gursky, D. (2000, December/2001, January). Supply and demand: The teacher shortage: How bad is it? What's being done about it? *American Teacher,* 12–13, 17.

Gutkin, T. B. (1980). Teacher perceptions of consultation services provided by school psychologists. *Professional Psychology, 11,* 637–642.

Gutkin, T. B. (1981). Relative frequency of consultee lack of knowledge, skill, confidence, and objectivity in school settings. *Journal of School Psychology, 19*, 57–61.

Gutkin, T. B. (1986). Consultees' perceptions of variables relating to the outcomes of school-based consultation interactions. *School Psychology Review, 15*, 375–382.

Gutkin, T. B. (1999a). Collaborative versus directive/prescriptive/expert school-based consultation: Reviewing and resolving a false dichotomy. *Journal of School Psychology, 37*, 161–190.

Gutkin, T. B. (1999b). The collaboration debate: Finding our way through the maze: Moving forward into the future: A response to Erchul (1999). *Journal of School Psychology, 37*, 229–241.

Gutkin, T. B., & Conoley, J. C. (1990). Reconceptualizing school psychology from a service delivery perspective: Implications for practice, training, and research. *Journal of School Psychology, 28*, 203–223.

Gutkin, T. B., & Curtis, M. J. (1982). School-based consultation: Theory and techniques. In C. R. Reynolds & T. B. Gutkin (Eds.), *The handbook of school psychology* (pp. 796–828). New York: Wiley.

Gutkin T. B., & Curtis, M. J. (1990). School-based consultation: Theory, techniques, and research. In T.B. Gutkin & C.R. Reynolds (Eds.), *The handbook of school psychology* (2nd ed., pp. 577–611). New York: Wiley.

Gutkin, T. B., Henning-Stout, M., & Piersel, W. C. (1988). Impact of a district-wide behavioral consultation prereferral intervention service on patterns of school psychological service delivery. *Professional School Psychology, 3*, 301–308.

Gutkin, T. B., & Hickman, J. A. (1988). Teachers' perceptions of control over presenting problems and resulting preferences for consultation versus referral services. *Journal of School Psychology, 26*, 395–398.

Halpin, A. (1966). *Theory and research in administration.* New York: Macmillan.

Happe, D. (1982). Behavioral intervention: It doesn't do any good in your briefcase. In J. Grimes (Ed.), *Psychological approaches to problems of children and adolescents* (pp. 15–41). Des Moines, IA: Iowa Department of Public Instruction.

Haring, N. G., & Eaton, M. D. (1978). Systematic instructional procedures: An instructional hierarchy. In N.G. Haring, T.C. Lovitt, M. D. Eaton & C. L. Hansen, (Eds.), *The fourth R: Research in the classroom.* Columbus, OH: Charles E. Merrill.

Haring, N. G., Lovitt, T. C., Eaton, M. D., & Hansen, C. L. (1978). *The fourth R: Research in the classroom.* Columbus, OH: Charles E. Merrill.

Harris, A. M., & Cancelli, A. A. (1991). Teachers as consultees: Enthusiastic, willing, or resistant participants? *Journal of Educational and Psychological Consultation, 2*, 217–238.

Harris, K. R. (1985). Definitional, parametric, and procedural considerations in timeout interventions and research. *Exceptional Children, 51*, 279–288.

Hayes, S. C. (1981). Single case experimental design and empirical clinical practice. *Journal of Consulting and Clinical Psychology, 49*, 198–211.

Hayes, S. C., Nelson, R. O., & Jarrett, R. B. (1986). Evaluating the quality of behavioral assessment. In R. O. Nelson & S. C. Hayes (Eds.), *Conceptual foundations of behavioral assessment* (pp. 463–503). New York: Guilford.

Heller, K., & Monahan, J. (1977). *Psychology and community change.* Homewood, IL: Dorsey.

Henning-Stout, M. (1993). Theoretical and empirical bases of consultation. In J. E. Zins, T. R. Kratochwill & S. N. Elliott (Eds.), *Handbook of consultation services for children: Applications in educational and clinical settings* (pp. 15–45). San Francisco: Jossey-Bass.

Hersch, C. (1968). The discontent explosion in mental health. *American Psychologist, 23*, 497–506.

Hintze, J. M. (1998). Review of *School Consultation: Conceptual and Empirical Bases of Practice. Journal of Educational and Psychological Consultation, 9*, 165–169.

Hiralall, A. S., & Martens, B. K. (1998). Teaching classroom management skills to preschool staff: The effects of scripted instructional sequences on teacher and student behavior. *School Psychology Quarterly, 13,* 94–115.

Hobbs, N. (1963). Strategies for the development of clinical psychology. *American Psychological Association Division of Clinical Psychology Newsletter, 16,* 3–5.

Hobbs, N. (1964). Mental health's third revolution. *American Journal of Orthopsychiatry, 34,* 822–833.

Hobbs, N. (1966). Helping disturbed children: Psychological and ecological strategies. *American Psychologist, 21,* 1105–1115.

Hoff, K., & Zirkel, P. (1999, December). The IDEA's final regulations: Our Top Ten list for school psychologists. *NASP Communique, 28*(4), 6–7.

Hollingshead, A. B., & Redlich, F. C. (1958). *Social class and mental illness: A community study.* New York: Wiley.

Holtgraves, T. (1992). The linguistic realization of face management: Implications for language production and comprehension, person perception, and cross-cultural communications. *Social Psychology Quarterly, 55,* 141–159.

Holtgraves, T., & Yang, J. (1990). Politeness as universal: Cross-cultural perceptions of request strategies and inferences based on their use. *Journal of Personality and Social Psychology, 59,* 719–729.

Horner, R. H. (1994). Functional assessment: Contributions and future directions. *Journal of Applied Behavior Analysis, 27,* 401–404.

Hughes, J. N. (1986). Ethical issues in school consultation. *School Psychology Review, 15,* 489–499.

Hughes, J. N. (1992). Social psychology foundations of consultation. In F. J. Medway & T. P. Cafferty (Eds.), *School psychology: A social psychological perspective.* Hillsdale, NJ: Erlbaum.

Hughes, J. N., Erchul, W. P., Yoon, J., Jackson, T., & Henington, C. (1997). Consultant use of questions and its relationship to consultee evaluation of effectiveness. *Journal of School Psychology, 35,* 281–297.

Hughes, J. N., & Falk, R. (1981). Resistance, reactance, and consultation. *Journal of School Psychology, 19,* 134–142.

Hughes, J. N., Grossman, P., & Barker, D. (1990). Teacher expectancies, participation in consultation, and perceptions of consultant helpfulness. *School Psychology Quarterly, 5,* 167–179.

Hyman, I., Duffey, J., Caroll, R., Manni, J., & Winikur, D. (1973). Patterns of interprofessional conflict resolution on school child study teams. *Journal of School Psychology, 11,* 187–195.

Idol, L., & West, J. F. (1987). Consultation in special education (Part II): Training and practice. *Journal of Learning Disabilities, 20,* 474–494.

Ingraham, C. L. (2000). Consultation through a multicultural lens: Multicultural and cross-cultural consultation in schools. *School Psychology Review, 29,* 320–343.

Iscoe, I. (1993). Gerald Caplan's conceptual and qualitative contributions to community psychology: Views from an old timer. In W. P. Erchul (Ed.), *Consultation in community, school, and organizational practice: Gerald Caplan's contributions to professional psychology* (pp. 87–98). Washington, DC: Taylor & Francis.

Iwata, B. A., Dorsey, M. F., Slifer, K. J., Bauman, K. E., & Richman, G. S. (1994). Toward a functional analysis of self-injury. *Journal of Applied Behavior Analysis, 27,* 215–240. (Reprinted from *Analysis and Intervention in Developmental Disabilities, 2,* 1–20, 1982.)

Iwata, B. A., Pace, G. M., Dorsey, M. F., Zarcone, J. R., Vollmer, T. R., Smith, R. G., Rodgers, T. A., Lerman, D. C., Shore, B. A., Mazaleski, J. L., Goh, H., Cowdery, G. E., Kalsher, M. J., McCosh, K. C., & Willis, K. D. (1994). The functions of self-injurious behavior: An experimental-epidemiological analysis. *Journal of Applied Behavior Analysis, 27,* 215–240.

Jackson, P. (1968). *Life in classrooms*. New York: Holt, Rinehart & Winston.

Jenkins, J. R., & Pany, D. (1978). Standardized achievement tests: How useful for special education? *Exceptional Children, 44*, 448–453.

Johnson, P. (1976). Women and power: Toward a theory of effectiveness. *Journal of Social Issues, 32*(3), 99–110.

Jones, E. E., & Pittman, T. S. (1982). Toward a general theory of strategic interaction. In J. Suls (Ed.), *Psychological perspectives of self* (Vol. 1, pp. 231–263). Hillsdale, NJ: Erlbaum.

Joyce, B., & Showers, B. (1981). Improving inservice training: The messages of research. *Educational Leadership, 39*, 379–385.

Kavale, K. (1990). Effectiveness of special education. In T. B. Gutkin & C. R. Reynolds (Eds.), *Handbook of school psychology* (2nd ed., pp. 868–898). New York: John Wiley.

Kazdin, A. E. (1980). Acceptability of alternative treatments for deviant child behavior. *Journal of Applied Behavior Analysis, 13*, 259–273.

Kazdin, A. E. (1994). *Behavior modification in applied settings*. Pacific Grove, CA: Brooks/Cole.

Kelly, J. G. (1993). Gerald Caplan's paradigm: Bridging psychotherapy and public health practice. In W. P. Erchul (Ed.), *Consultation in community, school, and organizational practice: Gerald Caplan's contributions to professional psychology* (pp 75–85). Washington, DC: Taylor & Francis.

Kern, L., Childs, K. E., Dunlap, G., Clarke, S., & Falk, G. D. (1994). Using assessment-based curricular intervention to improve the classroom behavior of a student with emotional and behavioral challenges. *Journal of Applied Behavior Analysis, 27*, 7–19.

Kern, L., Mauk, J. E., Marder, T. J., & Mace, F. C. (1995). Functional analysis and intervention for breath holding. *Journal of Applied Behavior Analysis, 28*, 339–340.

Kinsala, M. G. (1985). An investigation of variables affecting perceived consultation outcome: A utilization of expert and referent power theory (Doctoral dissertation, Texas Women's University, 1984). *Dissertation Abstracts International, 45*, 3922B.

Kipnis, D. (1994). Accounting for the use of behavior technologies in social psychology. *American Psychologist, 49*, 165–172.

Kirby, J. H. (1985). *Consultation: Practice and practitioner*. Muncie, IN: Accelerated Development.

Kounin, J. (1970). *Discipline and group management in classrooms*. New York: Holt, Rinehart & Winston.

Kratochwill, T. R., & Bergan, J. R. (1990). *Behavioral consultation in applied settings: An individual guide*. New York: Plenum.

Kratochwill, T. R., & Stoiber, K. C. (2000). Empirically supported interventions and school psychology: Conceptual and practice issues - Part II. *School Psychology Quarterly, 15*, 233–253.

Kratochwill, T. R., VanSomeren, K. R., & Sheridan, S. M. (1989). Training behavioral consultants: A competency-based model to teacher interview skills. *Professional School Psychology, 4*, 41–58.

Kruger, R. H. (1984). The effects of problem-related stress, consultant's approach, and consultant's source of social power on teacher reactions to behavioral consultation (Doctoral dissertation, University of Cincinnati, 1983). *Dissertation Abstracts International, 44*, 3637A–3638A.

Lalli, J. S., Browder, D. M., Mace, F. C., & Brown, D. K. (1993). Teacher use of descriptive analysis data to implement interventions to decrease students' problem behaviors. *Journal of Applied Behavior Analysis, 26*, 227–238.

Lambert, N. M. (1976). Children's problems and classroom interventions from the perspective of classroom teachers. *Professional Psychology, 7*, 507–517.

Lentz, F. E. (1988). On-task behavior, academic performance, and classroom disruptions: Untangling the target selection problem in classroom interventions. *School Psychology Review, 17*, 243–257.

Lentz, F. E., & Daly, E. J. (1996). Is the behavior of academic change agents controlled meta-physically?: An analysis of the behavior of those who change behavior. *School Psychology Quarterly, 11,* 337–352.

Levinson, H. (1972). *Organizational diagnosis.* Cambridge, MA: Harvard University Press.

Lewin, K. (1952). Group decision and social change. In G. E. Swanson, T. M. Newcomb, & E. L. Hartley (Eds.), *Readings in social psychology* (2nd ed., pp. 459–473). New York: Holt, Rinehart & Winston.

Lieberman, M. A., Yalom, I. D., & Miles, M. B. (1973). *Encounter groups: First facts.* New York: Basic Books.

Lippitt, G., & Lippitt, R. (1986). *The consulting process in action* (2nd ed.). San Diego, CA: University Associates.

Lipsey, M. W., & Wilson, D. B. (1993). The efficacy of psychological, educational, and behavioral treatment: Confirmation from meta-analysis. *American Psychologist, 48,* 1181–1209.

Lloyd, J. W., Singh, N. N., & Repp, A. C. (Eds.). (1991). *The regular education initiative: Alternative perspectives on concepts issues and models.* Sycamore, IL: Sycamore.

Lortie, D. C. (1975). *Schoolteacher: A sociological study.* Chicago: University of Chicago Press.

Lundervold, D., & Bourland, G. (1988). Quantitative analysis of treatment of aggression, self-injury, and property destruction. *Behavior Modification, 12,* 591–617.

Mace, F. C., & Lalli, J. S. (1991). Linking descriptive and experimental analyses in the treatment of bizarre speech. *Journal of Applied Behavior Analysis, 24,* 553–562.

Maher, C. A., & Bennett, R. E. (1984). *Planning and evaluating special education services.* Englewood Cliffs, NJ: Prentice-Hall.

Mannino, F. V., & Shore, M. F. (1971). *Consultation research in mental health and related fields.* Public Health Monograph No. 79. Washington, DC: U.S. Government Printing Office.

Mannino, F. V., & Shore, M. F. (1975). The effects of consultation: A review of the literature. *American Journal of Community Psychology, 3,* 1–21.

Mansfield, W., Alexander, D., & Farris, E. (1991, November). *Teacher survey on safe, disciplined, and drug-free schools.* Washington, DC: National Center for Education Statistics, U.S. Department of Education, Office of Educational Research and Improvement (#NCES 91–091).

Marks, E. S. (1995). *Entry strategies for school consultation.* New York: Guilford.

Martens, B. K. (1993a). A behavioral approach to consultation. In J. E. Zins, T. R. Kratochwill & S. N. Elliott (Eds.), *Handbook of consultation services for children: Applications in educational and clinical settings* (pp. 65–86). San Francisco: Jossey-Bass.

Martens, B. K. (1993b). A case against magical thinking in school-based intervention. *Journal of Educational and Psychological Consultation, 4,* 185–189.

Martens, B. K. (1993c). Social labeling, precision of measurement, and problem solving: Key issues in the assessment of children's emotional problems. *School Psychology Review, 22,* 308–312.

Martens, B. K. (1996). *Helping teachers design effective school-based interventions.* Invited workshop at the Syracuse City School District Summer Academy for School Psychologists, Syracuse, NY.

Martens, B. K., & Ardoin, S. P. (in press). Training school psychologists in behavior support consultation. *Child and Family Behavior Therapy.*

Martens, B. K., Deery, K. S., & Gherardi, J. P. (1991). An experimental analysis of reflected affect versus reflected content in consultative interactions. *Journal of Educational and Psychological Consultation, 2,* 117–132.

Martens, B. K., Eckert, T. L. (2000). The essential role of data in psychological theory. *Journal of School Psychology, 38,* 369–376.

Martens, B. K., Eckert, T. L., Bradley, T. A., & Ardoin, S. P. (1999). Identifying effective treatments from a brief experimental analysis: Using single-case design elements to aid decision making. *School Psychology Quarterly, 14,* 163–181.

Martens, B. K., Erchul, W. P., & Witt, J. C. (1992). Quantifying verbal interactions in school-based consultation: A comparison of four coding schemes. *School Psychology Review, 21*, 109–124.

Martens, B. K., Hiralall, A. S., & Bradley, T. A. (1997). A note to teacher: Improving student behavior through goal setting and feedback. *School Psychology Quarterly, 12*, 33–41.

Martens, B. K., & Kelly, S. Q. (1993). A behavioral analysis of effective teaching. *School Psychology Quarterly, 8*, 10–26.

Martens, B. K., Kelly, S. Q., & Diskin, M. T. (1996). The effects of two sequential-request strategies on teachers' acceptability and use of a classroom intervention. *Journal of Educational and Psychological Consultation, 7*, 211–221.

Martens, B. K., Lewandowski, L. J, & Houk, J. L. (1989). Correlational analysis of verbal interactions during the consultative interview and consultees' subsequent perceptions. *Professional Psychology: Research and Practice, 20*, 334–339.

Martens, B. K., & Meller, P. J. (1990). The application of behavioral principles to educational settings. In T. B. Gutkin & C. R. Reynolds (Eds.), *Handbook of school psychology* (2nd ed., pp. 614–634). New York: Wiley.

Martens, B. K., Peterson, R. L., Witt, J. C., & Cirone, S. (1986). Teacher perceptions of school based interventions. *Exceptional Children, 53*, 213–223.

Martens, B. K., Steele, E. S., Massie, D. R., & Diskin, M. T. (1995). Curriculum bias in standardized tests of reading decoding. *Journal of School Psychology, 33*, 287–296.

Martens, B. K., Witt, J. C., Daly E. J., & Vollmer, T. (1999). Behavior analysis: Theory and practice in educational settings. In C. R. Reynolds & T. B. Gutkin, (Eds.), *Handbook of school psychology* (3rd ed., pp. 638–663). New York: John Wiley & Sons.

Martin, R. (1978). Expert and referent power: A framework for understanding and maximizing consultation effectiveness. *Journal of School Psychology, 16*, 49–55.

Martin, R., & Curtis, M. (1980). Effects of age and experience of consultant and consultee on consultation outcome. *American Journal of Community Psychology, 8*, 733–736.

McDougal, J. L., Clonan, S. M., & Martens, B. K. (2000). Using organizational change procedures to promote the acceptability of prereferral intervention services: The school-based intervention team project. *School Psychology Quarterly, 15*, 149–171.

McDougall, L. M., Reschly, D. J., & Corkery, J. M. (1988). Changes in referral interviews with teachers after behavioral consultation training. *Journal of School Psychology, 26*, 225–232.

McKee, W. T., & Witt, J. C. (1990). Effective teaching: A review of instructional environmental variables. In T. B. Gutkin & C.R. Reynolds (Eds.), *The handbook of school psychology* (2nd ed., pp 823–894). New York: John Wiley.

Medway, F. J. (1979). How effective is school consultation?: A review of recent research. *Journal of School Psychology, 17*, 275–281.

Medway, F. J., & Updyke, J. F. (1985). Meta-analysis of consultation outcome studies. *American Journal of Community Psychology, 13*, 489–504.

Merrell, K. W., & Shinn, M. R. (1990). Critical variables in the learning disabilities identification process. *School Psychology Review, 19*, 74–82.

Meyers, J. Parsons, R. D., & Martin, R. (1979). *Mental health consultation in the schools.* San Francisco: Jossey-Bass.

Miller, D. L., & Kelley, M. L. (1994). The use of goal setting and contingency contracting for improving children's homework performance. *Journal of Applied Behavior Analysis, 27*, 73–84.

Mintzberg, H. (1983). *Power in and around organizations.* Englewood Cliffs, NJ: Prentice-Hall.

Morison, P. (1992). Testing in American schools: Issues for research and policy. *Social Policy Report, 6*, 1–27.

Motta, R. W., Little, S. G., & Tobin, M. I. (1993). The use and abuse of human figure drawings. *School Psychology Quarterly, 8*, 162–169.

Mrazek, P. J., & Haggerty, R. J. (Eds.) (1994). *Reducing risks for mental disorders: Frontiers for preventive intervention research.* Washington, DC: National Academy Press.

Neef, N. A., Mace, F. C., & Shade, D. (1993). Impulsivity in students with serious emotional disturbance: The interactive effects of reinforcer rate, delay, and quality. *Journal of Applied Behavior Analysis, 26*, 37–52.

Nevin, J.A. (1988). Behavioral momentum and the partial reinforcement effect. *Psychological Bulletin, 103*, 44–56.

Ng, S. H., & Bradac, J. J. (1993). *Power in language: Verbal communication and social influence.* Newbury Park, CA: Sage.

Noell, G. H., & Witt, J. C. (1996). A critical reevaluation of five fundamental assumptions of behavioral consultation. *School Psychology Quarterly, 11*, 189–203.

Noell, G. H., & Witt, J. C. (1999). When does consultation lead to intervention implementation? Critical issues for research and practice. *Journal of Special Education, 33*, 29–35.

Noell, G. H., Witt, J. C., Gilbertson, D. N., Ranier, D. D., & Freeland, J. T. (1997). Increasing teacher intervention implementation in general education settings through consultation and performance feedback. *School Psychology Quarterly, 12*, 77–88.

Noell, G. H., Witt, J. C., LaFleur, L. H., Mortenson, B. P., Ranier, D. D., & LeVelle, J. (2000). Increasing intervention implementation in general education following consultation: A comparison of two follow-up strategies. *Journal of Applied Behavior Analysis, 33*, 271–284.

North Carolina Professional Practices Commission. (1995). *Something must be done: Attracting and retaining a quality and diverse teaching force in North Carolina.* Raleigh, NC: Author.

North Carolina State Department of Public Instruction, Exceptional Children Division. (2000). *Procedures governing programs and services for children with disabilities.* Raleigh, NC: Author.

Northup, J., George, T., Jones, K., Broussard, C., & Vollmer, T. R. (1996). A comparison of reinforcer assessment methods: The utility of verbal and pictorial choice procedures. *Journal of Applied Behavior Analysis, 29*, 201–212.

O'Keefe, D. J., & Medway, F. J. (1997). The application of persuasion research to consultation in school psychology. *Journal of School Psychology, 35*, 173–193.

Ost, D. H. (1991). The culture of teaching: Stability and change. In N. B. Wyner (Ed.), *Current perspectives on the culture of schools* (pp. 79–93). Brookline, MA: Brookline Books.

Owens, R. G. (1981). *Organizational behavior in education* (pp. 3–40). Englewood Cliffs, NJ: Prentice-Hall.

Parsons, R. D., & Meyers, J. (1984). *Developing consultation skills.* San Francisco: Jossey-Bass.

Perry, C. L., Williams, C. L., Veblen-Mortenson, S., Toomey, T., Komro, K., Anstine, P., McGovern, P., Finnegan, J., Forster, J., Wagenaar, A., & Wolfson, M. (1996). Project Northland: Outcomes of a community wide alcohol use prevention program during early adolescence. *American Journal of Public Health, 86*, 956–965.

Peterson, F. M., & Martens, B. K. (1995). A comparison of behavioral interventions reported in treatment studies and programs for adults with developmental disabilities. *Research in Developmental Disabilities, 16*, 27–41.

Peterson, L., Homer, A., & Wonderlich, S. (1982). The integrity of independent variables in behavior analysis. *Journal of Applied Behavior Analysis, 15*, 477–492.

Pfeiffer, S. I. (1980). The school-based interprofessional team: Recurring problems and some possible solutions. *Journal of School Psychology, 18*, 388–394.

Pfeiffer, S. I. (1981). The problems facing multidisciplinary teams: As perceived by team members. *Psychology in the Schools, 18*, 330–333.

Piersel, W. C., & Gutkin, T. B. (1983). Resistance to school-based consultation: A behavioral analysis of the problem. *Psychology in the Schools, 20*, 311–320.

Plisko, V. (1984). *The condition of teaching.* Washington, DC: National Center for Education Statistics.

Ponti, C. R., Zins, J. E., & Graden, J. L. (1988). Implementing a consultation-based service delivery system to decrease referrals for special education: A case study of organizational considerations. *School Psychology Review, 17*, 89–100.

Powell, R. A., Martindale, B., & Kulp, S. (1975). An evaluation of time-sampling measures of behavior. *Journal of Applied Behavior Analysis, 8*, 463–469.

Prout, H. T. (1983). School psychologists and social-emotional assessment techniques: Patterns in training and use. *School Psychology Review, 12*, 377–383.

Pryzwansky, W. B. (1974). A reconsideration of the consultation model for delivery of school-based psychological services. *American Journal of Orthopsychiatry, 44*, 579–583.

Pryzwansky, W. B. (1977). Collaboration or consultation: Is there a difference? *Journal of Special Education, 11*, 179–182.

Pryzwansky, W. B. (1986). Indirect service delivery: Considerations for future research in consultation. *School Psychology Review, 15*, 479–488.

Ramage, J. (1979). National survey of school psychologists: Update. *School Psychology Digest, 8*, 153–161.

Ramirez, S. Z., Lepage, K. M., Kratochwill, T. R., & Duffy, J. L. (1998). Multicultural issues in school-based consultation: Conceptual and research considerations. *Journal of School Psychology, 36*, 479–509.

Rappaport, J. (1981). In praise of paradox: A social policy of empowerment over prevention. *American Journal of Community Psychology, 9*, 1–25.

Raven, B. H. (1965). Social influence and power. In I. D. Steiner and M. Fishbein (Eds.), *Current studies in social psychology* (pp. 371–381). New York, NY: Holt, Rinehart & Winston.

Raven, B. H. (1992). A power/interaction model of interpersonal influence: French and Raven thirty years later. *Journal of Social Behavior and Personality, 7*, 217–244.

Raven, B. H. (1993). The bases of power: Origins and recent developments. *Journal of Social Issues, 49*, 227–251.

Raven, B. H., & Kruglanski, A. W. (1970). Conflict and power. In P. G. Swingle (Ed.), *The structure of conflict* (pp. 69–109). New York, NY: Academic Press.

Raven, B. H., & Litman-Adizes, T. (1986). Interpersonal influence and social power in health promotion. In Z. Salisbury, S. Kar & J. Zapka (Eds.), *Advances in health education and promotion* (pp. 181–210). Greenwich, CT: JAI Press.

Raven, B. H., Schwarzwald, J., & Koslowsky, M. (1998). Conceptualizing and measuring a power/interaction model of interpersonal influence. *Journal of Applied Social Psychology, 28*, 307–332.

Reid, E. R. (1986). Practicing effective instruction: The exemplary center for reading instruction approach. *Exceptional Children, 52*, 510–519.

Reimers, T. M., Wacker, D. P., & Koeppl, G. (1987). Acceptability of behavioral interventions: A review of the literature. *School Psychology Review, 16*, 212–227.

Reppucci, N. D., & Saunders, J. T. (1974). Social psychology of behavior modification: Problems of implementation in natural settings. *American Psychologist, 29*, 649–660.

Reschly, D. J. (1988). Special education reform: School psychology revolution. *School Psychology Review, 17*, 459–475.

Reschly, D. J., Tilly, W. D., & Grimes, J. P. (Eds.) (1999). *Special education in transition: Functional and noncategorical programming.* Longmont, CO: Sopris West.

Reschly, D. J., & Wilson, M. S. (1995). School psychology practitioners and faculty: 1986 to 1991–92 trends in demographics, roles, satisfaction, and system reform. *School Psychology Review, 24*, 62–80.

Reynolds, C. R. (1981). The fallacy of "Two years below grade level for age" as a diagnostic criterion for reading disorders. *Journal of School Psychology, 19*, 350–358.

Reynolds, C. R., Gutkin, T. B., Elliott, S. N., & Witt, J. C. (1984). *School psychology: Essentials of theory and practice.* New York: Wiley.

Roberts, L. A. (1985). School psychological consultation outcomes and perception of consultant power base (Doctoral dissertation, University of Connecticut, 1984). *Dissertation Abstracts International, 46*, 382A.

Robinson, J. A., & Falconer, J. (1972). Mental health consultation to schoolteachers. In J. Zusman & D. L. Davidson (Eds.), *Practical aspects of mental health consultation* (pp. 88–95). Springfield, IL: Thomas.

Rogers, L. E., & Farace, R. V. (1975). Analysis of relational communication in dyads: New measurement procedures. *Human Communication Research, 1*, 222–239.

Rosenfield, S. (1992). Developing school-based consultation teams: A design for organizational change. *School Psychology Quarterly, 7*, 27–46.

Rosenfield, S. (2000). Crafting usable knowledge. *American Psychologist, 55*, 1347–1355.

Rosenfield, S., & Gravois, T. A. (1999). Working with teams in the school. In C. R. Reynolds & T. B. Gutkin (Eds.), *Handbook of school psychology* (3rd ed., pp. 1025–1040). New York: Wiley.

Sandoval, J., Lambert, N., & Davis, J. (1977). Consultation from the consultee's perspective. *Journal of School Psychology, 15*, 334–342.

Sarason, I. G., & Sarason, B. R. (1986). Experimentally provided social support. *Journal of Personality and Social Psychology, 50*, 1222–1225.

Sarason, S. B. (1971). *The culture of the school and the problem of change.* Boston, MA: Allyn & Bacon.

Sarason, S. B. (1982). *The culture of the school and the problem of change* (2nd ed.). Boston: Allyn & Bacon.

Sarason, S. B. (1996). *Revisiting "The culture of the school and the problem of change."* New York: Teachers College Press, Columbia University.

Sarason, S. B., Levine, M., Goldenberg, I. I., Cherlin, D. L., & Bennett, E. M. (1966). *Psychology in community settings: Clinical, educational, vocational, social aspects.* New York: Wiley.

Saudargas, R. A., & Lentz, F. E. (1986). Estimating percent of time and rate via direct observation: A suggested observational procedure and format. *School Psychology Review, 15*, 36–48.

Schein, E. H. (1969). *Process consultation: Its role in organization development.* Reading, MA: Addison-Wesley.

Schlenker, B. R. (1980). *Impression management: The self-concept, social identity, and interpersonal relations.* Monterey, CA: Brooks/Cole.

Schulberg, H. C., & Killilea, M. (1982). Community mental health in transition. In H. C. Schulberg & M. Killilea (Eds.), *The modern practice of community mental health: A volume in honor of Gerald Caplan* (pp. 40–94). San Francisco: Jossey-Bass.

Schulte, A. C., Osborne, S. S., & Erchul, W. P. (1998). Effective special education: A United States dilemma. *School Psychology Review, 27*, 66–76.

Shapiro, E. S., & Derr, T. F. (1987). An examination of overlap between reading curricula and standardized achievement tests. *The Journal of Special Education, 21*, 59–67.

Sheridan, S. M., & Kratochwill, T. R. (1992). Behavioral parent-teacher consultation: Conceptual and research considerations. *Journal of School Psychology, 30*, 117–139.

Sheridan, S. M., Kratochwill, T. R., & Bergan, J. R. (1996). *Conjoint behavioral consultation: A procedural manual.* New York: Plenum.

Sheridan, S. M., Kratochwill, T. R., & Elliott, S. N. (1990). Behavioral consultation with parents and teachers: Applications with socially withdrawn children. *School Psychology Review, 19*, 33–52.

Sheridan, S. M., Welch, M., & Orme, S. F. (1996). Is consultation effective? A review of outcome research. *Remedial and Special Education, 17*, 341–354.

Shinn, M. R. (1986). Does anyone care what happens after the refer-test-place sequence: The systematic evaluation of special education program effectiveness. *School Psychology Review, 15*, 49–58.

Shinn, M. R. (1989). *Curriculum-based measurement: Assessing special children*. New York: Guilford.

Shinn, M. R., Rosenfield, S., & Knutson, N. (1989). Curriculum-based assessment: A comparison of models. *School Psychology Review, 18*, 299–316.

Short, R. J., Moore, S. C., & Williams, C. (1991). Social influence in consultation: Effect of degree and experience on consultees' perceptions. *Psychological Reports, 68*, 131–137.

Showers, B. (1990). Aiming for superior classroom instruction for all children: A comprehensive staff development model. *Remedial and Special Education, 11*, 35–39.

Singer, J., Bossard, M., & Watkins, M. (1977). Effects of parental presence on attendance and input of interdisciplinary teams in an institutional setting. *Psychological Reports, 41*, 1031–1034.

Singh, N. N. (1990). Effects of two error-correction procedures on oral reading errors: Word supply versus sentence repeat. *Behavior Modification, 14*, 188–199.

Sirotnik, K. A. (1983). What you see is what you get—consistency, persistency, and mediocrity in classrooms. *Harvard Educational Review, 53*, 16–31.

Skinner, C. H., McLaughlin, T. F., & Logan, P. (1997). Cover, copy, and compare: A self-managed academic intervention effective across skills, students, and settings. *Journal of Behavioral Education, 7*, 295–306.

Smith, D. K. (1984). Practicing school psychologists: Their characteristics, activities, and populations served. *Professional Psychology: Research and Practice, 15*, 798–810.

Smith, M. L., & Glass, G. V. (1977). Meta-analysis of psychotherapy outcome studies. *American Psychologist, 32*, 752–760.

Stein, L. I. (1971). Male and female: The doctor–nurse game. In J. P. Spradley & D. W. McCurdy (Eds.), *Conformity and conflict: Readings in cultural anthropology* (pp. 185–193). Boston: Little, Brown.

Stenger, M. K., Tollefson, N., & Fine, M. J. (1992). Variables that distinguish elementary teachers who participate in school-based consultation from those who do not. *School Psychology Quarterly, 7*, 271–284.

Stoiber, K. C., & Kratochwill, T. R. (2000). Empirically supported interventions and school psychology: Rationale and methodological issues—Part I. *School Psychology Quarterly, 15*, 75–105.

Stokes, T. F., & Baer, D. M. (1977). An implicit technology of generalization. *Journal of Applied Behavior Analysis, 19*, 349–367.

Stoner, G., Carey, S. P., Ikeda, M. J., & Shinn, M. R. (1994). The utility of curriculum-based measurement for evaluating the effects of methylphenidate on academic performance. *Journal of Applied Behavior Analysis, 27*, 101–113.

Sugai, G. M., & Tindal, G. A. (1993). *Effective school consultation*. Pacific Grove, CA: Brooks/Cole.

Supply and demand: The teacher shortage: Teacher recruitment: Pulling out all the stops. (2001, March). *American Teacher, 10–11,* 17.

Swanson, J. M. (1992). *School-based assessments and interventions for ADD students*. Irvine, CA: K.C. Publishing.

Szasz, T. S. (1960). The myth of mental illness. *American Psychologist, 15*, 113–118.

Tagiuri, R., & Litwin, G. H. (1968). *Organizational climate: Explorations of a concept*. Boston, MA: Harvard University Press.

Tannen, D. (1994). *Talking from 9 to 5: Women and men in the workplace: Language, sex, and power*. New York: Avon Books.

Tardy, C. H. (1994). Counteracting task-induced stress: Studies of instrumental and emotional support in problem-solving contexts. In B. R. Burleson, T. L. Albrecht, & I. G. Sarason (Eds.), *Communication of social support: Messages. interactions relationships, and community* (pp. 71–87). Thousand Oaks, CA: Sage.

Telzrow, C. F. (1999). IDEA amendments of 1997: Promise or pitfall for special education reform? *Journal of School Psychology, 37,* 7–28.

Telzrow, C. F., & Tankersley, M. (Eds.) (2000). *IDEA Amendments of 1997: Practice guidelines for school-based teams.* Bethesda, MD: National Association of School Psychologists.

Tharp, R. G., & Wetzel, R. J. (1969). *Behavior modification in the natural environment.* New York: Academic Press.

Thurlow, M. L., & Ysseldyke, J. E. (1982). Instructional planning: Information collected by school psychologists vs. information considered useful by teachers. *Journal of School Psychology, 20,* 3–10.

Tindall, R. H. (1979). School psychology: Development of a profession. In G. D. Phye & D. J. Reschly (Eds.), *School psychology: Perspectives and issues* (pp. 3–24). New York: Academic Press.

Tombari, M. L., & Bergan, J. R. (1978). Consultant cues and teacher verbalizations, judgments, and expectancies concerning children's adjustment problems. *Journal of School Psychology, 16,* 212–219.

Touchette, P. E., MacDonald, R. F., & Langer, S. N. (1985). A scatter plot for identifying stimulus control of problem behavior. *Journal of Applied Behavior Analysis, 18,* 343–351.

Tracey, T. J., & Ray, P. B. (1984). Stages of successful time-limited counseling: An interactional examination. *Journal of Counseling Psychology, 31,* 13–27.

Trickett, E. J. (1993). Gerald Caplan and the unfinished business of community psychology: A comment. In W. P. Erchul (Ed.), *Consultation in community school, and organizational practice: Gerald Caplan's contributions to professional psychology* (pp. 163–175). Washington, DC: Taylor & Francis.

Trickett, E. J., Dahiyat, C., & Selby, P. M. (1994). *Primary prevention in mental health: An annotated bibliography 1983–1991* (NIH Publication No. 94–3767). Washington, DC: U.S. Government Printing Office.

Ullmann, L. P., & Krasner, L. (1969). *A psychological approach to abnormal behavior.* Englewood Cliffs, NJ: Prentice-Hall.

United States Department of Education. (1987). *Ninth annual report to Congress on the implementation of the Education of the Handicapped Act (Vol. I).* Washington, DC: U.S. Department of Educational Series, Special Education Programs.

Vernberg, E. M., & Reppucci, N. D. (1986). Behavioral consultation. In F. V. Mannino, E. J. Trickett, M. F. Shore, M. G. Kidder, & G. Levin (Eds.), *Handbook of mental health consultation* (DHHS Publication No. ADM 86–1446, pp. 49–80). Washington, DC: U.S. Government Printing Office.

Von Brock, M. B., & Elliott, S. N. (1987). The influence of treatment effectiveness information on the acceptability of classroom interventions. *Journal of School Psychology, 25,* 131–144.

Walster, E. & Festinger, L. (1962). The effectiveness of "overheard" persuasive communications. *Journal of Abnormal and Social Psychology, 65,* 395–402.

Walster, E., Walster, G. W., & Berscheid, E. (1978). *Equity theory and research.* Boston, MA: Allyn & Bacon.

Webster, R. E., McInnis, E. D., & Craver, L. (1986). Curriculum biasing effects in standardized and criterion-referenced reading achievement tests. *Psychology in the Schools, 23,* 205–213.

Weinstein, C. S. (1991). The classroom as a social context for learning. *Annual Review of Psychology, 42,* 493–525.

Welch, M., & Tulbert, B. (2000). Practitioners' perspectives of collaboration: A social validation and factor analysis. *Journal of Educational and Psychological Consultation, 11,* 357–378.

Wickstrom, K. F., & Witt, J. C. (1993). Resistance within school-based consultation. In J. E. Zins, T. R. Kratochwill, and S. N. Elliott (Eds.), *Handbook of consultation services for children: Applications in educational and clinical settings* (pp. 159–178). San Francisco, CA: Jossey-Bass.

Witt, J. C. (1990). Collaboration in school-based consultation: Myth in need of data. *Journal of Educational and Psychological Consultation, 1,* 367–370.

Witt, J. C. (1997). Talk is not cheap. School is not cheap. *School Psychology, 12,* 281–292.

Witt, J. C., Daly, E. M., & Noell, G. (2000). *Functional assessments: A step-by-step guide to solving academic and behavior problems.* Longmont, CO: Sopris West.

Witt, J. C., & Elliott, S. N. (1985). Acceptability of classroom management strategies. In T. R. Kratochwill (Ed.), *Advances in school psychology* (Vol. 4, pp. 251–288). Hillsdale, NJ: Erlbaum.

Witt, J. C., Erchul, W. P., McKee, W. T., Pardue, M. M., & Wickstrom, K. F. (1991). Conversational control in school-based consultation: The relationship between consultant and consultee topic determination and consultation outcome. *Journal of Educational and Psychological Consultation, 2,* 101–116.

Witt, J. C., Hannafin, M. J., & Martens, B. K. (1983). Home-based reinforcement: Behavioral covariation between academic performance and inappropriate behavior. *Journal of School Psychology, 21,* 337–348.

Witt, J. C., Noell, G. H., La Fleur, L. H., & Mortenson, B. P. (1997). Teacher usage of interventions in general education: Measurement and analysis of the independent variable. *Journal of Applied Behavior Analysis, 30,* 693–696.

Witt, J. C., & Martens, B. K. (1983). Assessing the acceptability of behavioral interventions used in classrooms. *Psychology in the Schools, 20,* 510–517.

Witt, J. C., & Martens, B. K. (1984). Adaptive behavior: Tests and assessment issues. *School Psychology Review, 13,* 478–484.

Witt, J. C., & Martens, B. K. (1988). Problems with problem-solving consultation: A re-analysis of assumptions, methods, and goals. *School Psychology Review, 17,* 211–226.

Witt, J. C., Martens, B. K., & Elliott, S. N. (1984). Factors affecting teachers' judgments of the acceptability of behavioral interventions: Time involvement, behavior problem severity, and type of intervention. *Behavior Therapy, 15,* 204–209.

Witt, J. C., Miller, C. D., McIntyre, R., & Smith, D. (1984). Effects of variables on parental perceptions of staffings. *Exceptional Children, 51,* 27–32.

Witt, J. C., Moe, G., Gutkin, T. B., & Andrews, L. (1984). The effect of saying the same thing in different ways: The problem of language and jargon in school-based consultation. *Journal of School Psychology, 22,* 361–367.

Witt, J., C., Noell, G. H., LaFleur, L. H., & Mortenson, B. P. (1997). Teacher usage of interventions in general education: Measurement and analysis of the independent variable. *Journal of Applied Behavior Analysis, 30,* 693–696.

Witt, J. C., & Robbins, J. R. (1985). Acceptability of reductive interventions for the control of inappropriate child behavior. *Journal of Abnormal Child Psychology, 13,* 59–67.

Wolery, M., Bailey, D. B., & Sugai, G. M. (1988). *Effective teaching: Principles and procedures of applied behavior analysis with exceptional students.* Boston: Allyn & Bacon.

Wyne, M. D., & Stuck, G. B. (1982). Time and learning: Implications for the classroom teacher. *Elementary School Journal, 83,* 67–75.

Wyner, N. B. (Ed.) (1991). *Current perspectives on the culture of schools.* Brookline, MA: Brookline Books.

Yeaton, W. H., & Sechrest, L. (1981). Critical dimensions in the choice and maintenance of successful treatments: Strength, integrity, and effectiveness. *Journal of Consulting and Clinical Psychology, 49,* 156–167.

Yell, M. L., Drasgow, E., & Ford, L. (2000). The Individuals Education Act Amendments of 1997: Implications for school-based teams. In C. F. Telzrow & M. Tankersley (Eds.), *IDEA amendments of 1997: Practice guidelines for school-based teams* (pp. 1–27). Bethesda, MD: National Association of School Psychologists.

Yoshida, R. K., Fenton, K. S., Maxwell, J. P., & Kaufman, M. J. (1978). Group decision-making in the planning team process: Myth or reality? *Journal of School Psychology, 16,* 237–244.

Ysseldyke, J. E. (1979). Issues in psychoeducational assessment. In G. D. Phye & D. J. Reschly (Eds.), *School psychology: Perspectives and issues* (pp. 87–121). New York: Academic Press.

Ysseldyke, J. E., Christenson, S. L., & Thurlow, M. L. (1987). Factors that influence student achievement: An integrative review. *Remedial and Special Education, 10,* 21–31.

Ysseldyke, J. E., Christenson, S. L., Thurlow, M. L., & Bakewell, D. (1989). Are different kinds of instructional tasks used by different categories of students in different settings? *School Psychology Review, 18,* 98–111.

Ysseldyke, J. E., & Marston, D. (1990). The use of assessment information to plan instructional interventions: A review of the research. In T. B. Gutkin & C. R. Reynolds (Eds.), *The handbook of school psychology, second edition* (pp. 661–682). New York: John Wiley.

Ysseldyke, J. E., Pianta, B., Christenson, S., Wang, J., & Algozzine, B. (1983). An analysis of prereferral interventions. *Psychology in the Schools, 20,* 184–190.

Yukl, G., & Falbe, C. M. (1991). Importance of different power sources in downward and lateral relations. *Journal of Applied Psychology, 77,* 525–535.

Zigler, E., & Phillips, L. (1961). Psychiatric diagnosis and symptomatology. *Journal of Abnormal and Social Psychology, 63,* 69–75.

Zins, J. E. (1995). Has consultation achieved its primary prevention potential? *Journal of Primary Prevention, 15,* 285–301.

Zins, J. E., & Erchul, W. P. (2002). Best practices in school consultation. In A. Thomas & J. Grimes (Eds.), *Best practices in school psychology-IV*. Bethesda, MD: National Association of School Psychologists.

Zins, J. E., Kratochwill, T. R., & Elliott, S. N. (Eds.). (1993). *The handbook of consultation services for children: Applications in educational and clinical settings*. San Francisco: Jossey-Bass.

Zubin, J. (1967). Classification of the behavior disorders. In P. R. Farnsworth, O. McNemar, & Q. McNemar (Eds.), *Annual review of psychology* (Vol. 18, pp. 373–406). Palo Alto, CA: Annual Reviews.

Author Index

Albee, G. W., 9, 98, 213
Aldrich, S. F., 107, 118, 213
Alessi, G. J., 137, 213
Alexander, D., 145, 225
Algozzine, B., 63, 69, 101, 107, 153, 172, 213, 233
Allinder, R. M., 136, 220
Allington, R. L., 57, 213
Alpert, J., 6, 14, 141, 213
Andrews, L., 102, 133, 232
Anstine, P., 148, 227
Apter, S. J., 49, 62, 168, 209, 213
Archer, R. P., 175, 213
Ardoin, S. P., 109, 115, 129, 131, 136, 225
Armbruster, B. B., 173, 213
Astor, R. A., 76, 213
Ault, M. H., 130, 214
Axelrod, S., 52, 130, 214

Babinski, L. M., 160, 214
Baer, D. M., 127, 159, 230
Bahr, M. W., 23, 24, 100, 157, 208, 220
Bailey, D. B., 122, 124, 125, 179, 180, 232
Bakewell, D., 57, 168, 178, 209, 233
Bandura, A., 151, 214
Barker, D., 151, 152, 154, 223
Barlow, D. H., 109, 214
Barnett, D. W., 117, 218
Barone, S. G., 25, 214
Barry, B., 24, 214
Bass, B. M., 40, 214
Bauman, K. E., 131, 223
Baxter, L. A., 44, 214
Becker, W. C., 57, 121, 214
Bell, C. H., 89, 219

Bell, P. F., 173, 214
Benes, K. M., 210, 214
Benne, K. D., 19, 27, 28, 101, 215
Bennett, E. M., 92, 229
Bennett, L., 175, 219
Bennett, R. E., 89, 214, 225
Bennis, W. G., 89, 214
Bergan, J. R., 14, 15, 22, 34, 70, 71, 80, 82–86, 100, 108–110, 115, 148, 149, 156, 191, 198, 210, 214, 224, 229, 231
Berkowitz, L., 35, 214
Berkowitz, M. J., 130, 214
Berry, B. T., 146, 150, 217
Berscheid, E., 35, 231
Bijou, S. W., 130, 214
Blake, R. R., 89, 214
Bonstrom, O., 89, 221
Bossard, M., 53, 56, 107, 214, 230
Bourland, G., 128, 225
Bowlby, J., 72, 215
Boyer, J., 123, 217
Bradac, J. J., 44, 227
Braden, J. P., 152, 192, 218
Bradley, T. A., 116, 131, 136, 210, 225, 226
Brandenburg, N. A., 175, 215
Brehm, J. W., 37, 215
Brophy, J. E., 56, 142, 143, 180, 215, 221
Broussard, C., 130, 132, 227
Browder, D. M., 131, 224
Brown, D., 14, 15, 75, 76, 87, 93, 155, 156, 215
Brown, D. K., 131, 215, 224
Busse, R. T., 7, 161, 215

Cancelli, A. A., 26, 148, 222

Caplan, G., 3, 4, 9, 14–18, 21, 39, 41, 70–81, 90–93, 98, 99, 106, 149, 154, 155, 160, 183, 190, 199, 215
Caplan, R. B., 4, 14, 15, 17, 39, 41, 70–72, 75, 78, 93, 155, 160, 215
Carey, M. P., 63, 221
Carey, S. P., 137, 230
Carkhuff, R. R., 9, 215
Caroll, R., 56, 223
Carta, J. J., 118, 221
Carter, J., 156, 215
Casey, A., 89, 100, 157, 174, 221
Catalan, J., 111, 216
Cherlin, D. L., 92, 229
Chewning, T. G., 22, 23, 102, 103, 150, 208, 218
Childs, K. E., 131, 224
Chin, R., 19, 27, 28, 101, 215
Chowdhri, S., 121, 136, 220
Christenson, S., 12, 15, 56, 63, 69, 89, 100, 101, 107, 153, 157, 168, 174, 178–180, 204, 209, 210, 213, 216, 221, 233
Cialdini, R. B., 111, 216
Cienki, J. A., 36, 216
Cirone, S., 101, 226
Clark, E. G., 72, 73, 216
Clarke, S., 131, 224
Clonan, S. M., 62, 66–68, 70, 100, 157, 158, 176, 226
Cohen, M. D., 51, 216
Cohen, S., 75, 216
Cohn, M. M., 143–147, 216
Cone, J. D., 137, 216
Conoley, C. W., 39, 79, 90, 92, 93, 102, 105, 216, 218
Conoley, J. C., 15, 18, 20, 28, 39, 90, 92, 93, 102, 103, 105, 111, 112, 150, 216, 222
Cook, L., 15, 219
Corkery, J. M., 100, 108, 110, 135, 226
Costenbader, V., 67, 99, 100, 141, 206, 216
Covington, C. G., 103, 218
Cowdery, G. E., 131, 223
Cowen, E., 10, 73, 216
Craver, L., 173, 231
Creek, R. J., 121, 136, 220
Crimmins, D. B., 109, 129, 217
Crowe, D. S., 36, 217
Cubberley, E. P., 49, 217
Cullinan, D., 169, 218
Curry, L., 55, 56, 220

Curtis, M. J., 8, 36, 85, 99, 101, 102, 105, 106, 110, 118, 158, 217, 225, 226, 232

Dahiyat, C., 73, 231
Daly, E. J., 105, 109, 114, 123, 124, 128, 137, 177, 190, 208, 211, 217, 225, 226, 232
Daly, J. A., 12, 24, 183, 217
Daniels, L. R., 35, 214
Darby, B. L., 111, 216
Darch, C., 210, 220
Darling-Hammond, L., 146, 150, 217
Davis, C. J., 118, 221
Davis, H., 89, 217
Davis, J., 15, 47, 217, 229
Deery, K. S., 110, 113, 210, 225
Delmolino, L. M., 120, 217
Deno, S. L., 123, 219
Derr, T. F., 173, 229
deVoss, G. G., 57, 217
Dillard, J. M., 16, 217
Diskin, M. T., 63, 107, 111, 112, 133, 173, 204, 226
Dool, E. J., 124, 177, 217
Dorr, D., 10, 216
Dorsey, M. F., 131, 223
Dougherty, A. M., 15, 217
Douglass, D., 26, 219
Doyle, W., 57, 142, 217
Drasgow, E., 129, 165, 205, 217, 232
Duffey, J., 56, 223
Duffy, J. L., 16, 228
Dulan, J., 6, 220
Duncan, B. B., 76, 213
Dunlap, G., 131, 224
Dunst, C. J., 27, 114, 217
DuPaul, G. D., 128, 131, 175, 217, 219
Durand, V. M., 109, 129, 217
D'Zurilla, T. J., 80–83, 99, 217

Eaton, M. D., 123, 128, 180, 222
Eckert, T. L., 119, 131, 136, 225
Egan, G., 16, 217
Ehrhardt, K. E., 117, 218
Elam, S. M., 145, 218
Elliott, S. N., 5, 7, 11, 12, 20, 101, 107, 133, 156, 161, 215, 218, 228, 229, 231, 232, 233
Elmquist, D. L., 175, 218
Epstein, M., 133, 169, 218
Erchul, W. P., 4, 10, 16, 17, 21–23, 25–27, 31, 34, 36, 38–41, 43, 44, 46, 48, 72, 75, 78–80, 85, 86, 93, 97–99, 102, 103, 105, 106,

Erchul, W. P. (*cont.*)
    110–112, 114, 115, 149, 150, 152, 155, 160,
    190, 191, 204, 208–211, 215, 218, 219,
    223, 226, 229, 232, 233
Erikson, E. H., 74, 219
Ervin, R. A., 128, 131, 219
Espin, C. A., 123, 219
Eysenck, H. J., 9, 98, 219

Fagan, T. K., 5, 11, 12, 20, 49, 51, 205, 219
Falbe, C. M., 40, 233
Falbo, T., 39, 219
Falconer, J., 149, 229
Falk, G. D., 131, 224
Falk, R., 26, 37, 223
Farace, R. V., 22, 229
Farris, E., 145, 224
Fenton, K. S., 55, 233
Fernstrom, P., 6, 23, 24, 208, 220
Festinger, L., 39, 231
Fideler, E., 146, 150, 217
Fine, M. J., 154, 230
Finnegan, J., 148, 227
Flugum, K. R., 66, 219
Folger, J. P., 23, 102, 219
Ford, J. B., 41, 219
Ford, L., 205, 219, 232
Forness, S., 170, 175, 219
Forster, J., 148, 227
Fraser, S. C., 111, 219
Freedman, J. L., 111, 219
Freeland, J. T., 99, 116, 199, 208, 227
French, J. R. P., 19, 29–31, 34, 35, 112, 208, 219
French, W., 89, 219
Friedman, R. M., 175, 215
Friedrich, J., 26, 219
Friend, M., 15, 219
Friman, P. C., 128, 131, 219
Fuchs, D., 6, 23, 24, 100, 134–136, 157, 173,
    180, 204, 208, 210, 219, 220
Fuchs, L. S., 6, 23, 24, 100, 134–136, 157,
    173, 180, 204, 208, 210, 219, 220
Furlong, M. J., 12, 145, 220

Gallessich, J., 10, 15, 34, 87, 91, 149, 220
Galvin, G., 133, 218
Gansle, K. A., 134, 169, 221
Gelzheiser, L. M., 12, 220
George, T., 130, 132, 227
Gersten, R., 210, 220

Gettinger, M., 51, 57, 177–180, 220
Gherardi, J. P., 110, 113, 210, 225
Giangreco, M. F., 58, 220
Gilbertson, D. N., 99, 116, 199, 208, 227
Gilliam, J. E., 55, 220
Glass, G. V, 6, 9, 120, 230
Goffman, E., 44, 220
Goh, H., 131, 223
Goldbaum, J., 56, 220
Goldenberg, I. I., 92, 229
Goldfried, M. R., 80–83, 99, 217
Goldstein, A. P., 16, 115, 123, 158–160, 220
Goldstein, S., 55, 56, 220
Good, R. H., 121, 136, 173, 220
Good, T. L., 142, 143, 168, 221
Gopaul–McNicol, S., 12, 221
Gordon, R., 73, 221
Gouldner, A. W., 35, 221
Graden, J. L., 66, 67, 89, 100, 102, 157, 173,
    174, 210, 214, 221, 228
Grant, W. V., 49, 221
Gravois, T. A., 157, 205, 229
Greenwood, C. R., 118, 221
Gresham, F. M., 6, 7, 63, 99, 109, 118, 132–
    134, 141, 169, 171, 175, 176, 208, 218, 221
Grimes, J. P., 11, 228
Grissom, P. F., 211, 219
Grossman, H. J., 169, 221
Grossman, P., 151, 152, 154, 223
Gursky, D., 144, 221
Gutkin, T. B., 8, 11, 12, 16, 20, 24, 26, 52, 53,
    66, 67, 69, 85, 99, 101–103, 105–107, 111,
    112, 118, 133, 149, 151, 153, 157, 158, 209,
    210, 214, 216, 221, 222, 227, 228, 232

Haggerty, R. J., 73, 227
Hall, R. V., 118, 221
Halpin, A., 53, 70, 222
Hamlett, C. L., 136, 220
Hannafin, M. J., 53, 232
Hansen, C. L., 123, 222
Happe, D., 101, 222
Haring, N. G., 123, 180, 222
Harris, A. M., 26, 148, 222
Harris, K. R., 127, 222
Haselkorn, D., 146, 150, 217
Hayes, S. C., 109, 137, 214, 222
Heller, K., 15, 222
Helsel, W. J., 133, 218
Henington, C., 25, 223

Henning-Stout, M., 25, 66, 102, 157, 222
Hersch, C., 7–9, 98, 222
Hickman, J. A., 118, 152, 192, 218, 222
Higginbotham, H. N., 16, 220
Hightower, A. D., 73, 216
Hintze, J., viii, 222
Hiralall, A. S., 116, 117, 210, 223, 226
Hobbs, N., 8–10, 98, 223
Hoff, K., 11, 205, 223
Hollingshead, A. B., 8, 9, 223
Holtgraves, T., 44, 223
Homer, A., 134, 227
Horner, R. H., 129, 223
Houk, J. L., 210, 226
Hughes, J. N., 24–26, 37, 103, 151, 152, 154, 192, 218, 223
Hyman, I., 56, 223

Idol, L., 183, 223
Ikeda, M. J., 137, 230
Imhof, E. A., 175, 213
Ingraham, C. L., 16, 223
Isaacson, R. V., 10, 216
Iscoe, I., 88, 223
Iwata, B. A., 131, 223
Izzo, L. D., 10, 216

Jackson, P., 142, 150, 224
Jackson, T., 25, 223
Jarrett, R. B., 137, 222
Jenkins, J. R., 173, 224
Johnson, P., 38, 39, 224
Jones, E. E., 41, 224
Jones, K., 130, 132, 227
Joyce, B., 159, 224

Kalsher, M. J., 131, 223
Katz, L., 121, 136, 220
Kaufman, M. J., 55, 233
Kavale, K., 120, 121, 180, 209, 210, 224
Kazdin, A. E., 127, 133, 224
Kelley, M. L., 210, 226
Kelly, J. G., 92, 224
Kelly, S. Q., 58, 63, 107, 111, 112, 124, 126, 129, 133, 177, 179, 226
Kendell, G. K., 6, 99, 141, 208, 221
Kern, L., 128, 131, 219, 224
Killilea, M., 9, 10, 71, 215, 229
Killough, C. E., 211, 219
Kinsala, M. G., 36, 224

Kipnis, D., 26, 224
Kirby, J. H., 90, 224
Knitzer, J., 170, 175, 219
Knutson, N., 180, 230
Koeppl, G., 133, 228
Komro, K., 148, 227
Korinek, L., 127, 213
Koslowsky, M., 40, 228
Kottkamp, R. B., 143–147, 216
Kounin, J., 56, 224
Kramer, J. J., 210, 214
Krasner, L., 176, 231
Kratochwill, T. R., 5, 6, 14–16, 22, 34, 70, 71, 80, 82, 84–86, 100, 109, 115, 149, 156, 161, 210, 214, 215, 224, 228–230, 233
Kruger, R. H., 34, 36, 224
Kruglanski, A. W., 34, 228
Kulp, S., 137, 228

LaFleur, L. H., 114, 116, 117, 208, 227, 232
Lalli, J. S., 131, 224, 225
Lambert, N. M., 47, 108, 153, 224, 229
Langer, S. N., 130, 231
LaVelle, J., 114, 116, 208, 227
Leavell, H. R., 72, 73, 216
Lentz, F. E., 123, 137, 173, 211, 214, 217, 218, 224, 225, 229
Lepage, K. M., 16, 228
Lerman, D. C., 131, 223
Levine, M., 92, 229
Levinson, H., 89, 225
Lewandowski, L. J., 210, 226
Lewin, K., 41, 225
Lewis, S. K., 111, 216
Lieberman, M. A., 9, 225
Lippitt, G., 36, 225
Lippitt, R., 36, 225
Lipsey, M. W., 120, 121, 210, 225
Litman-Adizes, T., 38, 228
Little, S. G., 175, 226
Litwin, G. H., 53, 230
Lloyd, J. W., 11, 225
Logan, P., 82, 105, 230
Lorion, R. P., 10, 216
Lortie, D. C., 143, 146, 225
Lovitt, T. C., 123, 144, 222
Lundervold, D., 128, 225

MacDonald, R. F., 130, 231
Mace, F. C., 131, 132, 224, 225, 227

Maher, C. A., 89, 225
Manni, J., 56, 223
Mannino, F. V., 75, 101, 198, 225
Mansfield, W., 145, 225
March, J. G., 51, 216
Marks, E. S., 15, 89, 225
Marston, D., 122, 135, 179, 180, 204, 233
Martens, B. K., 12, 21, 26, 53, 58, 62, 63, 65–
    68, 70, 84–86, 100–103, 105–107, 109–
    119, 121–131, 133, 136, 137, 157–160, 169,
    173, 176, 177, 179, 204, 208, 210, 213,
    217, 218, 220, 223, 225–227, 232
Martin, R., 15, 26, 30, 31, 35, 36, 44, 47, 111,
    112, 118, 226
Martindale, B., 137, 228
Maruish, M., 175, 213
Massie, D. R., 173, 204, 226
Matson, J. L., 133, 218
Maxwell, J. P., 55, 233
Mazaleski, J. L., 131, 223
McCosh, K. C., 131, 223
McDougal, J. L., 62, 66–68, 70, 100, 157,
    158, 176, 226
McDougall, L. M., 100, 108, 110, 135, 226
McGovern, P., 148, 227
McInnis, E. D., 173, 231
McIntyre, R., 55, 56, 232
McKee, W. T., 22, 23, 63, 107, 151, 226, 232
McLaughlin, T. F., 105, 230
Medway, F. J., 6, 24, 99, 101, 226, 227
Meller, P. J., 121, 122, 125, 226
Merrell, K. W., 172, 174, 226
Mettler, D. W., 211, 219
Meyers, J., 12, 15, 38, 44, 103, 152, 192, 218,
    220, 226, 227
Miles, M. B., 9, 225
Miller, C. D., 55, 56, 232
Miller, D. L., 210, 226
Mintzberg, H., 29, 226
Moe, G., 102, 133, 232
Monahan, J., 15, 222
Moore, S. C., 36, 230
Morison, P., 51, 226
Morrison, G. M., 12, 145, 220
Mortenson, B. P., 114, 116, 117, 208, 227, 232
Motta, R. W., 175, 226
Mouton, J. S., 89, 214
Mrazek, P. J., 73, 227

Neef, N. A., 132, 227

Nelson, R. O., 109, 137, 214, 222
Neumann, A. J., 86, 198, 214
Nevin, J. A., 176, 227
Ng, S. H., 44, 227
Noell, G. H., 6, 7, 99, 114, 116, 117, 134, 190,
    199, 208, 211, 221, 227, 232
Northup, J., 130, 132, 227

O'Keefe, D. J., 24, 227
Olsen, J. P., 51, 216
Orme, S. F., 7, 100, 101, 229
Osborne, S. S., 204, 229
Ost, D. H., 148, 227
Owens, R. G., 50, 51, 53, 54, 57, 58, 70, 101,
    227

Pace, G. M., 131, 223
Pany, D., 173, 224
Pardue, M. M., 22, 23, 150, 232
Parsons, R. D., 15, 38, 44, 118, 226, 227
Pavelski, R., 12, 220
Peplau, L. A., 39, 219
Perry, C. L., 148, 227
Peterson, F. M., 125, 227
Peterson, L., 124, 134, 227
Peterson, R., 133, 218
Peterson, R. F., 130, 214
Peterson, R. L., 101, 226
Petrix, L., 67, 99, 100, 141, 206, 216
Pfeiffer, S. I., 55, 227
Phillips, L., 8, 233
Pianta, B., 63, 101, 107, 153, 233
Piersel, W. C., 52, 66, 67, 102, 107, 157, 209,
    222, 227
Piotrowski, C., 175, 213
Pitner, R. O., 76, 213
Pittman, T. S., 41, 224
Plisko, V., 144, 227
Ponti, C. R., 66, 67, 102, 210, 228
Powell, R. A., 137, 228
Prout, H. T., 170, 175, 228
Prusek, R. M., 12, 220
Pryzwansky, W. B., 6, 14, 15, 75, 76, 87, 93,
    155, 156, 215, 228
Puck, S., 23, 102, 219

Ramage, J., 170, 228
Ramirez, S. Z., 16, 228
Ranier, D. D., 99, 114, 116, 199, 208, 227
Rappaport, J., 26, 228

Raven, B. H., 19, 27, 29–48, 86, 97, 111, 112, 115, 190, 191, 208, 209, 211, 218, 219, 228
Ray, A. G., 40, 46, 86, 115, 209, 211, 219
Ray, P. B., 23, 231
Redlich, F. C., 8, 9, 223
Reid, E. R., 210, 228
Reifin, L. H., 117, 218
Reilly, R. R., 16, 217
Reimers, T. M., 133, 228
Repp, A., 11, 133, 218, 225
Reppucci, N. D., 15, 80, 82, 100, 111, 228, 231
Reschly, D. J., 11, 12, 63, 66, 100, 108, 110, 135, 163, 166–168, 171, 172, 180, 203, 204, 209, 219, 221, 226, 228
Reynolds, C. R., 11, 12, 20, 107, 173, 228
Richman, G. S., 131, 223
Robbins, J. R., 133, 232
Roberts, H., 6, 220, 220
Roberts, L. A., 36, 229
Robinson, J. A., 149, 229
Rodgers, T. A., 131, 223
Rogers, D. L., 160, 214
Rogers, L. E., 22, 229
Romanczyk, R. G., 120, 217
Rosenfield, S., 66, 157, 174, 180, 183, 205, 209, 210, 229, 230
Rosenshine, B., 173, 213
Rucker, C. N., 56, 220
Ryan, D. A., 211, 219

Sabatino, D., 169, 218
Salasin, S., 89, 217
Salvia, J., 173, 220
Sandoval, J., 15, 47, 217, 229
Sarason, B. R., 75, 229
Sarason, I. G., 75, 229
Sarason, S. B., 54, 58, 68, 92, 115, 148, 150, 229
Saudargas, R. A., 137, 229
Saunders, J. T., 82, 100, 111, 228
Schein, E. H., 62, 81, 229
Schlenker, B. R., 41, 229
Schulberg, H. C., 10, 71, 229
Schulte, A. C., 10, 14, 15, 72, 76, 87, 93, 155, 156, 204, 215, 219, 229
Schwarzwald, J., 40, 228
Sechrest, L., 128, 232
Selby, P. M., 73, 231
Shade, D., 132, 227

Shapiro, E. S., 173, 229
Sheridan, S. M., 7, 12, 15, 100, 101, 210, 211, 216, 219, 224, 229
Shinn, M. R., 106, 107, 127, 135–137, 168, 172, 174, 180, 209, 226, 229, 230
Shore, B. A., 131, 223
Shore, M. F., 75, 98, 101, 225
Short, R. J., 36, 230
Showers, B., 159, 160, 199, 224, 230
Silver, S. E., 175, 215
Silverstein, J., 14, 213
Singer, J., 11, 56, 230
Singh, N. N., 123, 225, 230
Sirotnik, K. A., 168, 230
Skinner, C. H., 105, 230
Slifer, K. J., 131, 223
Smith, D., 55, 56, 232
Smith, D. K., 203, 230
Smith, M. L., 6, 9, 120, 230
Smith, R. G., 131, 223
Snyder, T. D., 49, 221
Stecker, P. M., 23, 24, 208, 220
Steele, E. S., 173, 204, 226
Stein, L. I., 38, 39, 230
Stenger, M. K., 154, 230
Stevens, R. J., 173, 213
Stoiber, K. C., 5, 6, 224, 230
Stokes, T. F., 127, 159, 230
Stollar, S. A., 117, 218
Stoner, G., 137, 230
Strickland, B., 55, 56, 220
Stuck, G. B., 179, 232
Sugai, G. M., 15, 122, 124, 156, 179, 180, 215, 230, 232
Swanson, J. M., 199, 230
Swartz, J., 67, 99, 100, 141, 206, 216
Szasz, T. S., 7, 98, 230

Tagiuri, R., 53, 230
Tankersley, M., ix, 231
Tannen, D., 39, 230
Tardy, C. H., 75, 114, 230
Telzrow, C. F., ix, 163, 165, 231
Tharp, R. G., 31, 80–82, 100, 111, 231
Thurlow, M. L., 57, 69, 153, 168, 178, 179, 204, 209, 213, 231, 233
Tilly, W. D., 11, 228
Tindal, G. A., 15, 230
Tindall, R. H., 12, 231
Tobin, M.I., 175, 226

Tollefson, N., 154, 230
Tombari, M. L., 85, 86, 100, 108, 110, 191,
   214, 231
Toomey, T., 148, 227
Tose, J., 175, 219
Touchette, P. E., 130, 231
Tracey, T. J., 23, 231
Trickett, E. J., 73, 118, 231
Trivette, C. M., 27, 114, 217
Trost, M. A., 10, 216
Tulbert, B., 17, 231
Turco, T., 133, 218
Turnbull, A. P., 55, 220

Ullmann, L. P., 176, 231
Updyke, J. F., 6, 226

Van Someren, K. R., 100, 224
Veblen-Mortenson, S., 148, 227
Vernberg, E. M., 15, 80, 231
Vincent, J. B., 111, 216
Vollmer, M., 121, 136, 220
Vollmer, T., 12, 109, 114, 128, 130–132, 177,
   208, 223, 226, 227
Von Brock, M. B., 101, 231

Wacker, D. P., 133, 228
Wagenaar, A., 148, 227
Walster, E., 35, 231
Walster, G. W., 35, 231
Wang, J., 63, 101, 107, 153, 233
Watkins, M., 56, 230
Watson, M. R., 24, 214
Webster, R. E., 173, 231
Weinstein, C. S., 56, 231
Welch, M., 17, 101, 229, 231
West, J. F., 183, 223
Wetzel, R. J., 8, 31, 81, 82, 100, 111, 231
Wheeler, D., 111, 216
Whichard, S. M., 40, 86, 209, 219
Wickstrom, K. F., 22, 23, 101, 150, 231, 232

Wiemann, J. M., 24, 183, 217
Williams, C., 37, 230
Williams, C. L., 148, 227
Willis, K. D., 131, 223
Wills, T. A., 75, 216
Wilson, D. B., 120, 212, 210, 225
Wilson, M. S., 203, 228
Winikur, D., 56, 223
Wise, P. S., 5, 11, 12, 20, 49, 51, 203, 219
Witt, J. C., 11, 12, 20, 22, 23, 26, 53, 55, 56,
   63, 65, 85, 99, 101–103, 107, 109, 110,
   114, 116, 117, 124, 127, 128, 133, 158, 169,
   177, 190, 199, 208, 211, 217, 218, 226–
   228, 231, 232
Wolery, M., 122, 124, 125, 179, 180, 232
Wolfson, M., 148, 227
Wonderlich, S., 134, 227
Woodward, J., 210, 220
Wright, C., 150, 216
Wyne, M. D., 179, 232
Wyner, N. B., 148, 232

Yalom, I. D., 9, 225
Yammer, D. M., 6, 141, 213
Yang, J., 44, 223
Yeaton, W. H., 132, 232
Yell, M., 129, 165, 205, 217, 232
Yoon, J., 25, 223
Yoshida, R. K., 55, 233
Ysseldyke, J. E., 57, 63, 69, 101, 107, 122,
   135, 136, 153, 168, 178–180, 204, 209,
   213, 216, 231, 233
Yukl, G., 40, 233

Zarcone, J. R., 131, 223
Zelditch, M., 41, 219
Zigler, E., 8, 233
Zins, J. E., 5, 26, 66, 67, 80, 93, 102, 110, 118,
   156, 210, 217, 228, 233
Zirkel, P., 11, 205, 223
Zubin, J., 8, 233

Subject Index

Ability training approach, 121, 122
Activity segment: *see* Instructional arrangement
Allocated time, 178
Analog conditions: *see* Functional assessment
Aptitude X treatment interaction, 135
Assessment, of schools as organizations, 90–92
AVICTORY model, 91, 93

Basal curriculum, 52, 168, 173, 178
Behavior analysis
  limitations, 127–129
  principles, 122, 129
  procedures, 123–127
Behavioral consultation
  assumptions, 14–15, 82, 84–85, 99–102, 207
  interview objectives, 85–87, 100, 105, 108–110
  stages, 85–87
Behavioral contracts, 125, 126
Behavioral momentum, 176
Behavioral psychology, 8, 73, 82, 122–123
Behavioral regularities, 53–57, 65
Building teams, 63, 156–158; *see also* Multidisciplinary teams
Bureaucracy
  assumptions, 50–53
  principles of administration, 50–51

Caregivers, 103–117
Classical organizational theory, 50–53

Clients, 4, 7–9, 14, 26, 78–81, 83–85, 99–103, 105, 106, 117–118, 122, 148, 171
Client-centered focus, 79, 101, 103, 189
Clinical psychology, 10
Coaching, 99, 116–117, 159–160, 199, 208
Collaboration
  contrasted with consultation, 16–18
  as myth, 21–25
Communication
  lateral, 52
  vertical, 52
Community Mental Health Centers Act (P.L. 88-164), 10
Community mental health concepts, 10, 73–77
Compartmentalized instruction, 49
Conceptual relevance, 99, 120, 128–132
Confidentiality, 16–17, 80, 93, 94–96, 106
Consideration, 53–54, 70
Consultants
  as change agents, 18, 19
  internal/external distinction 14–15
Consultant–consultee relationship
  Caplan's view, 4, 80
  as cooperative, 25–26, 69, 88, 102, 208
Consultation
  barriers to, 66–68, 98, 107
  contrasted with collaboration 16–18
  contracting, 17, 89, 92–93
  effectiveness, 5–7
  history, 3–4, 7–10, 73–74
  integrated model, 15, 16, 18, 24, 70, 103–106, 207–210
  journals on, 5
  outcomes, 117–118

Consultation (*cont.*)
  paradoxes of, 68–70
  tasks of, 103–105, 207
Consultation Analysis Record, 87–88
Consultative interviews
  problem analysis, 86, 108–109
  problem evaluation, 86–87, 109–110
  problem identification, 85–86, 108
  tactics, 110
Consultees, 3–4, 14, 16, 20–23, 26, 28, 79–
    80, 83, 103, 141
Continuum of services: *see* Range of
    services
Core characteristics, 105–106, 158
Coupling
  pooled, 58
  reciprocal, 58
  sequential, 58
Crisis/Crisis model, 75, 99, 106
Crisis intervention, 10, 13, 75
Cross-cultural factors in consultation, 16
Curriculum-based measurement, 136, 211
Curriculum content validity, 173

Data–based decision making, 117, 119–120
Diagnostic and Statistical Manual (4th Ed.;
    DSM-IV), 8, 163, 168–172
Direct observation, 67, 85, 130, 137
Discrete categorization, 137
Disorders First Diagnosed in Infancy,
    Childhood, or Adolescence, 171
Divisions of labor, 51
Dominance, 22, 102
Domineeringness, 22, 102
Door-in-the-face intervention, 111
Due process requirements, 164–165
Duration recording, 137
Dyadic social influence, 24, 88

Ecological perspective, 179
Education of All Handicapped Children
    Act (P.L. 94-142), 11–12, 164, 175, 203
Educationally Related Support Services, 68
Effect size statistics, 6, 121, 122; *see also*
    Meta-analysis
Egalitarian virus, 25–26
Empirical data, 19
Empirical–rational approach to change, 27,
    101
Empirically supported interventions, 5–6

Empowerment philosophy, 26–27, 114
Enrichment programs, 60
Entry, in school consultation, 67, 89–96,
    114, 154, 207
Ethical Standards, of American
    Psychological Association, 120
Evaluation reports, 64
Event recording, 137
Exception principle, 70
Exclusionary criteria, 170–171

FAPE, 163, 165
Fifteen-minute consultations, 155–156
Focus groups, 67
Foot-in-the-door intervention, 111–112
Formative evaluation 24, 120, 135–136, 157
Functional assessment, 100, 108–109, 128–
    132, 158, 165, 190, 205

Gatekeeper role, within school psychology, 12
Generalization, 20, 78, 123, 127–128, 159–
    160, 199
Goals, 8, 11, 13, 36, 51, 64, 85–87, 92, 98,
    100, 102, 103, 105, 108–110, 112, 114,
    115–118, 127, 137, 150, 156–160, 164,
    169, 179–180, 207
Group norms, 53–54, 70

Handicapping conditions
  emotional disturbances, 52, 61, 85, 169,
    172, 174–177
  mental retardation, 61, 166, 169, 172
  specific learning disabilities, 161, 169,
    172–174
Home-based reinforcement, 52–53, 70, 112,
    126
Human relations movement, 50, 53–57
Human services consultation, 5; *see also*
    Consultation

IDEA 97, 11, 129, 161, 205–206
Implementation protocols, 117; *see also*
    Protocols
Inclusive Elementary and Special
    Education Training Program, 205
Individualized education programs (IEP),
    55, 61, 62, 64, 136, 164, 165, 203
Individuals with Disabilities Education Act
    (IDEA), 11, 12, 13, 55, 63, 126, 164,
    166–169, 175, 203, 205–206

Influence
  ethical concerns, 26–27, 88–89
  mode of, 46–47, 89
  power/interaction model, 44–48
Influencing agents, 27–30, 36, 37, 40–47
Initiating structure, 53–55
Instructional arrangement, 56–57
Instructional hierarchy
  acquisition, 123–124
  adaptation, 123
  fluency, 123
  generalization, 123
Instructional interventions, 67, 124, 125,
    174, 179
Instructional match, 180
Integrated model of school consultation,
    15, 16, 18, 24, 70, 73, 82, 89, 97, 103–
    106, 181, 183, 207–210; see also
    Consultation, integrated model)
Interpersonal influence: see Influence
Invoking the power of a third party, 40–41

Leader Behavior Description
    Questionnaire, 53–54
Leadership style, 53, 54, 90, 107
Least restrictive environment, 126, 165, 166

Mainstreaming, 11
Mental health collaboration, 17–18, 95; see
    also Collaboration
Mental health consultation
  assumptions, 4, 17, 73–74, 77–78, 98–99,
    208
  parables, 39
  sources of consultee difficulty, 80–81,
    148–150
  theme interference reduction, 80, 99, 208
  types, 78–79
Meta-analysis, 6–7, 120, 136
Motivation Assessment Scale, 109, 129–130,
    131
Multiaxial classification, 171
Multicultural factors in consultation, 16
Multidisciplinary teams, 11, 13, 55, 203, 204
Mutual help groups, 9, 77; see also Social
    support

Narrative ABC recordings, 130
Needs assessment, 67

Normative-re-educative approach to
    change, 27–28
Norm-referenced, 56, 63–64, 173, 204

"One Right Model" of public education, 168
Organization development model of
    consultation, 15, 89
Organizational behavior theory, 50, 57–58
Organizational climate, 53–54, 70, 90, 107
Outcome expectancy, 151–152

Paradox, 68–70, 147
Paraprofessionals, 4, 8
Parents, 8, 10, 53, 55–56, 59, 61, 64, 75, 83,
    91, 100, 119, 141, 145–146, 164–165,
    187, 190, 205, 212
Performance feedback, 116–117, 159–160
P.L. 94-142 the Individuals with Disabilities
    Education Act: see IDEA
Planning teams, 68, 157
Positive behavioral interventions/support,
    52, 165, 205
Power: see Social power
Power-coercive approach to change, 28
Prereferral intervention programs, 50, 66,
    100, 157, 210
Prereferral intervention teams, 141, 157
Prevention
  population-oriented, 10, 13, 73, 74–75, 89
  primary, 5, 21, 73–75, 77, 118
  secondary, 21, 75, 118
  tertiary, 74–75, 118
Problem attributions, 107
Problem solving, 14, 16, 18, 25, 69, 73, 76,
    79, 82–85, 99–100, 103–108, 112–114,
    148, 152, 154, 190, 198, 199, 207, 210
Professional support, 14, 18, 29, 69, 97, 105,
    113–115, 207
Programmatic isolation, 58
Prompting, in errorless learning, 57, 116,
    123, 124, 125, 129
Prompting, procedures for
  graduated guidance, 124
  least-to-most, 124
  most-to-least, 124
  prompt and fade, 124
  prompt and test, 124
  time delay, 124
Psychoeducational evaluation, 63–64, 161,
    204

Psychological services
direct/indirect distinction, 20, 103
Psychotherapy, 3, 4, 9, 13, 20, 81, 98, 160
Pull-out programs, 11, 50, 52, 58, 61, 166
Punishment
Type I, 126
Type II, 126
Push-in programs, 50, 61, 166

Range of services, 11, 166
Reactance, 37, 38
Recitation, 56
Reducing the power of a third party, 41
Refer-test-place sequence, 50, 62–64, 65, 67, 106, 209
Referral, 3, 55, 60, 62–63, 65, 66, 70, 153, 157, 158, 174, 209, 211
Regular education initiative (REI), 11, 212
Reinforcement
differential, 126
positive, 31, 121, 122, 125, 126, 129, 131, 132, 135
Reinforcer preference assessment, 130
Relational communication, 22, 103
Relational control, 102, 112, 158
Remedial assistance, 60
Resistance to intervention: see Behavioral momentum
Resource rooms, 52, 61, 166
Response cost, 126
Role structuring, 95, 189

SBIT project, 158
School-based intervention, 14, 21, 107, 115, 118, 119–123, 127, 133, 135, 137, 179, 180, 212
School psychology, 10, 12, 13, 20, 32, 149, 151
Scientific methods, 119
Scientist-practitioners, 14, 120
Scope and sequence charts, 178
Seatwork, 56, 57, 67, 108, 130, 143, 176, 186, 189
Self-contained classroom, 59–61, 175
Self-efficacy, 118, 151–152, 154
Single-case experimental research, 7, 109
Skill training approach, 121–122
Social influence, 14, 16, 18, 19, 24, 25, 29, 41, 47, 69, 88–89, 97, 104–105, 111–113, 115, 159, 189, 207, 208, 211; see also Influence
Social labeling, 176

Social power
bases of social power model, 19, 29–40, 208
coercive power, 29, 30, 31–34, 41, 42, 48
impersonal, 31–33
personal, 34
expert power, 29, 30
negative, 37
positive, 35–37
hard bases, 40, 46
informational power, 30, 31
direct, 33, 37–39
indirect, 37–39
legitimate power, 29, 31, 34
formal/position power, 34
legitimacy of equity, 35
legitimacy of reciprocity, 35
legitimacy of responsibility/ dependence, 35
referent power, 29, 30
negative, 37
positive, 35–37
reward power 29
impersonal, 31–33
personal, 34
soft bases, 40, 46, 88
Social support
emotional support, 77, 81, 114
instrumental support, 77, 81, 114
supporting teachers, 114, 115, 133
Special education, 5, 10–12, 21, 33, 35, 50, 52, 54, 55, 57, 58, 59, 60–68, 70, 90, 91, 93, 100, 102, 106, 147, 157–158, 164, 166, 167–168, 172–177, 203–205, 209
Staffing, 55, 64; see also Multidisciplinary teams
Stage-setting devices, 41–42, 46
Standards of practice, 169
State regulations, 64, 167, 168, 170, 171, 174, 176
Strategic interpersonal communication, 24, 183
Student Learning in Context model (SLIC), 179–181
Support: see Social support and Professional support)
Support services, 61–62, 68

Targets of influence, 29
Teacher consultant model, 166

Teacher-directed small groups, 56–57
Teachers
  challenges/constraints, 142–143, 144–146,
    178–179
  expectations for consultation, 150–153
  occupational role, 144, 150
  reasons for seeking consultation, 148–150
  recruitment issues, 146–147
  retention issues, 146–147
  rewards, 143–144
  salaries, 143–144, 147
  shortage of, 146–147
Time-out, 109, 114, 126, 127, 142, 201
Time sampling, 101, 137
Topic determination, 23

Treatment
  acceptability of, 111, 120, 133–134
  integrity of, 109, 117, 118, 120, 133, 134–
    135, 137, 199
  strength of, 120, 128, 132–133

Verbal praise, 112, 125, 126
Vocational Rehabilitation Act Section 504,
  164–165

YAVIS, 9
Year-round school, 161

Zero reject models, 11

About the Authors

WILLIAM P. ERCHUL is a Professor of Psychology and the Director of the School Psychology Training program at North Carolina State University. He received his B.A. in Psychology and Communication Arts from the Honors Program of the College of Letters and Science at the University of Wisconsin, and his Ph.D. in Educational Psychology with a specialization in School Psychology from the University of Texas. Dr. Erchul has written numerous journal articles on processes and outcomes of mental health and behavioral consultation, as well as edited the book, *Consultation in Community, School, and Organizational Practice*. Dr. Erchul, a Fellow of the American Psychological Association, has received various awards, including the Lightner Witmer Award, presented by the Division of School Psychology of APA in recognition of early career research contributions to the field of school psychology; the Excellence in Staff Development Award, presented by the North Carolina School Psychology Association; and the Outstanding Faculty Research Award, presented by NC State's College of Education and Psychology. He has served as associate editor of *School Psychology Quarterly*, guest editor of special issues of the *School Psychology Review* and the *Journal of Educational and Psychological Consultation*, and presently serves on the editorial boards of four journals. He is the current Vice President of Publications, Communications, and Convention Affairs of APA's Division of School Psychology.

BRIAN K. MARTENS joined the Psychology Department at Syracuse University in 1986, and is a Professor of Psychology and Director of Training for the School Psychology program. His scholarly record includes over 70 research articles, books, chapters, and invited reviews in the areas of applied behavior analysis and school consultation. Professor Martens received the Lightner Witmer Award from Division 16 of the

American Psychological Association for outstanding early research contributions in 1990 and is currently a Fellow of the Association and a member of the Society for the Study of School Psychology. He was named Outstanding Teacher of the Year at University College in 1995, was appointed to the board of directors of the Society for the Experimental Analysis of Behavior in 1995, and was named one of 90 distinguished alumni at the 90th Anniversary Celebration of Teachers College at the University of Nebraska in 1997. He has served as associate editor for the *Journal of Applied Behavior Analysis* (1993–1996) and *School Psychology Quarterly* (1991–1994) and currently serves as a guest associate editor or editorial board member of three journals.